D1395104

Media, Monarchy and Power

Neil Blain
Hugh O'Donnell

intellect™
Bristol, UK
Portland, OR, USA

intellect – European Studies Series
General Editor – Keith Cameron

Humour and History	Keith Cameron (ed)
The Nation: Myth or Reality?	Keith Cameron (ed)
Regionalism in Europe	Peter Wagstaff (ed)
Women in European Theatre	Elizabeth Woodrough (ed)
Children and Propaganda	Judith Proud
The New Russia	Michael Pursglove (ed)
English Language in Europe	Reinhard Hartmann (ed)
Food in European Literature	John Wilkins (ed)
Theatre and Europe	Christopher McCullough
European Identity in Cinema	Wendy Everett (ed)
Television in Europe	James A. Coleman & Brigitte Rollet (eds)
Language, Community and the State	Dennis Ager
Women Voice Men	Maya Slater (ed)
National Identity	Keith Cameron (ed)
Policing in Europe	Bill Tupman & Alison Tupman
Regionalism in the European Union	Peter Wagstaff (ed)
Spaces in European Cinema	Myrto Konstantarakos (ed)

First Published in Hardback in 2003 by
Intellect Books, PO Box 862, Bristol BS99 1DE, UK

First Published in USA in 2003 by
Intellect Books, ISBS, 5804 N.E. Hassalo St, Portland, Oregon 97213–3644, USA

A catalogue record for this book is available from the British Library

ISBN 1-84150-043-7

Series Editor:	Keith Cameron
Production Officer:	Peter Singh
Cover Photograph:	Sheila Clark
Copy Editor:	Holly Spradling

Printed and bound in Great Britain by The Cromwell Press, Wiltshire

CONTENTS

PART THREE – CELEBRITY, ROYALTY AND POWER

Acknowledgements

Some of the material in Chapter 3 and in the Conclusion appeared in an earlier form in 'Constructing the People's Princess: The State of Britain and the Death of Diana', in C. Cornut Gentille D'Arcy (ed.), *Cultural Confrontations*, University of Zaragoza, 1999. Aspects of the discussion in Chapters 2 and 5 were published earlier in 'Constructing the Citizen-King: monarchy, myth and modernity in the contemporary Spanish media', in the *International Journal of Iberian Studies*, Volume 9 Number 1, 1997. Part of the argument in Chapter 4 appeared in 'Royalty, modernity and postmodernity: monarchy in the Spanish and British presses', in *Acis: Journal of the Association for Contemporary Iberian Studies*, Volume 7 Number 1, 1994.

Many people helped us in the preparation of this book. We would like to thank in particular Salvador Cardús (Universitat Autònoma de Barcelona), Peter Dahlén (Bergen University), Tom Hutchison (Middle Tennessee State University), Fernando León Solís (University of Paisley), Roel Puijk (Lillehammer University College), Isabel Simões Ferreira (Instituto Politécnico de Lisboa), and Bob Spires (Middle Tennessee State University).

We are also indebted to Sverre Amundsen of *Aftenposten*, Filip Marsboom of *Gazet van Antwerpen*, Martijn Roessingh of *Trouw*, and Stéphane Renard of *Le Vif-L'Express* for their help.

Our thanks also go to Santiago Boland, Anna Bondesson, Lisa Douglas, Barbera Fransz, Maria Lamuedra, Svend Larssen, Caroline McElhone, Trude Nyhus, Joanne O'Donnell, Jim Rafferty, Eva van Walle, and David and Julie Becker of the Byrne Roberts B&B in Murfreesboro, Tennessee. We are likewise grateful to colleagues with whom we had the chance to discuss some of the ideas that appear here, at seminar presentations we made on various aspects of royalty and monarchy at Antwerp, Manchester Metropolitan, Stirling, Sunderland, and Glasgow Caledonian Universities.

We are also very grateful to the following for granting us permission to reproduce their cartoons in this book:
- Gallego y Rey for the cartoon from *Diario 16* on page 83
- Idigoras y Pachi for the cartoon from *El Mundo* on page 100
- Nicolas Vadot for the cartoon from *Le Vif-L'Express* on page 123
- Sus Damiaens (Canary Pete) for the cartoon from the *Gazet van Antwerpen* on page 131
- Inge Grødum, for the cartoon from *Aftenposten* on page 140, and
- Juan Ballesta for the cartoon from *Cambio 16* on page 200.

We are indebted to Sheila Clark for permission to use one of her very special royal photographs.

We would also like to express our gratitude to Keith Cameron for his constructive, concise, and very helpful comments on the draft work; and to Bill Scott, formerly our colleague at Glasgow Caledonian University, whose support was (as always) unstinting.

INTRODUCTION

Monarchy and Power

Britain is a state with a rather small-scale, fairly anonymous monarchy. No-one is much interested in the royal family. Occasionally they are on television, when the monarch has a birthday, or during special events like marriages or funerals. Sometimes they appear in lifestyle magazines but since they lead such ordinary lives they are less likely to figure than stars from the worlds of television, sport and pop. It is not unusual to encounter the complaint that they are a bit boring as a family, if worthy in their own way, though eyebrows have been raised by the engagement of the heir to the throne to the divorced daughter of a Russian businessman reputed to have Mafia connections. In general the media have more important matters to cover, though, and given their interest in serious questions the royal family are often absent from both screens and pages. Extended members of the royal family – the core group is very limited in size – are commoners and do ordinary jobs; there is little interest in their royal connections.

There was a time when the monarchy would have been treasured for its symbolic role in maintaining 'traditional' national values. These days, however, the country is so wedded to an idea of itself as a modern political democracy that many politicians and media editors are frankly a bit embarrassed at not living in a republic like the French. It is almost as compromising as having once had an upper chamber at Westminster which wasn't elected. Nonetheless, they reckon that the royal family – living as it does in a fairly ordinary way, and considering the work it does for trade and public relations – is a minor but useful enterprise organization whose balance sheet tends toward credit rather than debit. Debate rumbles on, but for the time being the UK will probably keep its monarchy, though in fact few would greatly regret its demise and many would hardly notice it.

Evidently this must be a description of a parallel universe, unless it is an imaginative projection a century or so into the future. It is very hard to imagine a British monarchy like this, or a Britain in which to situate it. That difficulty is mainly what motivates this book.

No such difficulty exists close by in Europe. If you're Scandinavian or you live in the Low Countries, imagining a monarchy like this is very easy. There, you've already got a monarchy pretty much as described, even if some are more 'ordinary' than others. At times they will figure more rather than less in the national consciousness – an unsuitable marriage, a drink problem – but generally they don't, much, figure at all. In Spain, where things are different again, there is a role for the monarchy as large, in its own way, as the role of the British monarchy in the UK, but it produces a set of cultural and political meanings which are quite unlike those generated by the British monarchy. In particular it is most important to the Spanish to understand their monarchy as 'modern', so some aspects of our parallel universe are already in place in Spain too.

1

Elsewhere in Europe monarchs are long gone. If you're French you can take as much interest (not necessarily all that much) as you like in the lives of the British or Monegasque royals, safe in the propriety of the republican consciousness. Across the Rhine, you could still, in a couple of regions of Germany, bump into one of your former royals: perhaps a Hohenzollern at your grocer's in Sigmaringen; the shop assistant may become a bit self-conscious, but you won't think much about it and your children won't even recognize them.

By contrast in Britain, when, sadly, Princess Margaret died, the BBC that Saturday morning devoted for a time both of its terrestrial television channels to continuous coverage of the event, giving that sense which might be conveyed in other countries after a political coup or during a civil war, of the displacement of alternative realities by one momentous single fact of national seriousness. (At the time of Diana's death this media process extended to the complete obliteration, for very long periods, of any world beyond hers.)

This sense of focus is not an easy achievement in the globalized, web-connected world, but obsession with royal events is a routine British media habit, even over minor misdemeanours by the Princes Edward or Harry. It is not that Margaret was a negligible figure in British culture, particularly for her own generation. During some phases of her life she fulfilled many public duties and was well-regarded, and in her youth she was the most glamorous ever of British royals. She was also a person often understood with sympathy as a victim, if in a strictly relative sense, of her royal identity. However, in later years she had become marginal, even as a member of the royal family in Britain. It is true that the BBC displays a special form of adhesion to royal events, but in easily privileging them over other events it is more typical than otherwise of the British media generally. (For example, the early ITN News on the evening of Margaret's death in February 2002 covered only that event, apart from a very short item on the Winter Olympics – in other words, no other news was delivered, at all.)

In the alternative United Kingdom (would it still be called a 'kingdom'?) with which we began, what could have happened to reduce the monarchy to its diminished and ordinary status? Could Britain have become a 'modern political democracy' – in the twenty-first century British politicians still spoke of this as an aspiration – and, thereafter, have turned reflectively to examine the monarchy, and found it truly anachronistic?

If so, how could Britain have managed to become 'modern' without in the first place dethroning its monarchy, and removing all the symbolic apparatus of hierarchical privilege which accompanies it? And that leaves other questions: for example, whether greater political maturity (in this parallel universe we have created) would be demonstrated by becoming a republic, rather than just placing the royal family on bicycles, as in some parts of Europe. Just the reverse might be true, in the sense that an adult democracy might care so little about its monarchy that it would be happy to let it alone in a minor role (though in which order this democracy would reach maturity, and reduce the role of its monarchy, is not clear).

Perhaps the world of the last thirty years, with its tendencies, not least in Britain, toward social fragmentation, depoliticization, and the sovereignty of consumer culture, is not the most fertile environment for republicanism. If there is a 'post-monarchist' dimension to new forms of consumer royalty, then at least consumption helps sustain the monarchic institution. It is difficult to imagine an equivalent 'consumer republicanism' (it will certainly have been a marketing feat should it ever catch on).

Another question concerns the likely engines of change in this parallel Britain; Europeanization, perhaps; or English decentralization – another imaginative leap; or a truly massive royal scandal or two, if such latter irruptions didn't indeed lead directly to a republic and remove the 'bicycling' option altogether.

In part this book was inspired by theoretical questions raised by the very difficulty of imagining a Britain able to produce a monarchy like the Belgian or Dutch or Scandinavian monarchies. There belongs to this argument a representative truism, to the effect that only Belgium can produce the Belgian monarchy. But it is also true that the British monarchy and the political situation which enables its continuance in its present state are abnormal when measured by European benchmarks. All the nations in our analyses produce from very different national histories monarchies more like each others' than like Britain's.

This is a theoretical and textual study of the way the media in a range of Western European countries construct accounts of the phenomena of monarchy and royalty. It speculates about how these accounts may be understood in relation to wider cultural questions, in the context of existing theories about culture. It also tries to suggest how these constructions of royalty and monarchy contribute to the circulation of ideas about the organization of society. The book is about both the British monarchy and royal family, and about European monarchies and royal families. It has been our intention to privilege neither Britain nor Europe, though the subject position taken is of the view from Britain (the nation in which we are in any case most clearly constituted as royal subjects).

In this sense we usually, though not exclusively, read conclusions about British culture from European culture, rather than the other way round. But we have produced a study in which our focus is nonetheless as much on Europe as on the UK.

At best it can only be a series of snapshots of a large and shifting subject. But we have tried to assemble our samples both with breadth, and with respect for consistent trends. The argument proceeds on the assumption that large-scale textual sampling from media sources provides significant evidence from the cultures thereby investigated. Over time (and our study has a longitudinal dimension) media producers necessarily adjust content and mode of address to consumers, in a fashion which enables the analyst to separate the typical from the aberrant, in that uneven dialogue which links media producers and audience.

One of the very large questions which we have to leave open is whether, even over a ten- or twenty-year period, the media's agenda and the views of the public can remain asymmetrical. It is a commonplace that different newspapers and even different television companies can produce politically varied news output, so one aspect of that question about ideological fit concerns the precise media source of the product. This analysis pursues with care questions about agenda-setting by specific media producers; and questions about the audience are raised continuously.

Yet there is also an overall flavour which emerges from a national media system. For example, the conservatism over the theme of monarchy which typifies the British media, despite very occasional editorials seriously critical of monarchy (nearly always in the broadsheet press, but not often found even there) is part of a broader pattern of ideological conservatism.

The matter of how reliable a reading from media sources can ever be, as a measurement of the nature of culture, is as contentious as any argument about any other form of sampling. For that reason we consider other research approaches to the 'culture of monarchy', such as the direct interviews with the public which some researchers have very productively attempted. However, given appropriate dimensions of breadth and longitude, sampling of media products provides valuable evidence of the nature of specific cultural periods. Sampling media texts comparatively is a method which arguably provides forms of sedimented cultural evidence lacking in other forms of measurement (its selectiveness has not prevented us from using it accurately for the purposes of prediction elsewhere).

This is an international study, almost all from European and British sources, though we include in Chapter 2 some American television material to extend the comparative dimension in a particular context. Though the British monarchy also nominally and sometimes controversially provides a head of state for other nations, this dimension of its role is not considered here.

What has been the principle of national selection?

Our underlying theme is difference between Britain and Europe: so we have not included other monarchies from around the world. We have not concerned ourselves with the Monegasque monarchy either, because we wish to consider monarchies in relation to significant political cultures, and as a symbol, the royal house of Monaco floats much more freely beyond considerations of political culture than the Dutch, Spanish, Belgian or Norwegian royal houses (the Grand-Ducal house of Luxembourg is, on the other hand, relatively restricted in its symbolic reach). Norway has been chosen among the Scandinavian monarchies partly for purposes of contrast with our other instances. Its monarchy was electorally reinstated in 1905 after Norway's lengthy periods of union with Denmark, then Sweden. But its recent history also afforded valuable comparative opportunities.

Another reason for concentrating on our group of nations is associated with the central theoretical mode of comprehension of cross-national difference which we propose, namely a linked model of modern and postmodern processes. This becomes overstretched when applied beyond certain boundaries. (The model is extensively outlined in Part One, especially Chapter 1.)

Our most cogent reason for our specific European focus, however, is the currency of the European question both for Britain and for the other monarchies in this study.

We can say therefore that we were led by a desire to propose the mediation of monarchy as a worthwhile theme in itself. But the research has been international, the more to comprehend the politico-cultural role of monarchy; and also because the cultures of monarchy and royalty provide insights into wider aspects of cross-national difference in Europe.

We leave some of the specific comparative argumentation about Britain and Europe until later, but what can be said for now is that we are – in the company, it can justly be claimed, of a growing number of British observers – struck by the persistence and substance of cultural differences between the UK on the one hand, and much of Europe on the other. Our hypothesis is that asymmetries in the development of aspects of both modernity and postmodernity are at the heart of these differences, and that it is by treating both phases in association that the clearest light can be shed on the matter.

A book which explored these differences between Britain and Europe might focus on quite other themes, of course, for example the management of transport, or the organization of food industries; so our book is in another sense a snapshot, in this instance of a much larger pattern of difference. We contend, however, that the inter-related realms of monarchy and royalty sediment this cultural difference in such a striking manner that they should no longer be ignored in their mediated form as the subjects of a developed study. From quite another set of concerns the study is overdue, that is to say, as a media-focused study. One of the most striking phenomena of 'actuality' media production is its obsessive focus on royalty, and this is an under-analysed domain.

We will not make too much of the distinction between monarchy as an institution and specific royal families as an instance. The concluding section develops some ideas about the distinction as it differentially emerges from British and European accounts, but it is not our view that there is a great deal to discover by developing it theoretically. Despite existing theorization of the two domains, media constructions and cultural reception alike of narratives about royal families fuse the two, albeit that British accounts are especially prone to do so. It is our belief that theoretical and practical distinctions between 'monarchy' and 'royalty' are neither difficult to understand nor especially illuminating to dwell upon. It is not difficult to separate monarchy as a constitutional phenomenon from royalty as a set of socio-cultural or personal/psychological attributes.

We believe that a comprehension of that distinction is clearly embedded in most public discussion of the monarchic/royal phenomenon, and that their fusion is not a sign of 'incomprehension' in public exchange, but rather of differential understanding; sometimes in the form of ideological manipulation on the media production side, and also of political contestation on the part of both media producers and audience. That is, there is a comprehension that in practice these two – let us call them 'processes' since they are active – are both implicated in (say) a discussion of the appropriate constitutional relationship between Crown Prince Haakon of Norway and Mette-Marit Tjessem Høiby, or between Charles and Camilla Parker-Bowles in the UK. Nonetheless, in the Conclusion we do incorporate a further consideration of the significance of this distinction – especially its lack in nearly all British discussion – into our remarks.

Nor can we conceivably seek, within an already busy agenda for this study, to make room for a justification of our privileging of the category of 'culture' over those of 'society', 'politics' or 'economics' (although all of these are present). In our discussion of the modern/postmodern model which underpins the argument, we note the very wide recognition since the 1980s of the expansion of the realm of culture within the envelope of the social, and of the deployment of the category of 'culture' as more central to many academic accounts than once it was. Our selectivities in this study have required to be plural and for the sake of lucidity it is in the 'cultural' realm that we locate most of the discussion, treating politics, society and economics 'culturally', while tacitly recognizing the existence of the other quite different perspectives which subject specialists in other fields might bring to our concerns.

To the question of 'power' we return quite specifically in Chapter 2 and in the Conclusion, often leaving it as an implicit category elsewhere. The contrasts which we demonstrate between continental conceptions of monarchy, and those extant in the UK, are framed in Europe precisely as arguments about political power. They are arguments about the legitimate functions of monarchy/royalty in societies to whom it matters that they can legitimately recognize themselves as politically modern. Furthermore, the perception of differential patterns of inequality in political power, and in the disposition of the means for a life of quality, across European societies, is what partly motivates this study. In particular we are interested in pursuing the distinction between British 'subjects' on the one hand and near-European 'citizens' on the other.

There is a productive argument to be had around the general proposition that a lack of empowerment is a stronger characteristic of British life than it is for our near-neighbours in Europe, even if there are many qualifications which have to be made about demographic sub-groups of these nationalities (in the sense, for example, that many white Londoners may be more empowered than many non-white Parisians).

In certain instances differences in empowerment can be seen in the light of legal and constitutional rights, or other objectively measurable differences – differences both in empowerment and in the quality of life with which it is associated – between Britain and Europe. Differences in legal rights, for example, may be illustrated by variability in employee rights, from country to country, to amenities such as maternity or paternity leave; or to trades union membership rights, or security of job tenure. There are also constitutional differences over rights of access to state information, for example, and other differences of constitutional definition, often not in favour of the UK population.

(European law now sometimes comes to the rescue of Britons who have been denied justice in their own country.)

Very large numbers of children in Britain are born into poverty at the same time as the gap between rich and poor has grown to incomparable proportions, and is still growing. These questions of social stratification are especially severe in the UK and in turn impact on less clearly codified 'rights' (for example, to safety on the streets and on public transport, to the availability of healthy food) which in Britain are likewise often less satisfactorily addressed than in Europe.

But there are domains in which it is yet more difficult to shed light, those areas of human experience in which power is symbolically constructed, in which power is an imagined presence or lack. The British are not very good at consumer militancy, for example. They do not readily become angry at some of the worst transport, health and education provision in the developed world, whereas the French, more demanding, are ready to take their expectations with them onto the streets at short notice.

Some British commentators like to talk about a new 'classlessness', yet British speech still overflows with class markers. Class origin is still an especially reliable predictor of health, and life expectancy, as well as educational attainment, among other outcomes. (Indeed if there is a universal in European discourse about the UK, it is about the oddity and inequity of its social stratification). But class is also very much a matter of subjective and inter-subjective feeling, and the British feel it strongly. Their film and television drama and much of their soap opera and situation comedy and many other media products, including advertising, are still class-driven. There is a very strong socio-economic dimension to product and services stratification in the UK.

The British media system is politically conservative, only by 2001/2002 starting to move a very little in its anti-Europeanism; still generally hostile to trades unions, any remnants of the British left, and any trace of republicanism; while valorizing employers, the City of London, and middle-class values. In the 1990s an increased exploitation of 'ordinariness' and working-class identities was visible, albeit arguably in a mode of condescension which militates against an optimistic interpretation. (Ordinariness is further discussed in relation to celebrity and royalty in Chapter 9.)

This media system is tolerant of New Labour for as long as it mimics Conservatism, and generally works in favour of existing social distinctions, including those between whites and non-whites; and men and women, the latter of whom, when a slightly greater number arrived at ministerial level in government after 1997, were promptly dubbed 'Blair's Babes', often by women journalists, a jingle endlessly repeated. We should not underestimate the material difference signalled by the inconceivability of such a formulation in the media of the European countries in this study, which is part of a pattern of differential discourses which are very revealing. (The Scottish media do not always entirely conform to this conservative model but have shifted toward rather than away from it.)

The two most sustained and serious studies of monarchic/royal phenomena in the UK so far available, Tom Nairn's *The Enchanted Glass* of 1988, to which all subsequent commentators owe a debt, and Michael Billig's *Talking of the Royal Family* (published in that year of royal separation, 1992) both draw from their analyses the sense of a cultural role of the royal family which is ultimately political, functioning as a part-guarantor of the maintenance of existing relations of power. Objections subsequently made to the effect that Nairn overstated the political significance of royalty in Britain have themselves to be countered, by reference not just to evidence such as the revelations of ideology at work, recorded in Billig's empirical study (considered later), but to the major continuous political project undertaken by those with interests in the maintenance of existing relationships of power in Britain: namely, to valorize the monarchy and the royal house in their justification of Britain as a given and fixed political disposition.

The latter stages of writing coincided with the revelation that as part of New Labour's preparations for Queen Elizabeth II's Golden Jubilee, Labour MPs had been urged to issue what was in effect a pro-forma press release including the sentiments that 'We love our Queen. She is a symbol of what makes Britain great. I think it's only appropriate that we show how proud we are to have her as our head of state' (*Sunday Telegraph*, 27 January 2002). Names and constituencies were to be filled in as appropriate. Thus does the force of a full decade of sometimes fierce public criticism of the royal family (albeit only personal!) evaporate in the heat of the approaching Jubilee.

The advantage of an element of longitudinal sampling in our study is to raise the possibility that there is less evidence than sometimes appears of steady movement away from monarchism in Britain, despite occasional outbursts from some media sources, and intermittently iconoclastic poll returns. We return to the question in more detail in the Conclusion and Afterword.

In common with other writers, we recognize limitations in the existing comprehension of the relationship between symbolic forms and the disposition of social and cultural power. We surmise that the fullest possible analysis of this relationship in our chosen domain would require further studies using the ethnographic approach of Billig's work, which by itself reveals much. Comparative cross-national empirical studies of political subjects and citizens would be the next logical step. That is not our work here.

The book is in three sections:

Part One: Modern and Postmodern Monarchy comprises three chapters. Two explore the cultural functioning of monarchy and royalty in a theoretical context with much textual material, examining them as both modern and postmodern phenomena. Chapter 1 is a theoretical discussion focusing on postmodernism theory and royalty, and draws its ideas and illustrative texts from a number of nations and cultures. Chapter 2 explores the ideological and 'post-ideological' implications of monarchs and royal families and their cultural functioning. It ends with an extended case study drawing material from British, Norwegian, Swedish and other sources. The third chapter in the opening section focuses on the UK, exploring the limits of media discussion of monarchy and its families, and questions of discrepancy, credibility and ideological conformity in media coverage.

Part Two: European Monarchies and the Media comprises five chapters analysing monarchic and royal events in Spain, Belgium, The Netherlands and Norway as constructed by the media; preceded by a general European study.

Part Three: Celebrity, Royalty and Power introduces new theoretical material to the discussion, to develop the theme at a stage in the argument where a full comparative treatment has already been established. (This has, we hope, avoided thematic and theoretical overload in the first two sections of what is, of necessity, a very wide-ranging study.) It comprises an extensive analysis of royalty and celebrity in Chapter 9. Chapter 10, the Conclusion, turns to questions of royalty and power, and to the institution of monarchy. Part Three also includes an Afterword on the developments of 2002 associated with the funeral of the Queen Mother; and the Golden Jubilee.

There is also appended a Note on Britain and Europe which provides further context for the volume's European themes.

The book analyses media coverage of royal and monarchic matters mainly over a ten-year period, roughly from the early 1990s until mid-2002, though its historical reference is considerably longer. Its analysis is of both press and television. The cast includes King Juan Carlos of Spain, the infanta doña Elena de Borbón y Grecia and don Jaime Marichalar; Prince Philippe, heir to the Belgian throne, and his bride Mathilde d'Udekem d'Acoz; Crown Prince Haakon of Norway and Mette-Marit Tjessem Høiby; and Crown Prince Willem-Alexander of The Netherlands, and Máxima Zorreguieta. Happily this part of the cast is largely seen in a positive matrimonial context, no matter how controversial. We have in the European context focused on the initial phases of matrimony, not in order to focus exclusively on royal weddings (there are many other instances in the book) but because a wedding in a royal house produces a sustained passage of symbolic activity.

The book also includes Camilla Parker-Bowles, Prince Philip, and the Queen Mother, among the British Royal Family; and we have placed in two or three chapters some passages of discussion about Princess Diana, who still actively inhabits much current European and British discussion of royal families and the institution of monarchy. In this sense the British marriage narrative, where it occurs, unhappily emphasizes later conflictual stages of matrimony, merely an accident of recent history (though no doubt the particular rate of recurrence of divorce in the British royal house is linked to pressures associated with its unique position). The passing of the Queen Mother is also discussed, in the Afterword, as is the year of the Golden Jubilee.

Though we examine textual evidence of the nature of uneven development of European postmodernization, the proposition which still most strikingly emerges from the different cultural understandings of monarchy and royalty which we encounter is this: Britain's is the only monarchy among those studied which is not required to justify itself by its contribution to political modernity. We explore this idea amidst much evidence in the book to the effect that political modernity is still difficult to place within the same paradigm as British identity.

Two terminological notes

1. 'Britain' is a synonym for 'the UK' in what follows, the variation being solely for stylistic reasons. If we use 'England' or 'Scotland' it is purposively. We have not addressed the complexities of the Irish situation, not because it is unimportant to us, but because the role of the monarchy in Northern Ireland is exceedingly complex, and because we do not presume to involve the Republic in these monarchic questions, any more than we have much involved its French or other European republican neighbours.

2. In the course of the book, a number of conceptual models are applied to the question of 'representation', which we sometimes prefer to term 'construction' to emphasize the fabricative force of media narratives, and all narratives. Within our related model of modernity and postmodernity we discuss 'ideology' and 'post-ideology' as concomitants, in parallel with 'signification' and 'post-signification'. We also deploy a wide range of concepts which seek to illuminate symbolic and other communicative processes in culture, including 'discourse', 'myth', 'narrative' and 'mode of address'. We make use of Ferdinand de Saussure's twinned concepts of *'langue'* and *'parole'* (here, experimentally, in the context of royal boudoirs). The emphasis on this terminological range shifts from chapter to chapter. Generally we explain these terms as we proceed. We have no doctrinaire preference for any single approach to the description of symbolic process. We are therefore happy to license our readers to reassign, or to broaden, any of these emphases from one part of the volume to another.

PART ONE
MODERN AND POSTMODERN MONARCHY

1.   Modern and Postmodern Monarchy

The relatively stable aesthetic of Fordist modernism has given way to all the ferment, instability and fleeting qualities of a postmodernist aesthetic that celebrates difference, ephemerality, spectacle, fashion, and the commodification of cultural forms

(David Harvey, *The Condition of Postmodernity*, 1989: 156)

Historical scenes have always been cleverly and cunningly 'staged' by certain men who were aiming for specific results

(Henri Lefebvre, 1947)

...with wild fervour but no sycophancy or fanaticism, all decent British people today give three loud cheers

(A.N. Wilson, on the Queen Mother's centenary, *Daily Mail*, 4 August 2000)

'Big Brother with a family tree'

(Dutch *NRC Handelsblad* on the Dutch monarchy, 16 May 2001)

There is a specifically temporal aspect of this study which is central to the understanding of the cultural politics of European monarchy. It concerns the matter of what might be historically new, both socially and culturally, about the last thirty or so years; that is, what might make the so-called postmodern phase of history special, which might help us to understand why royalty has become a phenomenon inseparable from transformations of *culture* into *media culture*; and also why it is closely bound into a new phase of *consumption* which many commentators have distinguished as the central feature of developed societies in their current phase. These questions of media culture and consumer culture, which are closely related, bear very importantly on our understanding of royalty as a political phenomenon.

The analysis and argumentation which follow pay especial attention to the distinction between modernity and postmodernity as categories within which to understand politico-cultural development generally and the functioning of royalty in particular. This book is concerned primarily with the recent history of monarchy as a media phenomenon, but that history has occurred within very dynamic social and cultural circumstances, and in order to grasp their significance it will be helpful to be clear about 'modern' and 'postmodern' aspects of recent history, and how they impact on an understanding of monarchy.

'Modern' in this book is a term which is used chiefly in its economic and political dimensions, and specifically in association with ideas prevalent in the phase of modernity, whose period is continuously debated, but was certainly well inaugurated by the second half of the nineteenth century (Berman, 1983: 15–36). It was in decline in some of its aspects from the First World War, yet further after the Second, but vigorous enough economically until the 1960s (Bell, 1973; Fussell, 1977: 36–74, 315–335; Habermas, 1991; Harvey, 1989: 173–188; Hutcheon, 1988; Huyssen, 1984; Lefebvre, 1991; Rose, 1991). It is understood as a historical period with a beginning, and – in its pure form – an end, so let us say very roughly, 1850–1970, with many qualifications.

The idea itself that modernity has 'ended' needs to be qualified. In fact, we require a flexible notion of historical period which enables us to propose that it is only in its most characteristic form that the 'modern' world gradually evolves into the 'postmodern' world in the 1960s and 1970s. It is true that after the 1960s some characteristics of the modern phase diminish. Most crucially, the economic world of modernity does radically change between 1965 and 1974, with very large consequences for the nature of culture. If we wish to understand why Princess Diana was a 'postmodern' phenomenon then we need to understand how her existence as an economic product (besides, of course, yet other facets of her postmodern nature) grew directly from the collapse of the modern economic world.

And of course the development of a postmodern phase of history involves new phenomena, not merely the decline of old dynamics – phenomena such as the intensive round of what has been called 'mediatization', which we may define as the process whereby more and more of culture becomes media culture. Diana's nature as a phenomenon was, and is still, intensively associated with the mediatization of culture. These two ideas – of radical economic change and exponential growth in the centrality of the media in culture – are developed further in the next section in relation to their bearing upon the development of monarchy in the media age.

Meanwhile, it is worth completing the claim that modernity, though it may have been in some sense displaced, has not 'stopped'. There are still, as we shall see, many aspects of contemporary society for which we shall require to invoke the presence of 'modern' forces. Indeed, this book will make something of our belief that 'postmodernization' may well have taken place at different rates in the different countries whose monarchies are our concern. In the sense we will be using it here, 'postmodernity' does not mean a separate new historical phase 'after' modernity, but rather a new phase continuous with modernity and running alongside what remain of modern forces in their attenuated form. We will not take issue with any readers who refuse the term 'postmodern' altogether. Some commentators have preferred to see the current epoch as a phase of 'late modernity'. If it is, then it is a modernity greatly changed. What is important is that we are able to perceive the growth of new and central features of society and culture since the 1960s, whatever we call them.

In fact the idea that there are often long transitional zones between overlapping historical periods is merely a commonplace. The surprise is that a number of anglophone commentators since the late 1980s have written as though the postmodern period had suddenly and uncomplicatedly just 'arrived', a tendency satirized by Charles Jencks in his ironic assertion that postmodernity began on 'July 15, 1972 at 3.32 pm' (Jencks, 1991: 23) which is when the Pruitt-Igoe apartment blocks in St Louis, Missouri – housing designed in 1951 which had failed its inhabitants – were dynamited; this was 'the death of modern architecture' (for a particularly useful history of usages of the term 'postmodern' and associated forms, see Rose, 1991).

Historians seldom oversimplify social and cultural transitions except in a cause. Fernand Braudel, rigorously avoiding simplistic thinking about the origins of the modern, records that a 'bourgeois of Reims' has noted in his diary, in 1632, that his grandfather wants a particular marriage for him, yet, says the grandson, 'it's not my grandfather who is getting married, it's me'. Braudel asks:

> Should we think that this is a language new for the time, the 'modern' attitude of a man of the seventeenth century? Or is it simply that of a man who, having been born in Champagne, enjoyed a certain traditional independence within the family?
>
> (Braudel, 1986: 109)

Commentators looking elsewhere, for example in literary sources, for historical evidence of 'modern' perceptions in culture, might in practice find it (like Marshall Berman) in attitudes to the modern phenomenon of the city in the second half of the nineteenth century in France or Russia (Berman, 1983). But in Britain, which industrialized early, Raymond Williams convincingly finds similar attitudes as early as Wordsworth's *Prelude*, begun in 1798 and finished in 1805 (Williams, 1985: 13–24). This evidence warns us to be alert to the complications of uneven development, in both modern and postmodern contexts (similar complexities of argument surround 'postmodernism' in the literary and visual arts).

In the same spirit, we might say that if Princess Diana may have been in some sense a 'postmodern phenomenon', then (even if proven) that does not at all necessarily imply that Princess Stephanie of Monaco – of a country with an entirely different history – represents a similar instance. It certainly does not mean that Princess Stephanie's mother, Grace Kelly, a personality arguably better understood as 'modern', can plausibly be presented as a prefigurement of Diana, nor that the Spanish royal family, to take another example, has been significantly postmodernized. Recent Spanish political history is remarkably different from Britain's and the countries' economic histories are different too.

Speaking (at the end of the 1980s) of the phenomenon of modernity, Fredric Jameson notes 'how differently the various academic disciplines, as well as the various national traditions, have framed it':

> ' "Modernism" has come only recently to France, "modernity" only recently to us, "modernization" belongs to the sociologists, Spanish has two separate words for the artis-

tic movements ("modernismo" and "vanguardismo"), etc. A comparative lexicon would be a four- or five-dimensional affair, registering the chronological appearance of these terms in the various language groups, while recording the uneven development observable between them.

(Jameson, 1991)

'Uneven development' in our argument about monarchy is a trait also of the modern and the postmodern as real processes in the overlapping domains of the world – economic, social, cultural, political, psychological – which they have (unevenly) colonized (Harvey, 2000: 53–94). Jameson's writing about postmodernity has made a feature of problematizing the relationship between the modern and the postmodern.

However, Charles Jencks for his part opines that:

the Marxist critics, such as Fredric Jameson and David Harvey, are a little hasty in calling our condition post-modern when, if the periodisation is going to be made in their terms, it might be more consistently termed Late-Modern (to correspond with their characterisation of the economic base as Late-Capitalist). Further confusion arises from equating the post-modern condition with the various post-modern movements, as if there were a total world system and culture.

(1992: 13)

Andreas Huyssen, speaking of 'uneven development', and focusing on cultural movements, argues that:

...the global view which sees the 1960s as part of the modern movement extending from Manet and Baudelaire if not from romanticism, to the present is not able to account for the specifically American character of postmodernism. After all, the term accrued its emphatic connotations in the United States; not in Europe. I would even claim that it could not have been invented in Europe at the time. For a variety of reasons, it would not have made any sense there.........West Germany was trying to reclaim a civilized modernity and to find a cultural identity tuned to international modernism which would make others forget Germany's past as predator and pariah of the modern world.....In the context of French intellectual life, the term 'postmodernism' was simply not around in the 1960s, and even today it does not seem to imply a major break with modernism as it does in the US.

(Huyssen, 1992: 48–49)

In Chapter 7, we analyse Norwegian press commentary on the relationship between the crown prince Haakon and his controversial bride-to-be (as she then was) Mette-Marit, overtly framed within references to the postmodernization of culture. When the prince confirmed the relationship, as we shall see, *Dagbladet* of 13 May 2000 carried an editorial entitled 'Postmodern monarchy' where the author argued that:

A modern monarchy must at regular intervals seek new legitimacy by showing that it has value for society. This is not easy to do at a time when political debate is subdued to the point of silence, all political views are moving towards the centre and ideologies have died out … in the long run it's doubtful if [the monarchy] can be sustained as a weekly-magazine monarchy.

In an article on 4 April 2001 calling for a move towards a presidency, the same newspaper wrote 'we are living in a postmodern era where mystique and the irrational have a new place in people's philosophy'. Even when the term 'postmodern' was not expressly used, it was frequently implicit in the debate. Thus *Dagbladet* on 15 April 2000 saw the prince's relationship as constituting:

the beginning of a comprehensive modernisation of the monarchy where openness, close-ness to the people and a strong social commitment are important elements. But it can also be the beginning of the end because the throne is increasingly experienced as a piece of furniture from IKEA.

We analyse in Chapter 7 an extraordinary article on the Norwegian engagement which explicitly constructs the imminent royal wedding as part of a consumer and media landscape from which it is indistinguishable, like fact and fiction themselves. As Norwegian society *postmodernizes* there are increasing calls from broadly left-wing sources for a *modernization* of the monarchy.

In Chapter 5 we note how, in parallel to the manner that the current king has been consistently constructed in Spain as the architect of the previous transition from 'pre-modernity' to modernity, his son is now being constructed as the key to a new transition from the modern to the postmodern.

Writers such as Jean-François Lyotard have gone so far as to suggest that the postmodern may be only a phase of the modern, or as Lyotard more audaciously suggested in the 1980s, a prerequisite for the renewal of the modern (Lyotard, 1984: 71–82): while Jameson's fundamental proposition that capitalism is at a 'late stage' has itself been open to question.

Rather than take an either/or approach to the matter of choosing to believe or disbelieve in a wholesale process of postmodernization since the 1960s it may be possible to recognize, first, that if the transitional period under such often fierce debate has been merely around twenty or thirty years, then by the standards of some transitional periods in history this would be the blink of an eye. To insist that the period 1974 (say) until the present was 'postmodern' in any straightforward sense probably ought to seem absurd – though it has not prevented many arguments being offered in such a spirit.

A final example of the need for flexibility is provided by the early publication of Daniel Boorstin's work on celebrity and 'pseudo-events', both of which are of much relevance in this study. Was Diana's funeral, as hysterically constructed by the British media, a pseudo-event? Boorstin published *The Image: A Guide to Pseudo-Events in America* in 1961, which is early in relation to the appearance of parallel French post-structuralist writing, though there is early work by, among others, Foucault around this period, as well as the deconstructive psychiatric writing of R. D. Laing (of course Pop Art had a 'deconstructive' dimension too). We examine some of Boorstin's ideas on celebrity in the Conclusion. He is one of many practitioners in a variety of domains of cultural production – such as Warhol in the visual and musical arts – who are hinge figures between the increasingly attenuated modernity of the 1950s and the postmodern world of the mid-to-late 1970s.

The notion of the 'postmodern' is perhaps best grasped as a transitional phase of the modern – whether on its way to extinction or renewal – in which the modern is sufficiently altered as to require the addition of a new conceptual range to help us grasp it. As Jameson says:

> I occasionally get just as tired of the slogan "postmodern" as anyone else, but when I am tempted to regret my complicity with it, to deplore its misuses and its notoriety, and to conclude with some reluctance that it raises more problems than it solves, I find myself pausing to wonder whether any other concept can dramatize the issues in quite so effective and economical a fashion.

(1991: 418)

'Double-coding' of the modern and postmodern: a concrete explanation

For the benefit of readers whose familiarity with postmodernism theory is limited, this short explanation of a possible plural approach to contemporary culture focuses on the architectural field, where much of the conceptual material of 'postmodernism theory' was developed. Writers on architecture and urban design were innovators of the theorization of postmodern culture. In this short section we are going to propose a plural approach to reading culture, which we thereafter apply to the phenomenon of monarchy. We will then indicate how these ideas can be used in understanding culture generally and monarchy in particular.

If this illustration of how culture can be simultaneously 'modern' and 'postmodern' is helpful, then perhaps our readers will forgive us if we concentrate – for fewer than a dozen paragraphs – on what for this book is an architectural metaphor for monarchy, the more thoroughly to understand the latter.

Arguing about modern and postmodern characteristics in culture

The difficulty of reaching agreement over attributions of 'modern' or 'postmodern' traits has been seen in fierce architectural debate, none more so than over John Portman's Bonaventure Hotel in Los Angeles, which opened in 1977, and was the material focus of some of Fredric Jameson's early theorization of the postmodern in his very influential *New Left Review* article of 1984, in turn the basis for the later developed argument (Jameson, 1991). In an important passage of this article, Jameson reports on the interior space of the Bonaventure, in which the author (at a conference) has found himself lost. This is a widespread problem in the hotel and Jameson points out how shops in the complex close down because potential customers can't find their way back to them. For Jameson this becomes a new kind of space, literally (though he also sees it as a metaphor for a new space of invisible global capitalism). But other commentators responded to his article by arguing that the Bonaventure wasn't a postmodern building at all.

It has been enlisted, like other buildings, by proponents of arguments about when and where architecture is or is not postmodern; or high tech; or late modern. There have even been compromises suggested with respect to the Bonaventure that it is 'modern' on the outside and 'postmodern' on the inside. It will be plain that less physical embodiments of culture – like monarchy – may present an even tougher case.

But Charles Jencks arrived some time ago at an ingenious and flexible solution for reading buildings plurally. *Double-coding* (Jencks, 1991: 12) is proposed by Jencks in the 1970s to explain how buildings at certain historical periods have accommodated plural tastes and interpretations. Jencks points out that:

> the primary strategy architects have created to articulate the pluralism of culture is that of double-coding: mixing their own professional tastes and technical skills with those of their ultimate clients – the inhabitants. Double-coding exists at many levels and has done so in several periods: it may be an ancient temple which mixes abstract geometry and represen-tational sculpture, high and low art.
>
> (1991:12)

In fact the idea is broadened elsewhere in Jencks's work precisely in such a manner as to suggest its possible use beyond the domain of architecture:

> "I term Post-Modernism that paradoxical dualism, or double-coding, which its hybrid name entails: the continuation of Modernism and its transcendence" (1989: 10).

It has been suggested (Blain and O'Donnell, 1997; 1999) that this conception may be fruitfully extended into other forms of cultural analysis, including the field of political culture, where the dual characteristics appear not as the intention of any cultural producer, but as the inevitable result of overlap typical of a transitional period in history.

There might initially appear to be an awkward distance between this idea of 'double-coding' in architecture, and the broader definition which sees postmodernism, in culture as a whole, as 'the continuation of modernism and its transcendence'. It might seem yet further to the stage to which we wish to develop it, to the concepts of modernity and postmodernity as *historical periods* (which are of course larger categories than cultural styles within them such as modernism and postmodernism): that is, *postmodernity as the continuation of modernity and its transcendence.*

But in neither case is the distance too far, in fact. Jencks illustrates the growth of architectural *hybridity* (1991: 107), the characteristic which for him in fact makes architecture postmodern, now widely recognized as a central postmodern trait.

It is true that Jencks's specific architectural account of 'double-coding' will not directly help us with the postmodernization of economics, or the phenomenon of globalization.

But what we are appropriating from Jencks is a *structural principle*. The 'postmodernized' economic world does indeed display ongoing modern characteristics transcended by postmodern traits – we will see this plainly in the dual functioning of figures such as Princess Diana or King Juan Carlos.

It is therefore with this theoretical background in mind that we refer to postmodernity *as the continuation of modernity and its transcendence*.

This helps illuminate, to take one example, how royalty might conceivably be two apparently contradictory things, post-ideological, but also still ideological and political too. When we turn to consider how royal families are constructed by the mass media we encounter the possibility that their functioning is in large part 'post-ideological', in other words, it belongs to that phase of postmodernization in which politics is drained of much of its meaning, albeit differentially, in the developed world. We might not see in post-1970s media discourse about royal families much ideological intent at all, perceiving royalty only as media *product*; belonging thereby to that 'post-significatory' stage of media culture identified at the start of the 1980s by Jean Baudrillard, in which the ideological debates of the 1970s about power or hegemony are irrelevant, in a world now depoliticized, shorn of the previous underpinning of symbolic systems.

The Diana myth, and what in the new century is becoming the William myth, both exhibit strong symptoms of the postmodernized world. In that light, questions about 'what the media coverage means' begin to seem pointless, since so obviously it means only one thing, profit for media producers, otherwise mere sound and fury. It may come to appear solely an economic matter, not a political matter at all, nor even one carrying much symbolic significance.

And if a phenomenon belongs to the post-political, post-ideological, post-significatory world of postmodernity (might go the argument) then it is not possible to stitch it back into a theory about the world of politics, the modern world.

To avoid this either/or approach (which seems to us ahistorical) we find it necessary to deploy the dual model. Without pretending that the foregoing developments have not occurred (an option even yet sometimes exercised in the social sciences) we can nonetheless deal with the obvious fact that monarchic institutions and royal houses are ideological and political phenomena too – so much so in parts of Europe that their postmodernization is still at an early stage.

Various political and ideological propositions still asserted about monarchies are:
- that they are obstructive, obsolete fragments of an older order who interfere with the fullest realization of a citizens' democracy (can arise in more than one country)
- that they are a minor but worth-preserving extra layer of constitutional protection of democracy (Britain, diminishing)
- that their specific national form is a signal of a modern political democracy, or at least worth debating as a changing index thereof (Spain, The Netherlands, Belgium, Norway)
- that they are a truly significant safeguard of democratic rights (Spain)

Structurally in a sense these are the same proposition: *monarchy is politically important.*

What we need 'double-coding' for is to preserve this sense of monarchy alongside the foregoing, 'post-ideological' interpretation.

This 'double-coding' is not just about 'decoding' either, it is about 'encoding' too. Since – speaking, say, of the princes William or Harry in Britain – their construction as media-cultural phenomena has occurred in a world characterized by modern and postmodern processes, they must be 'decoded' plurally too.

The 'postmodernization' of royalty?

When Harvey talks of 'the relatively stable aesthetic of Fordist modernism' (Harvey, 1989: 156) he refers to the existence of a society and culture (and a psychology and aesthetics) produced by a production-orientated society, one phase of whose origins lie in Henry Ford's version of mass production techniques initiated at Dearborn, Michigan, in 1914. The society and culture based on mass production developed into its most typical form in the wake of the Second World War and the signs of change were not generally apparent until well into the 1960s. The year of crisis, however, was 1973. Looked at from a perspective accommodating Western Europe, North America and Japan, economic historians have characterized the later part of this period (1965–1973) as one in which the weakness identified by Harvey as 'rigidity' (in production, capital investment, labour practices, state commitments) compounded other problems (such as saturation of internal markets and rising inflation) to create a dangerous state of affairs which saw in 1973 a crash in property markets across the world; which was also hit by severe ill effects from oil price increases, and embargo, as a consequence of the Arab-Israeli war. If, to simplify matters, the USA and countries in Europe and elsewhere could no longer support their economies merely by large-scale production of white goods for kitchens, and motor cars, then among the other implications of such a state of affairs was the need for new forms of consumption.

Royal families from this time on will appeal for privacy in vain if they happen to live in countries where they are attractive commodities in the context of the growing media industries.

Many writers on postmodernity have seen the increasing emphasis on consumption as the key aspect of postmodern society and culture. When production is no longer the chief goal of developed societies – because producing is not a problem, as it was in the thinking, for example, of Henry Ford – then the problem becomes redefined as the need to create consumption (Baudrillard, 1993). 'Flexible accumulation' is 'characterized by the emergence of entirely new sectors of production, new ways of providing financial services, new markets, and, above all, greatly intensified rates of commercial, technological, and organizational innovation': Harvey further notes that 'the half-life of a typical Fordist product was, for example, from five to seven years' (1989: 156) but that by the end of the 1980s the half-life of 'thoughtware' industries products such as video games and computer software programmes, has dipped below eighteen months.

In other words, vast new ranges of goods and services require to be developed from the early 1970s, a number of these products and services being characterized by very short time-spans in their marketability (we may have a useful lever here with which later to try to approach the difference between Diana and Madonna, or David Beckham and Prince William).

Of the concomitants of this new round of economic activity, 'mediatization' is probably itself an instance. Despite growth in the colonization of culture by media culture even in the 1960s (and arguably well before), both the range and intensification of the process take large steps from the 1970s and against the post-1973 backdrop of a shift from the production of goods to services. Mediatization, though, is only one of the post-1973 developments which will shed light on our subject.

Fredric Jameson (1991: 48) discusses the sense in which 'everything in our social life – from economic value and state power to practices and to the very structure of the psyche itself – can be said to have become "cultural" in some original and yet untheorized sense'. The idea is of a growth in culture, in some sense a filling of social space by more and more culture. We will require to consider several features of contemporary responses to royalty in this light; such as the massive growth in public consumption of celebrity, the growth of public emotion, new 'Latin' habits of marking death in Britain, and other indexes of 'culturalization'. This last in turn makes consumption, and media consumption, more salient in our lives.

This involves a process through which more and more of our lives become 'cultural', while more and more of that culture is 'media culture'. Much of that, instead of being 'lived', is merely, from this point of view, 'consumed' as a range of commodities.

And beside 'mediatization' and 'culturalization' let us add 'aestheticization'. A number of countries have seen the development and rapid growth of innumerable 'lifestyle' and 'makeover' television shows, magazines, press features and supplements, and websites devoted to activities associated with aesthetic process, alongside the ever greater interpenetration of design and fashion consciousness and general culture. This implies the colonization of more and more of the population by forms of aesthetic consciousness; along with intensification, at an individual level, of aesthetic awareness.

The popularity of royal family members becomes closely bound up with aesthetic success. The extent to which Diana's media-domination was a specifically aesthetic triumph (to triumph over Charles's suits and Anne's hair was not in itself the main challenge) has probably been underestimated.

More importantly, 'consuming' royalty as a media product becomes, as the 1980s and 1990s unfold, more and more obviously bound up with a growth in public appetite for *sensation*, which reaches an apparently pathological stage with the death and funeral of Princess Diana, and which as a phenomenon we consider below in several contexts.

We note in Chapter 8 how the imminent Dutch royal wedding is merchandised in 2001, with condom manufacturers Durex publishing a full-page advertisement in a number of dailies on 1 April, describing itself as 'likely supplier to the court', the lottery producing adverts of a frog wearing a crown with the words 'kiss here' printed over its mouth, and a sufficient number of products and services being marketed that a prize – the Golden Crown – is organized for the most creative and humorous advert relating to the royal engagement and wedding.

To sum up these features of the world after 1973: alongside more 'flexible accumulation', necessitated by severe recession partly caused by system rigidity, develops

- more culture, more of which is
- media culture, which helps to lead to
- new forms of aestheticization and sensation-seeking, all of which lead to:
- more consumption

We have spoken of 'aestheticization' but one might expect a very sharp rebuttal of that claim from some observers, mindful that precisely what was claimed of media culture in the 1990s, and in its own restricted code, was that it was 'dumbing down'. However, although judgements on what constitutes aesthetic activity are still (especially in the UK) produced in part by values associated with demographic factors like class, the terrain on which all such judgements are offered has changed almost beyond recognition in the last thirty to forty years. The clear gap between 'high culture' and the 'popular' is celebratedly narrowed in the 1960s by The Beatles, by Andy Warhol and David Hockney and many another cultural producers. This is in part understandable as the rehabilitation of popular taste.

Popular culture moves irresistibly toward the centre ground of culture generally from as early as the 1950s, invading not just the concert hall and the quality newspaper but the art film and the museum. By the 1990s, we find that pop groups like the Spice Girls celebrate, above all, *ordinariness*, and, especially in the British context, working-class ordinariness; in marked distinction to the almost extraterrestrial aloofness of pop figures like Michael Jackson a decade earlier, as well as royal families, who thereby come under pressure to popularize. This dynamic leads among other formulations to Tony Blair's 'people's princess' characterization of Diana: and among other consequences to the really very misplaced depiction of Diana as 'ordinary' compared to the rest of the monarchy.

This celebration of the ordinary becomes a prime economic weapon in the hands of the media in Britain, providing us not only with an explanation for a range of attitudes marshalled in the public construction of royalty, but also an analytical lever with which to raise the matter of differences between Britain, and European countries where ordinariness may be demanded of current royalty.

So, the 'aestheticization' of the postmodern era has to be reconceived in the popular context (it is not an aesthetic advance of which the Frankfurt School or the high modern élites would have approved, indeed arguably it represents the realization of their worst nightmares). Enhanced aesthetic awareness in the 1980s and 1990s is easily dismissed as a rise in nothing other than sensationism. But in fact craving for sensation, as we will see, is only part of the development. From a less élitist perspective there is much to celebrate in new forms of aesthetic consciousness (beyond our concerns here). We merely note how the uneven growth of popular/populist taste impacts on royal families and issues of monarchy.

In a way strangely, this may not at all be associated with populism in political consciousness. Indeed we will find in the UK, particularly, a rather extraordinary conjuncture of the presence of populist taste, in public and media culture, with a marked absence of apparent desire to subvert the political order.

Of course, the very group of industries most obviously associated with these new expansions of (originally) economic activities, and characterized by very rapid growth, is the media sector. It is in the wake of the 1973 world recession that we might quite logically expect to see entirely new kinds of intensification in that older process, the manufacture of celebrity. We might, in that case, not be at all surprised to find new developments in the manufacture of royal celebrity.

The phenomenon of the film star had been quite literally invented by Carl Laemmle in 1910, four years before Henry Ford started making cars at Dearborn. It is often true of the postmodern phase that its characteristics can be found in earlier periods. Media stardom belongs to that category. What is distinctive about the postmodern phase, in such instances, is the intensification, centralization and augmented importance of these traits.

This is true likewise of globalization in its postmodern sense, a phenomenon with a much older history; interpenetration of cultures has always taken place. The new round of globalization inaugurated by factors such as the space race of the 1950s and 1960s, and also by developments in media technology and transportation in the 1960s, is greatly intensified after 1973 as an increasingly trans-national capitalism uses new forms of technology to bypass and subordinate the previously sovereign nation state (even the United States) and to diminish it in the minds of its inhabitants, likewise. During the 1970s the world becomes very much larger than the state. We will argue that this needs to be clearly understood in an enquiry into the nature of monarchy. And something else has meanwhile taken place, as it were 'inside' the state, which likewise helps to alter the relationship between national 'citizens', the state, and the world.

'Representation crisis', sovereignty – and sovereigns

Dick Hebdige speaks at the end of the 1980s of a 'crisis of representation' having grown in Europe between the end of the Second World War and 1968, seen in part as 'the retreat from the first person plural "We" – the characteristic mode of address of the voice of liberation during the heroic age of the great bourgeois revolutions' (1988:187). We return shortly to the question of who 'we' are, so to speak, in two brief introductory case studies focusing on a specimen eulogy to the British Queen Mother on her one hundredth birthday; and also on an extract from the funeral coverage of Diana.

Because if there has indeed been a retreat from an assured sense of collective identity, there are nonetheless sections of the media very keen to reassert it. Attitudes toward royalty are a central part of the ideological production of the British media (in particular): and it is our intention to retain a vigorous hold, in these analyses, of the concept of ideology, albeit in a postmodern environment in which it has become unfashionable.

Additionally, we select these two British royal figures as initial examples since the nature of their myths as media creations vividly illustrates the elements of 'constructedness' in royal accounts. This is true individually but even more so if we consider their relationship. They were seemingly the two most popular British royal figures of the late twentieth century. But – very awkwardly – they had a poor personal relationship whose distance was caused by conflictual understandings of the royal function. One was an embodiment of traditional monarchic values and the other (supposedly) a challenge to them. Yet the media preferred to deal with this difficulty by omission (two such lovable and admirable royals should have got on together).

Hebdige notes the political disenchantment after 1968 arising, among other factors, from events such as the Hungary invasion of 1956. In a world now already sufficiently globalized for cross-national influences to be rapid, we might add to Hebdige's examples developing American political disaffection from the 1960s onward caused by assassinations (of John Kennedy in 1963, of Malcolm X in 1965, of Bobby Kennedy and Martin Luther King in1968); by the Vietnam war and the Kent State killings in 1970; by Watergate. The symbolic meaning of the United States for cultures like Britain and France was also altered, adding to a widespread sense of an inadequacy of representative systems. It was no accident that Britain like other cultures in the late 1960s had to import symbolically a political figure like Che Guevara, or that so many were happy to display, with whatever sense of irony, their copies of Mao Tse-tung's *Little Red Book*. (To balance this version of events, we need to acknowledge that there were other demographic groups in Britain in the 1960s more likely to glorify the Queen Mum or the Duchess of Kent. But disaffection was a powerful new trend.)

The extent to which political models were losing their credibility after the 1970s is expressed by Jean Baudrillard in his travelogue *America*, in which, referring to the age of Ronald Reagan, he notes that 'governing today means giving acceptable signs of credibility': 'political weaknesses or stupidity', he notes, 'are of no importance' (Baudrillard, 1989: 109).

But there is a second strand of intention in Hebdige's phrase ('representation crisis').This highlights the Nietzsche revival sparked off a decade or so after the end of WW2 in the work of Foucault and others, and which becomes an important aspect of political thinking in the 1970s and 1980s.

Hebdige quotes Jean-Luc Godard's Nietzschean caveat that 'in every image we must ask who speaks'. The idea that symbolic activity is always in someone's interests was not new even in Nietzsche (if it has any modern originator it is Giambattista Vico in his early eighteenth century *Scienza Nuova*) but it is arguably new, like other postmodern phenomena, when it becomes a central principle of culture.

There is nowadays a widespread state of affairs in which distrust, disbelief, disenchantment, dislike, are reflex actions rather than exceptional responses when society is faced with the blandishments of organized politics. Worse still, perhaps, is frivolousness: many American political commentators believed by 2000 that male electors had voted for George Bush because he was a 'nicer guy to have a drink with' than Al Gore. Many among the young in several countries increasingly ignore party politics entirely. In Europe, a royal family, whether it is a family in some sense close to the centre of a nation's attention, like the British and Spanish royal families, or further toward the peripheries, like the royal houses of Scandinavia, become particularly interesting in these circumstances. Does a draining away of meaning from political parties and institutions, and a loss of belief in social amelioration generally, help us in part to understand the apparent emotional investment in a Diana or Prince William figure?

Meanwhile it is important to remember the loss specifically of national sovereignty, a process which accelerates so rapidly that by the 1980s the European nation state has become something of a shadow of itself fifty or a hundred years earlier. In part the European Union becomes justified in debate after the 1980s chiefly on the grounds that it is large enough to reassert a sovereignty unattainable at national level.

Hard on the heels of any questions about royal families amidst these processes is another, which is the issue of how *general* the loss of belief in traditional centralized political processes really is. It is not so difficult to see it at work in the Britain or the United States of the last twenty years and more. But we have already raised the probability that postmodern development has been uneven, like modern development. In a country like Spain, which has recent memories of what it is like to be deprived of democratic rights, and whose monarchy, as will be seen, has 'representative' functions in more than one sense different from Britain's royal family, it will be too glib to speak of 'representation crisis' as though this were the same phenomenon across the developed world.

In the next section of this introduction we consider the general question of 'constructedness' in media accounts of monarchy by briefly looking at one or two moments of Diana's funeral.

Meanwhile let us illustrate some of the issues in the foregoing discussion. Large sections of the British media have been unmoved (not very surprisingly!) by the urgings of post-structuralists since the 1960s to abandon faith in the confident subject of post-Cartesian philosophy – including its plural version. Abandon that old-fashioned collective 'we', and sales slide, and ideology goes out the window – not likely in the *Daily Mail*.

'We' and the Queen Mother: constructing accounts of British monarchy

'We' still exists as a central category in many British media accounts of royalty, in a society which – in this construction – is bafflingly unafflicted by the complications of ethnicity and multi-culturalism, the fractures of intra-British nationalisms, gender conflict, of misunderstandings of age, of ever steeper gulfs between rich and poor, of the growth of a large indigenous underclass, of the growing mutual miscomprehension between country and city – and other clear signals that no collective subject can be found in the United Kingdom of the twenty-first century, not even royal subjects.

When it was the Queen Mother's one hundredth birthday none of this mattered.

'Why We Love Her', proclaims A. N. Wilson (*Daily Mail*, 4 August 2000). It is true that a conservative columnist writing in the *Daily Mail* must do so at least partially in a reflexive spirit, so that we should be careful when characterizing the form of exchange taking place between newspaper and reader. That is to say, London newspapers like the *Daily Telegraph* and the *Mail* are aware of themselves as right-wing newspapers espousing traditional values. Feature writers, leader writers and columnists address a readership with known demographic characteristics. 'Why We Love Her' is probably not conceivable in *The Guardian*, in the sense that such a headline would puzzle its readers, who might suspect satirical intent, though, as will become apparent, the British press may be more similar than differentiated in their overall approbation of the British monarchy, even if there is variation in the terms of that endorsement.

But if Wilson is in any sense striking a traditionalist pose here it is different in degree rather than kind from the position taken by many other British media commentators, who persistently retrieve a respectful subject position with regard to the monarchy, 'retrieve' it in the sense that they must be positive about the royal family, in recent years, in the midst of potentially dissenting voices (though that 'dissent' is a very relative matter). If all that is happening between Wilson and the readers of the *Daily Mail* is a kind of sub-cognitive exchange of comforting prejudice, then it is still significant that it is this kind of exchange of prejudice and not any other kind. The position Wilson adopts is broadly, as a subject position, of a piece with, for example, the dress code adopted by royal correspondents on television. If Wilson has his twinset and pearls on here, he is only conforming to what in most of the British media is the requisite fashion code (even if some occasionally allow themselves some mildly discordant festoon – a burgundy tie worn by a TV presenter caused trouble at the passing of the Queen Mother, 20 months after Wilson's piece).

'Today is a day of days', he begins biblically, 'We celebrate someone, and something, unique and without parallel'. The Queen Mother is 'a remarkable human being' with 'prodigious reserves of charm', and 'an unparalleled ability to cheer people up'. Alas, 'it would not be Britain if the whingers and killjoys were not allowed their voice'. Wilson raises a variety of criticisms of the Queen Mother put by the 'killjoys', some of whom are apparently 'republicans who pose as serious grown-ups' in order to deride the 'babyish' qualities of the 'popular news outlets' when they dwell on royal matters. (He does not indicate where he has managed to find these republicans in Britain.) The lines of attack by killjoys are identified as (1) disapproval of royal stories pushing serious issues out of the headlines; (2) criticism of the Queen Mother's hedonistic lifestyle; and (3) dislike of the Queen Mother's behind-the-scenes manipulativeness. These must presumably be very weakly founded criticisms because Wilson does not deign to answer the first two (even though royal stories do push important matters out of the news headlines in Britain all the time, as he admits later; and the Queen Mother's extravagance is later acknowledged). He answers the third criticism by referring to accusations dating back to 1936 (this avoids more recent questions surrounding the Queen Mother's frosty relationship with Diana).

But Wilson also reproduces in his eulogy an entire ideological cluster, as do most accounts of the monarchy and royal family.

First, what may appear to be a minor observation; he ends his piece by noting that 'all decent British people today give three loud cheers', which rather puts the rest of us in our place, a process John Thompson refers to as 'fragmentation', an ideological strategy used alongside 'unification' (Thompson, 1990: 59–73). Wilson also notes how the Queen Mother 'thoroughly enjoyed being the Queen of England', further problematizing the 'we' of the heading, given the Queen Mother's Scottish identity.

Wilson argues, interestingly, that 'unlike other popular public figures, whether royal or political', the Queen Mother produces no 'cult of personality' since she never gives interviews and since biographies of her are 'largely fiction'. Tom Nairn, writing in the late 1980s before exposure to royal interviews was quite as great as it has latterly become, observes that:

> What the theatre of Royal obsession sustains is not (real) personality, therefore, in the ordinary sense of individuality or idiosyncracy. It projects perfectly *abstract* ideas of 'personality', which are received and revered as some kind of emblem. (1988: 48)

But in fact as media coverage of royal lives has become more detailed and assembles some sort of serial consistency with respect to the behaviours of a Diana, a Fergie or a Sophie, or of their spouses; and as more and more of royal personality is observed talking in front of, or directly to camera, or even presenting TV programmes – the abstraction takes on concrete structure. Then again, some might take issue with Nairn even on the royal facts of the matter as known in the 1980s, given that concrete facts about personality (of, say, Victoria; her son Edward; or Edward VIII) can be argued to have emerged over time. Complicating the question is the matter of the extent to which public figures knowingly construct personae.

If the Queen Mother has indeed avoided interviews throughout her life, the 'interloper' Diana, in having established a fleshed-out, if shapely, television and press personality is not however necessarily 'knowable' to her 'fans' of the 1980s and 1990s, since she, as in the instance of other royal personalities, may be seen as complicit in forms of personality fabrication with the expert myth-creators of the media.

(Besides, we need to consider the extent to which, in the first place, abstract ideas of personality may or may not have been characteristic of many forms of stardom.)

Wilson proceeds rapidly to enfold Europe in his ideological strictures. He suggests that the Horse Guards parade to celebrate the Queen Mother's one hundredth birthday is really a sort of anti-parade, in that, having started with the 'splendid pageantry of Parry's "I Was Glad"', it turns into a 'village parade, with corgis, figures from Dad's Army and the rest'. This strained observation then engenders the thought in the columnist that the anti-parade has been completely unlike the 'sinister pomps' which were the birthday parades of Stalin, Hitler 'or even of General Franco'. The British underwent the same hardships as other nations in the 1930s, Wilson observes, but only the others reacted by subjecting themselves to 'monstrous regimes'. History has got rid of these 'monsters', but Britain has retained until the millennium the 'jolly, rather P. G. Wodehouse figure' (i.e. the Queen Mum) who – in Wilson's account – rescued the constitutional monarchy during the Abdication Crisis.

Europe has been reduced to its essential features (Stalin, Hitler, Franco) and Britain to its (the Queen Mother).

The constructed quality of the account, as with most such accounts, is very marked. For example, the Queen Mother, as already noted, frequently referred to as Scottish in London media accounts, here becomes a characteristically English, Wodehouse, figure and has been 'Queen of England'. Contradictions abound. The Queen Mother enjoys no 'cult of personality' – which is in a sense quite true, and which is considered further in chapters below – yet Wilson appeals throughout to a consensual agreement over her attractive personality traits.

While berating the Queen Mother's critics he acknowledges the accuracy of their criticisms, for example, they 'hint that they know the size of the old lady's overdraft'. In fact, in this formulation, Wilson is criticizing them for presumptuously pretending to know what only an insider would know (he is snobbishly dismissing their presumption).

Here we encounter a specific question about the 'knowability' of royalty, which is a question of the authenticity of sources; which can be illustrated further by a royal furore some eight months after Wilson's eulogy. A *Daily Telegraph* serialization of biographical material on Prince Philip, reported in the tabloids and broadcast media the next day – the *Daily Express* refers to it as 'a semi-authorised warts-and-all article' – leads to widespread repetition of the assertion that Prince Philip believes that Charles is 'unfit to be king' because he is 'light-weight', lacks dedication and discipline, and is 'precious' and 'extravagant' (*Telegraph* 22 May, 2001; *Express*, 23 May). As a consequence Charles is 'understood to be sad and upset that his father allowed his closest confidantes to speak about their difficult relationship' (*Daily Mail*, 23 May).

The authenticity of royal 'information' is frequently an unknown quantity, in this instance as in so many, making reference to 'sources close to Prince Philip' or the refusal of St James's Palace 'to be drawn', which is however offset by the statement that 'privately Charles was understood to be 'upset' and 'dismayed'' (*Express*). Over on the *Mail*, 'Charles has refused to let his office be drawn on the development' but 'is understood to be sad and upset'. The serialized work, referred to as 'a biography' and a '10,000 word biography' by the *Daily Mail*, is called an 'article' and a 'devastating report' by the *Express*, while BBC News Online (23 May) refers to it in quotes as a 'biography' and reports a 'Buckingham Palace spokeswoman' as retorting that 'the duke said no such thing. These remarks are made by a reporter and have been wrongly attributed to the duke'. The BBC observes that the journalist who wrote the piece had been 'said to have been given access to a number of high ranking courtiers'.

We might note in passing that both the *Express* and the *Mail* give banner front-page headlines to the story.

This particular royal storm produces a revealing moment on BBC's Breakfast News on the day after the *Telegraph* piece. Royal Correspondent Jennie Bond is questioned by an interviewer, Jeremy Bowen, who has a serious journalistic background, and is a wilfully unconventional television presenter given to placing colleagues in situations of mild embarrassment.

The Queen Mother has, it appears, always – right up to her one hundredth year – referred to her son-in-law Prince Philip as 'the Hun', which Bond admits has long been 'rumoured', though she is plainly very uncomfortable talking about it, not least, no doubt, because of potential collateral offence to viewers. Bowen presses her nonetheless, but seeing that she is not going to co-operate, he ends by asking rather maliciously, 'does she refer to him as 'the Hun' affectionately, then?' 'I don't know, *I don't know!*' exclaims Bond, and Bowen lets her off the hook.

'Not knowing' generally does not form part of the persona of specialist reporters and given the premium attached to something as certain as 'knowledge' about this distant and highly manipulative family, 'not knowing' is paradoxically both relatively likely, but also difficult to admit. In this case Bond very understandably wants to stop the conversation. Therefore even her statement that she 'doesn't know' is open to doubt. Perhaps she knows perfectly well and can't admit it. The moment dramatizes issues both of knowability and propriety, matters which form part of the interpretative context which has to be considered by media readers when judging royal 'facts'.

Only a handful of the British public, A. N. Wilson concludes in his article of the previous year, begrudge the Queen Mother 'the supposedly extravagant perks of lavish meals and bets placed on the gee-gees'. This slippage now acknowledges that she is, in fact, rather self-indulgent. The idiomatic 'gee-gees' shifts the tone to that of the complicit approval of fellow punters. The behaviour is no longer 'supposed' but acknowledged, nor is it seen as culpable: now it is only the act of condemning such behaviour as extravagance which is criticized.

Wilson invokes 'expensive' carpets (actually a mere £13,500) purchased for the Deputy Prime Minister John Prescott, as extenuating collateral – 'all people in public life cost money'. This is an explicitly party political jibe but its force, like all anti-Prescott jibes, derives from his working-class identity, John Prescott being a relatively rare working-class presence in the New Labour cabinet of 1997–2001 and thereafter, and the politician chosen by New Labour visibly to exemplify its Old Labour credentials. The subtextual meaning of this reference is that it is particularly absurd that a former marine cabin steward should have public money spent on him: whereas it is the Queen Mother's birthright.

As can be seen so far, that 'we' in the title is at best a limited collective, in this actually very divisive article.

But the really major contradiction in Wilson's account is one which exemplifies a habit so pervasive in media constructions of the British monarchy as to belong to its deep structure. We shall stay briefly with this article to introduce a much larger theme.

Negotiating British subjecthood: contingent loyalty and serial realignment
Wilson observes that the Queen Mother has 'enough charm for ten people' and comments that 'in her family' she sometimes 'has need of it'.

> At the recent opening gala of the Royal Opera House in London a whole contingent of the Royal Family entered the Royal Box. The entire house stood and clapped. Only the Queen Mother turned to acknowledge the applause with a wave and with her jolly smile.

On the one hand, Wilson seems to be saying that the rest of the royal party is charmless and bad mannered; yet we know he is pleased that the Queen Mother bothered to 'save' the institution of monarchy in 1936, and he has already berated 'republicans', so we know that his emphatic contrast is not intended to imply disapproval of the monarchy.

Yet if the Queen Mum's birthday parade was not a parade, but a jolly Wodehousian affair with corgis and pensioners, has something been elided in the trajectory of contrast in Wilson's article, which moves so swiftly from the Queen Mother, to Hitler and Stalin and their 'sinister pomps'? Is there nothing in between? Where would the rest of the British Royal Family be found on this spectrum from lovability to monstrosity – when parading, as they often do?

For although Her Majesty the Queen does not go in for 'sinister pomps', there is much ceremonial surrounding the British monarchy and indeed for many it appears to be a centrally identifying characteristic. One of the respondents in Billig's social psychological study of British people talking about the royal family (see below) ruminates thus on British pomps: 'I think that you realise at the time, even watching it on telly, that all that pomp and pageantry, probably you couldn't see, find, anywhere else in the world', to which his wife adds 'for definite, for absolute definite you couldn't' – her husband further observes that people 'come from all over the world just to see little brief snatches of it' (Billig, 1992: 38).

Wilson's distinction between the Queen Mother's kind of ceremonial and other kinds of ceremonial seems unintentionally to implicate the world's centre of pomp (Britain) but becomes displaced suddenly onto Hitler, Franco and Stalin, thereby leaving a very interesting gap in his logic which parallels the manner in which many journalists, in the Britain of the last twenty and more years, deal with an irrepressible recognition of the multiple failures of British society by displacing them onto Europe; much as the awfulness of English football supporters abroad can be conveniently blamed on the Belgian police or some other hapless continental agent.

More serious British commentators strike the balance between British and European pomp more accurately: 'the Scandinavian royals saw the trap and lowered their profile for survival. Ours have not been able to forswear their pomp', observes Peter Preston (*Guardian*, 18 June 2000). In fact 'pomp' is often used neutrally or admiringly by the media. For example, when South African president Thabo Mbeki made an official visit to the UK in June 2001, a BBC reporter referred to 'the full pomp of a state welcome' (1.00 News, 12 June 2001).

There is an unspoken criticism, in the praise lavished on the Queen Mother, of the behaviour of the rest of the family, and criticism which extends well beyond their undemonstrative behaviour at the Royal Opera House. (We will leave for the time being the extraordinary sociological fact, assuming that the columnist has not been exaggerating, that, in this age of 'classlessness' and 'loss of deference', 'the entire house stood and clapped'. This is of a piece with the casual way in which the media attest the existence around the royal family, as we have seen above, of apparently large numbers of 'courtiers', without this becoming especially salient as sociology, politics or anthropology).

It seems that at this moment in the royal box, the Queen Mother is lovable *structurally*, that is, she is lovable because of the unlovability of the rest of the family, though perhaps in the latter instance only at this moment. And here we have identified a central principle of the British media's account of royalty, which is that some elements of the royal balance sheet are always in credit with the media (the Queen Mother, despite difficulties with her bank, nearly always in this sense in credit) while others are in the red. Some are in general framed negatively (Prince Edward) and some usually framed positively (the Princess Royal) but journalists and editors play them off one against the other – and with no particular degree of ideological consistency, and not much loyalty. Potentially, the British royals can all change places. The basis for realignments of sympathy is usually contingent. On the occasion of A. N. Wilson's observations on the royal gala night, the rest of the family were a dour bunch, but of course they are capable individually, and even in subordinate groups, of immense charm, depending on which feature article, leader, or news report they are figuring in, and what are its purposes and contexts: for example Charles and his sons might be very charming on the slopes at Klosters while posing for a photo shoot.

The relational valorization of the Queen Mother in the A. N. Wilson piece will, in generic terms, that is, in its representativeness of a widespread journalistic trait, be obsolete by the end of the article, as by the end of all such articles. In general, the British press, which much more than television or radio creates space for this sort of evaluative coverage, does not require itself to be consistent in these judgements either from feature to feature, or, as will be seen, even inside the covers of one edition of a newspaper. This is particularly true of tabloid newspapers. (The *Mail*, though tabloid in format, is well upmarket of a newspaper such as the *Sun* and presents a relatively consistent ideological line for that and other reasons.)

Three main observations can be made about the UK tabloid press account of royalty. One is that accounts present little discursive consistency, either between newspapers nor even within newspapers, the latter neither from edition to edition nor even at times within editions. This leads to the second observation, namely that tabloid accounts of royalty are much more complex than may seem to the case. The third observation is that the inconsistency and complexity of these accounts are probably rather less important than the huge quantity of coverage which royalty receives. In fact, the vast quantity of newsprint produced on royalty stories, itself tends to become the chief meaning of newspaper coverage, and especially tabloid coverage: one could describe this chief meaning in various ways (we return to this in the conclusion) but at its simplest it is 'here is a topic which is of more importance to you/us than any other'.

The *Sun* (10 December 1992), on the morning after the Charles/Diana separation explicitly sets up the two as rivals in different camps, plainly sensing many a story in the months and years to come. It deploys a bizarre mixture of signifiers. The page one headline is 'THRONE ALONE', and this wordplay on film and television programme titles is continued by pages' 2–3 subheading 'Winner takes all', while the main pages' 2–3 heading is 'VICTORY FOR DI' with a calendar style subheading 'Dec 9: V-Di'.

Yet the leader adopts a tone of respectful sympathy: 'The whole nation will feel sympathy for Charles and Diana as they confirm what many of us have feared for so long....There will be concern for the children, William and Harry, who must try to understand at a tender age what many adults find difficult to comprehend'. Most of the leader – but we shall return to something else in this leader – adopts this tone, and it ends with 'There are no rights and wrongs when two hearts are broken'. That is on page 6.

On page 9, however, in marked contrast, the columnist Richard Littlejohn describes Charles as 'a weak, dismal, arrogant little man with a third-rate intellect' and Diana as 'a little gold-digger'.

A month or so later on the front page of the *Sun*, in the wake of the Camillagate revelations, we perceive, above the main headline, 'Another Royal scandal....How much more can WE take' – the WE stressed – while the *Daily Star* of the same day leads its page one with 'PALACE OF PORKIES: scandal of the royal cover-up'. So we should be clear, first of all, that it will be impossible to point to unitary positions on the question of royalty in the tabloid press.

But we have suggested already that the question of tabloid coverage is really very complex. In the Richard Littlejohn piece referred to, in the morning after the announcement of the separation, he refers to how Charles:

> took Diana and used her as breeding stock. Once she had delivered sons and heirs he dumped her. Yet all the time the palace publicity machine fed the myth that this really was a fairy-tale marriage. They were held up as the perfect couple, an example to the nation. When the newspapers began to discover that all was not well in the royal bedchamber it was dismissed as fiction. But the tabloids were right all along. Charles and Di were living a lie.

Instead of dwelling overmuch on the rich irony of the tabloid press blaming anyone other than the tabloid press for the dominance of the 'fairy-tale' motif – the phrase appears in descriptions of the marriage elsewhere in this very edition of the *Sun* – let us instead note the sense of reflexivity here. We referred earlier to the leader in this edition: it manages to propose that 'It is a shame that a sad day was cheapened by those who seek to blame all this on the Press'. This sentence is a breathtakingly inverted piece of logic, all the more expert because of its brevity, but the most significant aspect of these references, in the leader and the Littlejohn piece, is that the *Sun* and the tabloid press generally are introduced as a further 'character' in the royal narrative.

Five pages further on the *Sun* reproduces, in miniature, eighteen front pages between June and December 1992 dealing with the Charles and Diana marriage alone (there were more, which it does not reproduce here). Leaving aside any questions about the suitability of the tabloids' tone of self-righteousness, what is more interesting is the way in which the *relationship* between the tabloids and the Royal Family itself becomes a topic in royal coverage. In the Camillagate *Sun* there is a piece entitled 'THE *SUN* SENT CHARLES A FAX: How we got sucked into Royal war' about a piece which Charles apparently persuaded the newspaper to drop. The *Sun* is not alone in this self-aware posture during the period.

So in addition to serial realignments in loyalties to members of the Royal Family, we now observe the tabloid press as a further character in the narrative, with its own persona, here, of exaggerated self-righteousness.

While it is true that the press has a long history of self-reference, two other factors are at play here. First, at the time of the Dianagate and Camillagate revelations there were proposals afoot to protect privacy from the press: the tabloids were particularly glad to accuse leading politicians and the Royal Family of cheating and hypocrisy, after it emerged that some small part of their 'invasion' of royal privacy might have been royally inspired. The post-Camillagate *Sun* even carries a distinctly paranoid leader, 'Why today we gag ourselves', beginning 'The *Sun*, the paper which campaigns for your right to know, is in a bizarre position'. It suggests that someone is just waiting for it to publish what it knows about the tapes in order to pounce on it.

Leaving aside the question of whether or not the *Sun* had at this point any information to be discreet about, the interesting moment in the leader is where it agonizes:

> Why, then, are we gagging ourselves? Why this self-denial? Simple. We're worried that

we're being set up. Being given enough rope to hang ourselves. Wouldn't the Establishment just love that?

Across at the *Daily Star*, the leader on the same day says: 'Nobody could deny a serious rift between the heir and his future consort was of legitimate public interest. *Except the Establishment*. The marble-mouths, who hide their steel claws in velvet gloves, simply didn't want you to find out what – it is now clear – had been common knowledge for months in the snobby world of Royal circles and politics. *So they framed the newspapers*' (*Daily Star*, 13.1.93).

Several aims are being accomplished here. One is of course the traditional tabloid objective of pursuing the populist agenda of mass-market newspapers, and another, in this instance, is to pre-empt legal reforms. More significantly, though, both leaders seek to position their newspapers against something called the Establishment while they themselves are identified with the powerless: the *Star* is quite explicit at the end of the same leader: 'what a stark example of what could happen to the free flow of information if our masters DID get a tribunal to censor and censure us'. In Part Three we consider how to interpret this posture, which is a constant of tabloid self-reference, and how it relates to broad questions of political power.

Of course, diversity of opinion is a strength, and no doubt it is a compliment to a newspaper if it contains conflicting evaluations of dimensions or individuals within the extended royal family. But the serially inconsistent, rapidly shifting realignment and contradictory judgement which emerges from the British press on its royalty – just because of the scale of the coverage they receive and the enormous scale of the inconsistency and contradictoriness and incoherence produced – does raise inevitable questions about the kind of 'ideological' functioning of the press in this area of British life. A minimal degree of continuity and coherence is required for ideological functioning.

Why should this process of juxtaposition so inevitably occur between one royal and another, or between one group of royals and another?

First of all it seems that there may be at work some form of negotiation of subjecthood. In a culture in which serious republicanism is still not really a discoverable strand, the only measure short of absolute subjecthood is to appear to be critical of the Royal Family by expressing limited negative judgement (interpersonal judgement of course, as distinct from critique of the monarchic institution). By extending at the same time comparative approval to other dimensions or parties associated with the monarchy, it is possible to construct a simulacrum of a critical space while remaining monarchist. If as a journalist you are unsure of the critical mass of approbation or disapproval of the monarchy among the community whom you imagine to be your readers, this sort of hedging of bets is a good move. In some newspapers you may thereby avoid the danger of editorial censure.

Some members of the Family become fair game in this respect, Prince Edward and his hapless bride Sophie having been good for scapegoating at the turn of the century. As we shall see, Diana herself occupied such a role in the period before her death. This structural system of continual realignment is very flexible, and with only two or three actors, not all of whom need even be alive, it can – dramaturgically – become sustainingly complex.

The narrative demands made by the British media on the British royals are infinite and eternal. Given the indefinite run of their performance, and in so many theatres, every device for changes of emphasis in the finite script has to be seized. The formats of 'fairy tale' and 'soap opera' discussed below are, in the first form limited, and in the second, profligate with material (see in particular Chapter 4).

So, another reason for this process of intra-familial juxtaposition is to sub-cultivate small narrative plots, or to extrude limited narrative strands, by creating or building on existing counter-loyalties: generally to maximize the potential for interest of limited narrative material, on the principle that friction creates heat. As well as seeking to avoid the appearance of complete, abject, slavering subjecthood, British journalists also extend the narrative infinitely, which is after all their living. (This conflictual device takes its place among others, as will be seen; one of which is a kind of *serial amnesiac refiguration'* in which 'fairy tale' and 'soap opera' metaphors are endlessly recycled in contexts in which – were any longitudinal dimension retained – they would be instantly rejected as incoherent. However, as can be seen in Chapter 4 and elsewhere, this constructive approach is by no means an exclusive British media characteristic.)

At times this intra-categorial distinction has taken the form of acknowledgement of the worth of 'the main royals' accompanied by disapprobation of 'the hangers-on', though these do not seem to be fixed categories for some royals; one television documentary on Prince Philip tends to characterize the 'Mountbattens' as opportunistic outsiders, depicting Philip as a sort of human stratagem of family advancement of his uncle, Louis Mountbatten. Other than the Queen herself, her late mother and elder two children, and William (and the unruly Harry) no-one has been exempt from being repositioned on the media sliding-scale of 'true royalty'.

Just as often, structural relationships are set up between (e.g.) Sophie and Anne, or Queen Elizabeth and the late Princess Margaret, or Prince Charles and Prince Philip. Relativity here serves the function of enabling criticism while awarding praise, as well as setting up tensions whose purposes are to sustain the royal narrative.

In this sense royalty itself, and its institutional form the monarchy, become in themselves abstractions, because although the Queen can never be notionally separated from her royal status, like almost everyone else in the Family she can be criticized, sometimes quite sharply. In this case another member of the Family will be invoked to preserve the propriety of monarchy as an institution, so that the institution is always greater than the sum of its parts. If necessary, previous monarchs can be invoked, or future monarchs, and the system of representation is so flexible that if the future monarch (Charles) is seen as unsuitable by a section of public commentators, his son (William) can then be imaginatively inserted into the role, so that even if all the current constituent human elements of the British monarchy were portrayed as thoroughly unsuitable, the future would be bright anyway – were it so wished by the conservative British media!

Elsewhere we consider a question which naturally arises from these distinctions, but which requires to be raised here. Is the Queen, as with her late Mother, in Britain always ultimately recuperated as a worthwhile or even lovable personage, because of the intensity of her royal essence, the particularly undiluted blueness of blood? Or does the argument proceed from the assumption that the worth of the essential royals is derived from strengths of personality, which validate their royal powers? If they are worthy queens and kings, is their worth intrinsic to their royal nature? There must be a suspicion that arguments which seem to derive from their 'suitability for the role' in fact proceed from monarchist requirements, that is from the requirement that monarchs, unless, like some past English and British monarchs, so howlingly unsuitable as to be irrecoverable by either contemporary judgement or history, be judged fit to rule; even if, as has happened in the case of Edward VII, it is decades after his death before he becomes even partially recuperable. In this respect, Prince Charles's future transformations in media accounts will be particularly interesting.

Later in our study we raise the possibility of other processes at work in these structural realignments of sympathy or condemnation; for example 'displacements' of various kinds in which opinions or prejudices (say, against vegetarians, or carnivores; or town or country; or merely the sartorially fashionable or unfashionable) are reworked as arguments for or against Prince Charles, the Princess Royal, or whoever else. Life would have been easier for the heir to the throne had he cropped his hair, worn Armani suits and grown a clipped beard. In postmodern culture, depth is not always the most important dimension: but indeed deeper prejudices, to do with multi-culturalism, say, or gender, can work themselves round into becoming determinants of position-taking on royal matters.

Meanwhile we may note, also, some other potential contradictions emerging from within the spectrum of 'royalness' across which the family are placed by the media.

Ultimately both the Queen and Queen Mother have figured as relatively immune to criticism from media sources because of their identification with the monarchic form itself, from which 'incomers', 'interlopers' and 'hangers-on' can be discursively severed. Billig notes that the families interviewed in his study unanimously observe the convention over nomenclature when it comes to the Queen:

> Royalness is not derived from God's grace. Sometimes it appears as a characteristic of biology and blood. Perhaps it is expressed automatically in the universal habit of not calling the Queen familiarly by her first name. There is Philip, Margaret, Charles and Diana but no Elizabeth – only 'the Queen'. This is a habit which no participant commented upon and none avoided.
>
> (1992: 114)

But, interestingly, where the strongest critical commentary has been directed toward these two centrally monarchic figures, it is again as part of a relational judgement, in this case by juxtaposition with Diana. Had she not been royal Diana would not have been in Nairn's sense 'glamorous': "glamour' is the old Scottish word for magical enchantment, the spell cast upon humans by fairies, or witches' (Nairn: 214). Diana was invested with glamour because of her royal marriage. But she was nonetheless, both before and after her death, reinvented as an excluded figure of tragedy whose 'outsider' status had been constantly maintained by the core group of royals (which, in fact, included the Queen Mother), many media accounts even forgetting or disguising her aristocratic origins in order to reinforce a strong discursive strand in which she was a figure of the people. Her royal status became paradoxically the cause of public interest in her, while its contingent retraction by media commentators became the means to extol values the media intermittently sought to associate with her, by way of constructing limited 'criticism' of the Family from which she could conveniently be dissociated; or with whom she could, at the will of the journalist, be reintegrated.

Of course, structurally speaking, the force of each of these two versions is derived from contrast with the other. When seen happily with a group of (other) royals, contrast could be drawn with Diana's (normal) tendency to be increasingly lonely: photographed in literally splendid isolation in front of the Taj Mahal, an epic sense of isolation was derived thereby from the (abnormal) absence of (royal) family, particularly her husband. That this flexibility of approach can involve actual contradictions in the dimension of the real is seldom a major problem with royal reportage.

It might seem that if media accounts of the British royal family have tended to make arbitrary associations, between individual family members and sets of values – decency, kindness, openness, concernedness, responsibility and other attributes, and their obverse (often really the main concern) – then it will indeed be difficult to argue that the British media propose any view of royalty and monarchy *consistent* enough to be termed an 'ideology'.

And there is another problem with an 'ideological' form of explanation for royalty, such as Tom Nairn's late 1980s account of the British monarchy as a central symbol round which a pseudo-modern set of identities coalesce, in a British state which is actually stuck in a backward condition in which 'early modern' traits co-exist with feudal remnants. This difficulty is not a 'modern' difficulty but a 'postmodern' difficulty, and not one of interpreting the politico-cultural functioning of the royal family, but more challengingly, as seen earlier in this chapter, a difficulty over the concept of ideology itself as it appears in an age of socio-cultural fragmentation. This is putatively characterized by a sovereignty of consumption, which includes the colonization of the media by a value system which takes seriously only celebrity, sensation, and shopping.

Can something as coherently political as a conservative value system – held by some media owners, some editors, and some journalists, and seeking to impose itself on the beliefs of viewers or readers – really emerge from a media now largely subsumed as an instrument of consumption? Moreover, can this still be imagined in a postmodernized culture now deemed by many precisely as 'post-ideological'? This is the question handled in the next chapter of this opening section.

Let us finally again note that the structure within which the (predominantly) UK-focused royal examples above are understood, that is, in relation to the categories of the modern and the postmodern, holds good for the UK. In Spain, Norway, Belgium and The Netherlands, we gather local evidence for different patterns of development, analysed in the central section of this book.

2. The Ideological Realm

South African President Thabo Mbeki has handed over in person a cow to the king of the small mountain kingdom of Lesotho, Letsie III. President Mbeki incurred the fine by failing to attend the king's wedding last year. King Letsie described the nervous-looking Friesian cow he was presented with as 'a magnificent beast'... 'We have come here today with this beast to say that hopefully this would please Your Majesty', President Mbeki told the king. 'We will always respect your views and your opinion, and we are now paying this fine because as Africans, it is the correct thing to do', he said. Once a powerful force in Lesotho, the monarchy now plays a largely symbolic role.

(BBC News Online, 19 April 2001)

...everyday life inescapably secretes a true 'everyday knowledge' ('co-naissance') that the subtle Machiavelli called 'the thinking of the public square'.

(Michel Maffesoli, *The Time of the Tribes*, p. 148)

Ideology and 'post-ideology'

The development of theory about 'representation' took some radical turns from the late 1960s and in no writer's work more than Jean Baudrillard's. He moves from an 'economistic' view of social and cultural processes – that is to say, an interpretation of events in which economic activity, as in Marx's accounts, is the motor behind other processes – in the late 1960s and early 1970s, to an increasingly radical, and to some, outlandish, theoretical stance, from which he re-theorizes post-1960s society in a striking fashion.

In works such as *L'Echange symbolique et la mort* (1976) he begins constructing an argument about the breakdown of symbolic activity in contemporary Western society. This is an idea related, in certain thematic aspects, to central currents of French philosophical and social thought from the 1960s onward, and in some respects, as we noted in the previous chapter, prefigured by work by Daniel Boorstin (Boorstin, 1961). However, in Baudrillard's account the deconstructive turn is found in a particularly radical form when compared to parallel work by post-structuralist contemporaries, and it produces a considerably more theorized version of media culture than can be found in Boorstin.

Baudrillard suggests that the production of signs has reached such overwhelming volume and density by the latter part of the twentieth century that their relationship to the objective world is in doubt, excepting only the crucial sense in which such 'post-signifying' activity, or pseudo-communication, has been reduced to economic activity, one of a number of technologies of an all-conquering consumer system. (As with much 'post-Marxist' French theory since the late 1960s, it is not invariably difficult for the reader to re-insert Marx as a term in the argument.) Boorstin's emphasis on the fabrication of media events cannot be said to radicalize their conception to this extent. This is not necessarily, of course, a weakness in Boorstin.

Television in this perspective becomes the world, the system of signs having replaced their erstwhile objects (Baudrillard, 1983, 1993; Gane, 1993) in a world whose coherence is only the coherence of consumption. In this perspective, not only would the 'outpouring of grief' (see below) at Diana's funeral need to be very carefully distinguished in its guise as 'media reality' from its social and cultural and psychological existence, but also from its nature as a mere consumer experience. The form of consumer society which Baudrillard's writing depicts is one in which consumption is omnipresent in both private and public spheres: some of those writing under his influence are given to depicting identity itself as constructed by acts of purchasing, and 'empowerment' only as the periodic power to spend money in shops at the moment of transaction, or, perhaps, to turn up as a spectator at a royal funeral.

Whereas 'ideology' in the sense used by Marx and Engels is a phenomenon whose maintenance enables unequal societies to be perpetuated – by misrepresenting the nature of socio-economic and political reality – 'ideology' in Baudrillard's version of the late twentieth century is not only superfluous but unimaginable. It is superfluous because there is no longer any resistance to inequality in a developed world in which shopping and watching royal weddings on television has replaced political consciousness: and in any case unimaginable because the conditions of symbolic exchange which underwrite it no longer exist.

Though many commentators in the anglophone world have reacted to Baudrillard's ideas with hostility or disdain, the most thoughtful polemical responses (for example, Norris, 1990, 1992) offer a mixture of logical rejections of some of Baudrillard's propositions alongside the recognition that (along with his prescience over many socio-cultural developments of recent years) he has been right to suggest that there are literally new problems raised by the question of representation in the contemporary world. It is here that Baudrillard's theoretical drive can be seen as a very useful complement to Boorstin's political grasp. It is not after all unreasonable to raise a question about the capacity of the concept of ideology, whose roots are in a very different kind of era, to handle the highly mediatized world of the late twentieth century and beyond.

Ideology, in its negative sense, which implies that a misrepresentation of the world prolongs a 'false consciousness' within which those who are dominated by others misrecognize their oppressed state, further suggests a clear-cut distinction between 'reality' and 'representation' which is placed under severe strain by the sheer volume of sign-production from the 1970s onward. In a country such as Britain in which many newspapers devote most of their output to discussing what happens on television, and in the media world generally – in other words, in which the paramount distinction is often that between 'misrepresentation' and 'invention' – the domain of the 'real' is ever harder to locate.

Whether or not his readers reject, as exaggerated or theatrical, his claims that the real has been replaced by its images, Baudrillard was certainly right to signal the need, in the media age, to re-theorize the relationship between 'representation' and 'reality'. The manufacture of the former, in television, cinema, the press, in advertising, public relations and corporate communications, and – since the publication of *Simulacra and Simulations* in French in 1981 – in new technological media such as the Web, has become a central activity of many local and national economies. Sign-manufacture is what more and more students study or learn to do in universities.

Royal Families have Official Websites. Making images and signs and representations is a career for more and more workers, including one of the British Queen's own sons, her former brother-in-law, one of her cousins and yet other relatives. When the overwhelming focus of a historical phase is on the manufacture of signs – and not, as in eighteenth-century Europe, for example, on the understanding of reality – then it is necessary to review what has become of the latter. 'When the real is no longer what it used to be' says Baudrillard, 'nostalgia assumes its full meaning. There is a proliferation of myths of origin and signs of reality; of second-hand truth, objectivity and authenticity' (1988: 171).

Apply only that one short observation to the British royal family and witness a thousand fabricated narratives from myths of genealogy to dark rumours of assassination which mobilize notions of 'tradition', 'royal character', 'insider knowledge' and a host of other narrative components. Indeed, 'constructedness', a concept at the heart of the analytical drive of Foucault, Lyotard and others, as much as it is in Baudrillard's writing, has been a taken-for-granted term of historical analysis since the latter decades of the twentieth century. Many commentators who would not regard themselves as in any sense 'postmodernists', and who may in fact be very hostile to postmodernist versions of history, have nonetheless been very likely to approach 'facts' about the past (and present) as 'constructs' as distinct from 'truths'. In the British context this emphasis on 'constructedness' can be found in key works such as Patrick Wright's *On Living in an Old Country*, (Verso, 1985) or Eric Hobsbawm and Terence Ranger (eds.) *The Invention of Tradition* (Cambridge, 1992), as well as in aspects of work by Raphael Samuel, Linda Colley, Perry and Benedict Anderson, Tom Nairn and many others. It is not any novelty, by itself, in their emphasis on the 'construction' of understanding, but rather its adoption as a central premise of their analysis, which constitutes it as a feature of the postmodern phase.

In his schema of the 'four phases of the image' (1983) Baudrillard proposes that human culture reaches such an intensity of sign-production in the media age that previous ideas about signification, his first 'two phases' – namely that an image of something represents it, or that, as in the negative concept of ideology, it distorts it – are inadequate for a comprehension of new cultural processes. He argues that media signs more typically conceal an absence of the real, or relate to no object at all, in other words that 'reality' disappears from the equation. The distinction between the second phase, ideology, and Baudrillard's 'third phase', in which the image 'masks the absence of a basic reality' is the crucial stage in his suggested remodelling of sign-object relations in the media age.

We might suggest here, as examples, the assassination of Diana, or, to be consistent, her fatal accident; the mystery offspring of the British royals; the British heritage of the 'Windsors'. What is chiefly of interest in Baudrillard's schema is not so much the specifics of its proposals, but rather its convincing suggestion that there is a need to reconceptualize the problem. The 'third phase', to put it differently, is the space in which we are invited to rethink the inadequacy of working with the previous two categories. (His 'fourth phase', in which the sign 'bears no relation to any reality whatever: it is its own pure simulacrum', is, in the view of these authors, fanciful.)

In the third phase of the image, whether or not we accept Baudrillard's contention that it 'masks the absence of a basic reality', we can certainly agree that the relationship between sign and object in the highly mediatized world of the 1970s and beyond has become too complex for the concept of ideology, without further development, to be able to cope with it.

We will shortly illustrate 'constructedness' in a media context when we consider a fragment from the vast and still-expanding edifice of myth which surrounds Princess Diana. But it is worthwhile first confronting a taxing question. If we were to follow Baudrillard's lead in detecting a 'loss of the real' in postmodern society, could we simultaneously insist that royalty was *both* a 'post-significatory', 'post-ideological' phenomenon: and *also* an ideological phenomenon?

Wouldn't that be a contradiction? The answer seems obvious (yes). But we took care in Chapter 1 to define a plural view of contemporary society, in which both modern and postmodern socio-cultural strands are recognized as co-present, and we did so because what we will argue throughout and in the Conclusion is indeed that monarchy and royalty, as constructed in the media, do indeed operate both ideologically and post-ideologically. Far from this representing a contradiction, it represents the manner in which modern and postmodern society co-exist.

There is a view, best expressed by Tom Nairn (1988), to the effect that the British monarchy is politically very significant and that its most important feature is the way that it helps maintain Britain in a backward, only partly modernized condition. The latter aspect (in that brief paraphrase) did not look any less plausible at the beginning of the twenty first century, a time when innumerable overseas commentators were routinely picturing Britain as backward and even medieval. Part of this backwardness has been a disparity in the quality of life, as affected by income, housing and other factors, which grew rather than diminished over the first term of the New Labour government from 1997–2001. The classical sense of ideology as maintaining 'relations of domination' (Thompson, 1990) applies very well here. Britain, possessing an intractable underclass in which illiteracy, unemployment and misery are standard experiences, retains further socio-economic stratifications more pronounced than in many other European countries.

Were we to wish to explain the particular phenomenon which is the British media obsession with royalty, it might appear that we need look no further than its ideological function. Billig (1992) records how a mother and daughter in his empirical study, respectively a cleaner and a factory worker, 'in the evening imprisoned inside the small rented house' on an estate where the pavements are 'filled with litter from the nearby shops' and 'gangs of youths congregated on the street' sit 'talking about the hardships of the royal life' (1992: 142). Not being able to eat chips in the street ('again, chips were the metonym of the free spirit', says Billig) was the sort of freedom the Royal Family was missing. 'I bet they'd love to live the way we live', says the daughter, while Billig notes sombrely that 'outside the house, the gangs of the evening were gathering on the path to the chip shop'.

Though we may speculate that the equivalents of this mother and daughter might conceivably speak differently of the Royal Family ten and more years later, it is this topsy-turvy reality which has often been seen as the desired product of ideology. As late as the 1970s many commentators produced one refinement or another of the concept to explain how unequal and unfair societies could hold together without much use of state force. But the growth of a new postmodern consumer society of the kind glimpsed early by Baudrillard is not the only reason for the view of ideology thirty and more years later to have changed. Fragmentation and even 'atomization' of societies of the sort not only observed in Britain in the 1980s, but actively willed by Conservative Party ideologues, makes it much more difficult to speak of 'dominant ideologies' in the confident manner of the 1970s, in cultures fractured along a variety of fault lines.

As media consumers we are increasingly targeted in terms of what is demographically specific about us, not as members of an unrefined 'British public' or 'French public'.

Michel Maffesoli observes (the French original is in 1988) that:

> Television, because of its diffraction, is no longer the standard-bearer of a unique message applicable to all. Indeed, although what I am advancing here is just a tendency, it must be recognized that it is addressed increasingly to particular groups: groups based on age, region, cities, even neighbourhoods. Examples such as buildings which receive cable TV can only reinforce this process. What can this mean, except that the image is no longer distant, overarching, totally abstract, but rather it is defined by proximity?
>
> (Maffesoli, 1996: 138)

and Maffesoli's observations – we shall return to further implications of Maffesoli's argument in the Conclusion – may be extended to the manner in which newspapers, advertisers, public relations specialists and others, including website and mobile telephony producers and designers, target niche markets. 'Ideology', both for this reason and for that of its consumer-world backdrop, might seem, as a phenomenon, less central to explanations of social and cultural practice than it was as recently as the 1970s.

But though it has become more complicated to assess how ideology functions in contemporary societies it is still not possible to understand them without it. The field of sexual politics alone is one whose complications, like those from the domain of inter-ethnic relations, very much require the concept of ideology to make them comprehensible.

There is a very striking image emerging from an account in Billig's study, which is of the bar of the Snake Pass Inn in Derbyshire 'packed with disappointed men' on the day of Charles and Diana's wedding because no cafeteria was open, the staff having assumed that they would have a very quiet day – 'they'd thought everybody would be at home watching the television and the wedding', says Billig's male respondent (1992: 194), whereas this interviewee had said to the staff that they 'must be mad' because 'it's an ideal day for a man to leave his wife watching the wedding on the television, while he gets out and does his own thing'. He says that there were 'hundreds of men up there'. Rather poignantly the interviewee concludes 'it was a gorgeous day; oh, it was a fantastic day'.

But this was not a republican act by these men:

> The women's interest is protected from too much criticism, for the women are concerning themselves with the symbols of nationhood and family. Loyal men cannot attack the womanly interests without risking themselves being criticised as unpatriotic. Their absences on the great days are not radical statements. Instead, they affirm conventional masculinity, and, thereby, they affirm the conventions of that private realm which is being publicly celebrated on the television screen. (1992: 194)

Since the period during which Billig's respondents were sampled, the research having been completed by the end of 1989 (and as Billig himself notes in his new preface of 1998) public attitudes toward the Royal Family seem to change during the 1990s. So of course do beliefs associated with class and gender. We may speculate that the man who visited the Snake Pass Inn, who was in his early sixties when interviewed, represents a culture of working-class masculinity which was already changing as he spoke; the fear of being 'unpatriotic', and its mobilization in the context of attitudes to royal ceremonial, seem less likely occurrences a decade and a half later.

What is certain is that we can approach neither the original sentiment nor its obsolescence without the concept of ideology, there being ideologies in this set of sentiments which are associated with presumptions about masculine and feminine roles, social class, and national feeling. The ideological content of the original experience would be no less present in a contemporary account, even by a younger respondent whose socio-cultural formation was much more influentially located within postmodern consumer culture.

The ideological process would only be different, and perhaps more complicated, as we shall see in the instance of Diana's funeral. For example, during it a young couple are interviewed on television and asked why they have joined the crowd waiting for the funeral procession, and they say 'we were clubbing 'til five or six, and then we came on here'. Taken at face value this seems like a perfect 'post-ideological' statement by two self-indulgent, sensation-seeking products of a superficial consumer culture. It's a statement entirely consonant with what so many among the more pessimistic commentators on postmodernity call, echoing Jameson, 'depthlessness' in contemporary culture. But, to the extent that ideology proposes a 'view of the world' and a 'set of beliefs or attitudes', this is a very revealing statement both in its content and its omissions. Apart from reminding us of the aesthetic motives at work in responses to royalty, it directly contradicts the 'official' media version of crowd sentiments which we analyse below. By doing so it emphasizes the ideological nature of the BBC's version of events.

But it also tells us that, inhabiting the same world, we will be able to find people who relate to the phenomena of monarchy and royalty in a predominantly postmodern fashion; and others, those in the crowd to whom Diana was important, and because she was royal, who are ideological subjects, just as easily understood as victims of the topsy-turvy value world of Billig's mother and daughter who fret over the Royal Family's lack of opportunity to eat chips from newspaper wrappers in the street. But there were others, from neither the ranks of the sensation-seekers nor the politically oppressed, who were present out of mild curiosity, or because Diana might have done them, or their hospital or school, or an acquaintance, some kindness. We will not want to overemphasize either the ideological or the consumerist strand in the analysis, but we will try to create room for both of these and others.

Power

Ideology is about nothing if not power. To be the Royal Family with its immense privileges is in itself to enjoy the power to extract immense personal benefits, in return for symbolic capital, from the state. To have heavily disadvantaged members of the population sympathize with you because your life is so difficult, however ironic, is to embed that power. But the main power of monarchies lies in their symbolic functioning, which is why many states, including Lesotho, retain them, albeit that strictly speaking some may not have much choice, for example in Britain; actually because in the UK monarchy is so ideologically embedded that republicanism, which is periodically discussed in *Guardian* supplements or in journals, is not really a British phenomenon at all, but always itself heard as ideological, extremist or foreign. It is in this aspect of symbolic functioning more than any other that we shall see considerable differences in continental monarchies in their own countries, and also, in the instance of the particularly well-known British monarchy, in its reception in European countries.

The delicacy with which democratic states often continue to treat monarchies is explicable in terms of the advantages, in particular that of ancillary legitimization, which monarchy conveys upon government. When a prime minister, such as Tony Blair after winning the 2001 British general election, makes a ritual trip to the Palace to be received by the monarch, the symbolic meaning, though structurally quite incoherent, is chiefly one of propriety sanctioned by tradition and history. This is a curious fact. The Queen seems to be receiving the Prime Minister on behalf of the nation; like his civil servants, she has been there before him and will also survive him, but like them has no electoral mandate of any kind: no referendum on the monarchy has been offered to the electorate, only the results of opinion polls, which do still suggest support for the institution, though in certain aspects reduced over the decade from 1991 to 2001, rising again in 2002. Since the New Labour government was elected on the lowest electoral turnout since 1918, just as previous Conservative governments had been elected on a minority of votes cast, it might be said that when a British prime minister makes that triumphant journey to the Palace, there is some fragility in the proposition that a ritual of representative authority is being enacted.

These rituals are widespread. We began this chapter by noting a ritual, at roughly the same period as Mr Blair's visit to the Palace, in Lesotho. Norbert Elias describes another in Ghana:

> The guests were seated in a very wide circle. The hosts, local chiefs, were seated at one side of the circle. At the opposite side was seated the guest of honour, the delegate of the state president. In their toga-like traditional costumes they looked like Roman senators, dignified and proud. The ceremony began with the chiefs getting up from their seats and walking

with some of their followers slowly to the seats of the representatives of the state, presumably welcoming them to their festival. They returned to their seats. After a short interval the state representative and his staff got up and, walking through the whole circle, reciprocated the chiefs' visit, presumably thanking them for their invitation and expressing the good wishes of the head of state. What we saw was a symbolic representation of a certain equilibrium which had been reached in the long drawn-out tug-of-war between representatives of the two levels, of tribe and state. The president of the first African colony to become an independent state, while reserving more and more sources of real power for himself as head of state, wished to maintain as much as possible of the ceremonial power of tribal chiefs whom he regarded as a specifically African institution.

(Elias, 1991: 139–140)

'Ceremonial power', in the generic sense of 'symbolic power', relates to real power. At the beginning of the next chapter we review the interests of social élites who, benefitting from the present disposition of British society, will not tend to be motivated to support change to its vertical structure. (In the Conclusion we consider further aspects of 'power' as a concept in its relationship with monarchy.)

John B Thompson (1990: 59–73) suggests five modes – 'legitimation', 'dissimulation', 'unification', 'fragmentation' and 'reification' – as partial features of the operation of ideology. Focusing on 'the ways in which symbolic forms intersect with relations of power', Thompson seeks to explore 'strategies of symbolic construction'. Thompson characterises as critical conceptions those notions of ideology associated with negative judgements on ideological phenomena. However, Thompson also distinguishes another set of usages, 'neutral conceptions of ideology' to describe cases where ideology is simply intended to mean what we might call 'systems of belief', or 'sets of values'.

Although Marx's and Engels's development of the concept of ideology referred to domination of a ruling class, in contemporary usage the terms 'ideology' and 'hegemony' often make reference to competition in the symbolic domain among a variety of competing groups; but the symbolic competition is always pursued, in all such conceptions, in order to maintain or increase power.

One of Weber's grounds for legitimacy – tradition – is of central importance in the operation of the British monarchy. This is not merely an intermittently surfacing factor in British life. It is remarkably visible. It is possible to go to bed in Britain having watched television news broadcasts dominated by the latest Honours List, and wake up to the Trooping of the Colour. Since all royal events are significant to the British media this refrain of tradition is constant. Unification – 'a form of unity which embraces individuals in a collective identity, irrespective of the differences and divisions which may separate them' – will be seen at work during Diana's funeral (below); but in BBC coverage, and, in fact, not nearly so much in European or American constructions. Thompson's fifth category of reification, with its strategies of naturalization and eternalization, in the latter of which 'social-historical phenomena are deprived of their historical character by being portrayed as permanent, unchanging and ever-recurring' is in fact the very basis of the British rejection of republicanism, since royalty is seen as permanent and even naturalized. One of Thompson's other categories, 'fragmentation', which involves 'orientating forces of potential opposition towards a target which is projected as evil, harmful or threatening' is precisely what comes into operation against the merest stirrings in the UK of republicanism.

The category of 'discourse' – interpreted as a way of talking about the world which is the equivalent of 'ideology' as a way of understanding the world – has long been associated with power; in one recent trajectory from Nietzsche to Foucault. We briefly contextualize the term at the end of Chapter 3, and deploy it in a number of European contexts in the following chapters. We now consider a media event which brings some of these concepts together – the funeral of Diana.

After a detailed passage from BBC coverage, we compare its tendencies with those of transmissions from Sky and CNN, as well as Swedish and Norwegian accounts; and for further comparison extracts from CBS and NBC, to provide a North American dimension against which to read the primarily European accounts in this book.

Diana: constructing grief

The great scenes on the stage of history have never been 'representations' in the psychological and philosophical meaning of the word, as naïve people still believe; they were not the work of naïve people, expressing themselves 'with complete sincerity' and eager to speak the truth. They were more like theatrical 'performances' (and let us not forget the profound link that has always existed between theatre, acting and life itself); historical scenes have always been cleverly and cunningly 'staged' by certain men who were aiming for specific results. They were acts.

Henri Lefebvre (1991: 135)

BBC: eve of funeral; morning of funeral

On the eve of the funeral, *Diana, the People's Vigil* was presented on BBC by one of the channel's heavyweight presenters, David Dimbleby. It begins with a zoom out from the tower of Big Ben against a black sky: 'Big Ben in London telling us that it's just after half-past ten: and the thoughts of the whole country are turning towards this part of the city, to Westminster Abbey, whose west front is floodlit tonight...'.

After a short introductory sequence, there follows a montage of a dozen slow-motion soft-edged shots of Diana as mother; helper of the aged; with the sick; with Mother Theresa of Calcutta; punctuated here and there by shots of lilies, accompanied by a nostalgic popular piano track. This sequence ends with the title *Diana, the Nation's Vigil*, over a complex montage comprising a still of a serious-looking Diana to the left, with a shot of a bunch of lilies framing the right, in motion, over an abstract background, the latter shot dissolving into a live shot of the crowd (an intriguing editorial confection). After a further address from Dimbleby, of a nationally-unifying character, the reporter addresses the camera from the Mall.

Reporter 1: 'Well this is the scene in the Mall this evening, already hundreds of people lining the route prepared for a damp, possibly showery night, so that they can pay their respects tomorrow to Diana Princess of Wales. People have been coming from all over the country to really... be a symbol of a United Kingdom, a kingdom it seems already so

45

united in grief. People have all their own memories of Diana, they want to share them with other people, they talk about her constantly, they also are rather shocked and still have a lot of disbelief that such a young woman, such a vibrant, caring young woman has had her life cut so tragically short...' (this already presents a complex mixture of reporting and editorializing; as will be seen, we surmise that the reporter is uncomfortable at having to overrule a professional instinct merely to report – whereas the staging demands a clearly themed narrative).

At this point the reporter turns to her left, taking a pace or so backwards, to an obviously prepared vox pop: 'A family here, just behind me, they're already bedded down for this evening – can you tell me why you're prepared to stay the night here?', bending down to a young woman accompanied by two children in sleeping bags. 'It's just something I've got to do, just got to be here, pay my respects to Diana, she was, she's just, nobody will ever replace her, nobody could try, (I) mean we've just got to be here, it's the last thing, the only thing we can do.' This is delivered calmly and evenly, after which the reporter steps towards the young boys in the sleeping bags with 'And these are your sons down here, are they?' 'Yes they are.' 'What did Diana mean to you?' The boys deliver themselves politely and cheerfully, and with evident relief, of prepared statements. The younger says 'She was kind and she did a lot for other people' and then turns to his elder brother on cue, as does the reporter, and he says, 'She was a very special lady'. His younger brother grins with relief as the second response is given.

At its most plausible this interview is a mixture of what is no doubt a genuine enough response by the mother (though we cannot know this) and what seems like a piece of television rhetoric involving the children. This becomes yet clearer in the next phase of the interview. Continuing to address the elder, the reporter asks: 'Have you ever done anything like this before, camped out in the freezing cold?' 'No', he replies, as does his brother. 'Do you think you'd do it for anyone else?' the reporter asks the elder. 'Probably not', he replies, and the younger shakes his head with a smile which plainly says that he wasn't warned about this extension of the discussion, indicating that the interview has already exceeded its expected demands – the boys are plainly keen to acquit themselves well, and don't want to get involved in any more extemporized utterances. 'Well', says the reporter, standing up after a half-pause and moving off with a smile, 'some emotions there from two very young lads. And something of course that they'll remember for the rest of their lives as well'. It has to be said that there have been no emotions, as such, visible at all from either of the boys, who simply appear well brought up and anxious to complete a demanding task properly. But British television journalists have been well schooled to seek the emotional response as the *sine qua non* of any likely exchange, no matter how brief ('can you tell us how you feel' ?).

As for memories: Michael Billig's invaluable social psychological study (based on interviews conducted in late 1988 and throughout 1989 with families talking about the British royals) in one instance records a royalist mother trying to get her sceptical son to admit that he has watched royal weddings. He says he did but that 'I can't remember my feelings at the time, but I remember watching it on TV'. The mother does not really accept that he doesn't remember how he felt:

Then, she returned to the ceremonies. If Charles were to be crowned king, she said turning to her radical son, wouldn't you feel it was a memorable event, something to tell your grandchildren about? Hang on a minute, he replied, what have you told me about the Coronation of '53? 'We've never had reason to', she answered, 'I mean you've never said "Mum tell us about 1953"'. (Billig, 1992: 37–38)

There is an important difference between 'remembering your feelings' and remembering watching something on TV. This exchange shows the son trying to establish the not unreasonable claim that if royal events are really so important and symbolically enduring, then he would have expected to have thought about them a little during his life. Logically, had his mother thought the Coronation of 1953 important, she might previously have mentioned it.

Diana's funeral may be a different kind of event – we discuss Diana's qualities further in later chapters. The reporter now approaches a self-conscious looking group of women, walking round behind them as they are seated in a row stretching into the shot, on folding chairs, half-turned expectantly into the television lighting which picks them out as the reporter moves toward them. One or two members of the crowd move self-consciously back to create more space for her, and another cameraman is picked out behind the group: boys in baseball caps and sports clothes stand about looking, or move out the way. She takes a large breath: 'Friendships have been forged' – already at this point the reporter pauses and exhales loudly, which indicates that she is working fairly hard, and no doubt feeling the pressure – 'on days like this and I know that, eh, a number of people have just met up for the first time today, the mood' she says, without pause but with an increase in volume and pitch on 'mood' to indicate a major digression, 'is sombre, it's not gloomy, it's reflective, it's respectful, and it's chatty as well, I think people sharing their own memories and eh, the times that Diana had in her life', and then she bends to talk to two women from Northern Ireland, who have just met two other women from Wales, and she says 'You've met, I think, just today, haven't you?' (the 'I think': is a tic caused by her telepresenter's instinctive wish to dilute the impression of the interview being determined in advance). One of the Irish women is upset, albeit controlled: she ends 'it's when we don't see that beautiful face' and the reporter says 'You speak for the whole nation, I think'.

After an impromptu exchange with another woman the reporter then does what she can to conversationalize in tone something inevitably rehearsed: 'Without doubt I feel that... when Diana's coffin arrives at Westminster Abbey tomorrow morning' – there are significant pauses after 'coffin', 'arrives' and 'Westminster', and she appears once or twice to be searching for a term, but it is clear that she knows what she is going to say very exactly – 'it will have been borne through a tide of love and adoration from Kensington Palace right through to the great West Door'. She stops and looks at the camera and the director cuts back to Dimbleby. She has introduced a number of themes – community, national unity, compassion – which recur in the coverage, but she has also been attempting to fix the nature of 'the mood' in a manner repeated by a number of other presenters. The pattern is, as seems clear below, to establish a coherent narrative in the appropriate emotional – not, of course, political – terms (at one point the cameraman zooms in a little to exclude two sports-clothed young boys to the reporter's right, who stare at the camera): but at the same time there seems to be what might be interpreted as a genuine tension between the reporter's desire to give an accurate account of the 'mood' and the professionally understood need to give an 'appropriate' account. It is quite possible that this is an instance of an instinctively good reporter caught in circumstances in which her desire simply to report is compromised by the requirements of a specific form of television staging.

Here are two further examples of 'mood'-setting, but also of the reflexive tone of the moment, 'reflexive' in the sense that we see and hear journalists very clearly exploring their own constructions of the 'reality' which is being offered, just as the reporter does above.

At nine on the Saturday morning, just before the funeral procession moves off, reporter 2 reports from Kensington Palace. After a couple of preliminary remarks, she searches like the reporter the previous evening to define the 'mood' (there is always the notion that the mood is unitary) of the occasion. Reporter 2's variations in the rate of her utterance, her pitch, and her stress, are more considerable than those of many other reporters: her tone is very conversational, her attitude non-verbally demonstrative: 'The mood here... it's not really sombre, it's, it's quiet, it's reflective, you, you're struck by really the silence, despite the, the number of people here, the thousands of people on, on the streets' – at this point there is a dissolve from the reporter to a shot of two women talking to each other in a section of the crowd numbering around ten, perhaps designated to the director as 'strangers' by the maintenance of a significant distance between them, and a restraint in their non-verbal signals – 'people are talking quietly, there's a, a, a sense of camaraderie though, people happy to talk to each other, to strangers, about their stories, their thoughts, their feelings...' (as it happens, on the basis of even this selected shot most people aren't saying anything).

Reporter 3, immediately following reporter 2, says: 'The mood here I think has changed rather in that time (during the last hour) as well, what I described earlier as quiet and reflective has become rather more serious and I think there is an increasing sense of anticipation that, eh, this week of mourning is going to become *altogether more real* when people do see that funeral procession and the cortege and in particular of course the gun carriage go past. People are still silent, and sad'. This is over long shots of the crowd, who display a whole range of characteristics, though there is a moment of serendipity (during the funeral there were some very inappropriate crowd behaviours, which television directors would immediately try to exclude) when one of two young girls who have been smiling and talking falls quiet and reflective just as reporter 3 reaches his final words, creating an impressive moment.

Here it has become clear that the presenter is really quite worried that the crowd is not behaving 'appropriately' (not 'grieving' enough): and we have italicized a moment where reporter 3 seems to perceive a reality defect, which has something of the effect of listening to someone tear a gap in the fabric of television. Both reporters, like reporter 1, do indeed themselves seem torn, arguably between their instincts as journalists and their awareness of a television agenda which limits journalistic inquiry quite severely. (of course there are further dimensions to this discourse than it is appropriate to pursue here).

The unificatory discourses are not limited to standardization of emotion. 'Not just here in London' but also elsewhere (we are given lists, to start with, in Scotland, Glasgow, Edinburgh, Dundee, Dumfries, Crathie) and even in Northern Ireland, people are 'united' in 'grief'. Another reporter, reporter 4, begins 'Well, here in Northern Ireland the death of the Princess has, in a quite unprecedented way, united in grief an often divided community. Unionists and nationalists have come together to lay flowers in her memory at many focal points across the province, and to reflect on the loss of someone whose life and work touched so many in this corner of the kingdom.' 'Political and religious divisions have been firmly set aside in a week which has seen many people taking part in interdenominational church services.' It might seem that to claim that Northern Ireland is 'united in grief' and that religious divisions have been 'set aside' by the Princess's death verges as much on the distasteful as the inaccurate. Having discussed the Republic of Ireland's response, the report concludes 'In marking the passing of a princess, if in little else, all the people of Ireland will be united' (i.e. as *British* subjects). After Scotland and Ireland, Wales ('their Princess') concludes this unificatory tour of the national components of the United Kingdom, which has begun with a claim by David Dimbleby that:

> Tomorrow is the culmination of a week of mounting public grief after the sudden death of the Princess on Sunday in Paris. It all began with a few flowers being laid outside Kensington Palace. At the end of the week, it ended with a torrent of visitors with millions of bunches of flowers, many of them with moving messages attached to them. Our country discovering a shared grief for a Princess who seemed to touch them as no other person has.

This 'revelation' of how a limited display of emotion develops into a 'discovery' of 'shared' grief raises several questions, not least about the role of the media in turning the disposition of 'a few flowers' into the extraordinary displays which followed. Subsequent commentary on the funeral itself was provided in its entirety by David Dimbleby. His interpretation of the images displayed circled endlessly around terms such as 'mourning', 'grieving', 'love', 'adoration', all backed up by appropriate shots of 'mourners' in the crowd. Irrespective of what those present were actually doing, the streets were described as being 'thick with mourners'.

Other accounts and dissonant voices: Norwegian, Swedish and American versions

The question – in Machiavelli's terms, as invoked by Maffesoli at the start of this chapter – is: what was 'the thinking of the public square' while this performance was taking place?

We examine overseas accounts of the same event to look for clues, but we begin with Sky.

Our sample of Sky's coverage of the event is limited to the first hour of broadcasting before the procession proper began. However, even this relatively short extract is enough to highlight considerable differences from the BBC's report. The tone of Sky's coverage – despite the black suits of the two anchors in the studio – was much less funereal than the BBC's, in some ways relatively up-beat, mixing pre-prepared features with vox pops stressing the supposed changes which Diana, and in particular the reaction to her death, had brought to British society. There were reports from primary schools and secondary schools, with parents and even with visitors from abroad who had gone to watch the procession. María Miguel from Spain took the view that Diana 'had been very badly treated by the royal family'. 'Our royal family isn't like that at all', she added, 'and we're very fond of them'.

In 'Diana, the Final Farewell' she was described as a 'Princess of Pop', and we were informed that 'part of her appeal lay in her very modern image'. A long interview with royal photographer Jayne Fincher took us through various stages of Diana's relationship with fashion (for example, her *Dynasty* stage in 1985), and the accent was on this as a 'departure from tradition', on Diana as someone who was 'moving the monarchy into the twenty-first century'. Journalists interviewed in pre-shot features included not only Andrew Neil from the *Scotsman*, but also Andy Coulson, Showbiz Editor of the *Sun* (a newspaper much derided by virtually every other station whose coverage we were able to secure). While Neil mused:

> As you look at this scene outside Buckingham Palace, what does it say to you about New Britain and what Diana meant to that Britain? ... Diana was about the present, she was the only truly modern royal. Everything we're seeing out here has actually been determined by the people and so things will never be the same again.

Coulson informed viewers that Diana 'dripped showbiz', that 'This was completely new for a royal. Tradition had gone completely out of the window'. Royal biographer Anthony Holden also stressed how much she represented a 'radical change'.

There were, of course, the inevitable occasional references to the 'huge outpouring of grief', but by and large it was all much less focused than BBC coverage, more differentiated: a group of Scottish girls interviewed even announced 'we're not even royalists'. Sky was much more factual about the number of people attending being 'fewer than expected', suggesting just over one million as opposed to the figure of six million which had been widely accepted elsewhere, and commented on Archbishop Carey's warning about the dangers of 'making Diana superhuman'.

Norway

Norwegian coverage of the funeral was provided by the state-owned public-service broadcaster NRK and by the private channel TV2. NRK's first channel – NRK1 – was not only Norway's first television channel, starting in 1960, but was for over thirty year's Norway's *only* television channel until the appearance of TV2 in 1993. Though commercial in nature, TV2 is subject to a number of public-service obligations.

NRK's coverage was – as its viewers would expect – conservative in nature. As an on-screen clock on a plain blue background ticked its way slowly to 10 a.m. for the broadcast to start, viewers were treated only to plainsong. A female presenter wearing a black suit introduced live coverage from London, whose first few minutes as with the BBC consisted of an attempt to summarise the 'mood' among those who had spent the night on the streets of London waiting for the event. They were described as being from 'all ethnic groups' and as being 'young, old, rich, poor'.

Subsequent coverage was informed by three main discourses:
- explanatory, involving descriptions of the route, the main buildings passed, the personalities appearing on screen at different moments.
- historical, carried mostly by royal 'expert' Richard Hermann, covering a wide range of events and personages ranging from Edward the Confessor through Henry VIII to events such as the royal wedding of 1981. There was some attempt to provide a Norwegian perspective through references to King Haakon's relations with the British Government during the Second World War. The level of detail was at times astonishing, viewers learning that Crystal Palace contained over 300,000 panes of glass.
- of mourning; not especially vigorous, this manifested itself in occasional references to people coming 'from all over Great Britain to mourn together' and to a 'whole people in mourning'. These 'mourners' were described as coming from 'all races and social classes'.

Unexpected elements of NRK's coverage included its indirectly critical stance towards the British Royal Family, and its references to some problems of contemporary Britain. For example, the 'stiff upper lip' of the British royals was contrasted with the warmth and spontaneity shown by the 'people', and there was talk of the 'distance' which existed between the Royal Family and the British people, a distance which the Queen's speech the day before had, it was suggested, gone some way to abridge. There were also references to 'immigration problems' in 'run-down boroughs' inhabited by 'underprivileged people' and many references to the homeless, particularly in connection with Diana's charitable work. Despite its variety of approaches, NRK's commentary flagged as the broadcast went on, with increasingly long silences as the procession neared the Abbey, one of them lasting 2m 45s.

TV2

TV2's coverage was more varied in its approach, and also more youthful in tone. As well as taking the international feed from London, it frequently introduced on-screen frames where commentators at other points in the procession or in its studio in Bergen could discuss various aspects of the event, and during Elton John's song and the Archbishop of Canterbury's speech it edited in shots of Diana, with her children, or involved in various kinds of 'good works'. It also began summarising those of 'all ages and races' who had spent the night in London, and its commentary bore strong similarities to that of NRK1 (suggesting common sources). However its discourse of mourning was much more developed than on NRK1 with descriptions of 'an enormous sea of grieving people standing elbow to elbow on both sides of the Mall', the 'population's powerful participation in mourning' and 'people crying openly'. It also contained references to the 'dark side of British society', again in relation to Diana's charitable works.

The main difference between TV2 and NRK1's coverage, however, was the former's more developed level of political comment, and its questioning of received British media wisdom on the event. This took the form both of references to the Blair government's involvement in the staging of the funeral and its possible motives, and recurring criticism of the British Royal Family from various points of view. Indeed, after only four minutes royal 'expert' Carl-Erik Grimstad in the Bergen studio presented the event as an opportunity for the British Royal Family to 'modernize', contrasting its aloofness with the Norwegian Royal Family's relationship with the Norwegian people, described as a 'closeness which is completely different' from the British case, being 'deeper and more solid'. This was a theme coverage would return to regularly and develop, in particular, towards the end of the broadcast once the service in Westminster Abbey was over, where a remarkable exchange took place on the difference between the British Royal Family and its Norwegian and Scandinavian equivalents. In response to a prompt from the commentator that the British Royal family 'must change and become more like the Norwegian Royal Family or the Swedish Royal Family or the Danish Royal Family', Grimstad responded on being asked his opinion on the difference between the British and Scandinavian monarchies:

> Let's stick to the Norwegian monarchy. The Norwegian monarchy emerged in a way as a kind of opposition to an existing social system, or at least the modern Norwegian monarchy as we know it today, it was set up as a national... as part of a national movement on the side of the people, so to speak, and that is our social democracy. You can't say this of the British monarchy which is part of the earlier defenders of Empire, which has strong links with the upper class, which is closely linked with a political system which needs reforming... it will be interesting to see how Tony Blair tackles this situation in the future. Today he has come over as a strong defender both of the throne and of the monarchy...

This Norwegian discussion opens some substantial questions about the 'nation united in grief' discourses of the BBC's coverage.

Sweden

The Swedish coverage of the funeral we managed to obtain was provided by the public service broadcaster Sveriges Television, carried on its second channel SVT2 (coverage was also available on other channels).

SVT's coverage was much more interested than the Norwegian channels in the human-interest side of the Diana story, and was rather less disposed to a straightforward reproduction of the discourse of 'nation-uniting grief'. Reference was made to a 'party atmosphere' in parts of London the night before the funeral, and it was suggested that people had queued for long periods of time primarily in order to get a better view. Attempts were made to distinguish between the apparent grief felt by those lining the procession route and that felt by Diana's relatives, in particular her sons.

Diana despite being a 'fairy-tale figure' was also described as coming from the 'extreme upper class' and as being a glamourous jet-setter, and mention was made of the criticism which had been levelled against her because of her holidays on board Dodi Fayed's yacht in the Mediterranean earlier in the summer. Her attempts to manipulate the press were also raised, as was her public 'slanging match' (in English) with Charles via the media. However, perhaps the strongest thread was reference to her as a 'modern young woman', rollerblading through Hyde Park and taking her sons out to hamburger joints, taking a stand against the British 'stiff upper lip' (mentioned twice in English), as representing the 'young, modern, new Britain' and as challenging the ossified traditions of the English court.

The contrast between her style and that of the rest of the royal family was used as a prompt to discuss the difference between the British royals and their Scandinavian counterparts, London-based commentators Anders Lindqvist and Lee Persson discussing the fact that 'we can now see the royal family go out in the street among the people', which is perhaps a sign that Britain is 'developing into a "bicycling monarchy"'. 'They need to change', says Lindqvist, 'they need to be more like the Scandinavians'. Persson says that there have been 'quite serious republican noises both in the press and out in the streets in a way never heard before'. Asked by Lindqvist 'is there is a risk of Britain moving towards being a republic?', Persson responds to the effect that where once 'he would have said certainly not, now' he is unsure.

After the ceremony a very serious discussion ensued in Stockholm between anchorwoman Ingela Agardh and her six guests over a range of issues raised by the funeral. These included the role of the British media in the battle between Diana's and Charles's 'camps', the modern-day fixation with appearance, its relationship with pornography and the 'male gaze', the British tabloids, privacy laws in the UK as compared with those of both Sweden and France, and questions of symbolic leadership in society: no equivalent was imaginable on British TV.

The United States
CBS

For approximately the first hour CBS simply relayed Sky's coverage of early-morning London, complete with vox pops, more or less without comment. As the procession approached, however, it moved its own team into place. Subsequent coverage – starting at 4 a.m. Eastern Time – was anchored by veteran presenter Dan Rather assisted in the 'studio' (a room in a building overlooking Westminster Abbey) by the unlikely combination of British constitutional historian David Starkey of the London School of Economics and Ingrid Seward of *Majesty* magazine, and backed up by a wide array of on-the-spot reporters out and about at various points along the funeral route.

Coverage of the procession itself is best described as an electronic guided tour of the sights of London for Americans who had either already been there or were hoping to visit at some point in the future. A vast amount of historical and topographical detail was offered. Combined with this was an insistence on the momentousness of it all. It was, David Starkey intoned, 'bigger than VE day itself'. Dan Rather likened it to the funeral of J F Kennedy 'for any American of memory age in 63'. There were references to the 'sea of humanity', to the 'awesome and sombre silence', to the inevitable 'millions of mourners', to the 'nation united in grief', to the 'national day of mourning' involving 'all ages and races lining the route'. This was combined with a sustained attempt to deal with the problem of 'how difficult it is for Americans to understand what the Royal Family and the monarch represents to the British'. Starkey stated confidently that 'the monarchy is in fact the real fundamental essence of British nationhood ... it is responsible for the fact that we don't have the hateful, vehement nationalisms that have occasionally disfigured other European countries' (Northern Ireland was not considered).

However, anyone up early enough to have seen the previous uncut Sky footage must have been somewhat disorientated as David Starkey in particular now developed a strong 'break with tradition' narrative centred not on Diana – as had been the case with Sky and all the other channels analysed here – but on Margaret Thatcher, of whom both Diana and Tony Blair were presented as 'heirs' and acolytes. He returned to this point again and again. Margaret Thatcher was, he announced, 'the woman, along with Princess Diana, who had changed Britain most', Tony Blair was her 'heir', and all three represented a 'new' Britain. In particular he had no hesitation in highlighting Diana's 'leftish concerns' and her relationship with New Labour – and indeed how 'Tony Blair had very much taken the lead in managing public reaction' to her death – something which the BBC's nation-uniting discourse would have rendered impossible:

> Tony Blair is almost Diana's own generation, he understood her and his election victory represents again that very different new Britain for whom Diana was a goddess. Tony Blair is the political voice, Diana was the emotional voice and the two of them came together.

He later expressed the view that what Britain needed was 'something much more like Diana, much more like Tony Blair, that's outgoing, that seems somehow meritocratic, that isn't rigid and protocol-ridden'. In this new Britain, the monarchy had no option but to 're-invent' itself . Charles Spencer had 'fired the first warning shots in a battle for the soul of the monarchy'. But despite the need for change David Starkey announced on behalf of all Britons: 'We Britons are fond of inertia ... we don't want too much modernity too quickly. Charles is about the right mix'.

But there were more surprises in store. Reporter Tom Fenton regretted on behalf of the media having treated Diana's life as a 'soap opera' and not having concentrated enough on her charitable work while, when the issue of the 'cult' of Diana was raised, David Starkey intervened, despite having earlier described her as a 'Christian saint and athletic pagan goddess':

> Let me immediately confess to you, Dan, I'm a non-believer, What we're seeing now is a kind of invention of a religious cult. I didn't believe in Diana, I don't believe in Diana, and I won't believe in Diana.

No clearer example of the institutional limits of discourse is possible: it goes without saying that David Starkey could simply not have voiced these opinions had he been hired to commentate for the BBC.

NBC

While CBS teamed up with Sky for coverage of the funeral, NBC teamed up with ITN.

Our coverage here is limited to NBC's post-ceremony 'analysis' – which included recorded 'highlight' from both the procession and the ceremony – screened at 9 a.m. Eastern Time. Though there had been no commercial breaks at all prior to this, from this point on they became quite frequent. For the discussion anchors Katie Couric and Tom Brokaw were joined by a panel of three consisting of Jeffrey Archer, Andrew Roberts of the Times and Tina Brown of the New Yorker, these being later joined by fashion designer Valentino. Panel discussion was mixed with vox pops and reports from various parts of the procession route.

NBC was notably less deferential to the discourse of 'grief', preferring to refer instead to the 'incredible outpouring of affection' and the 'outpouring of love'. The event was described as a 'remarkable blend of tapestry and pop culture'. Tina Brown launched a stinging attack on the British tabloids, and blamed it all on Rupert Murdoch, whom she accused of treating 'the royal family like a commodity', a remark which was followed by a brief discussion of privacy laws in the UK and in France. Over and above her association with charitable works, Diana was also discussed at length as a 'fashion plate', a discussion in which Valentino took a leading part. As had also been the case with CBS, the tie-up between Diana and Tony Blair was made quite explicit, with Tina Brown arguing:

> It's arguable that his [Tony Blair's] election in May began to unlock the country from its emotion house arrest, which it's been in traditionally for so long. They were very much in sympathy, and she was very excited by his election.

International coverage
CNN

Coverage by CNN for its international audience differed from BBC coverage in a number of crucial ways. Though it primarily used the images provided by the BBC and ITN cameras, at various points along the funeral procession route and inside Westminster Abbey it combined these with some short feature-style reports of its own. While CNN was clearly aware of the narrative of 'outpouring of national grief' – it referred to it rather summarily on a few occasions – it made no attempt to use it as a framework for its coverage. Most of the images of 'grief' were passed over in silence, with no attempt to work them into a coherent narrative at all. And CNN quite explicitly challenged the 'one-nationness' of it all, pointing out – somewhat caustically – that royal events such as this were traditionally carried by the 'working class and the tourists', while the middle and upper-middle classes 'left for the country'. This sense of a demographically and ideologically quite varied Britain is entirely at odds with the BBC version.

In one of its early features CNN recycled a number of by now very well-established mini-narratives relating to Diana – how she was the 'royal rebel' preferring 'fun' to the stuffy conventions of the past, how she represented the 'younger generation', particularly of women, how she was simultaneously of the 'aristocracy' and of the 'people' – allowing itself, at the same time, the occasional critical note, referring at one point, for example, to Diana's 'sharp tongue'. To the extent that it attempted a 'grand narrative' framework at all, it used the by now very traditional 'historical narrative' (Blain and O'Donnell 1994).

However, perhaps the most striking feature of CNN's coverage was, oddly, its *refusal* of or *flight from* linguistic narrative. While it would be quite normal to expect relatively little commentary during the liturgy itself – a feature of both the BBC's and CNN's coverage of this part of the funeral – CNN's commentary on the procession of the cortege to the Abbey was often extremely laconic. At the simplest level, this was reflected in the many long periods during which nothing at all was said. There were a number of such periods lasting around a minute, several lasting around two minutes, two which lasted approximately three and a half minutes, one which lasted four minutes and twenty seconds, and one which lasted no less than five minutes and thirty seconds without a single word being spoken. It is not that there were no silences in the BBC's coverage – indeed there were, and occasionally of some length – but these were *strategic* in nature, occurring at key moments, and were themselves *part* of the narrative, whereas in CNN they were unpredictable and arbitrary. CNN's lack of *linguistic* commitment may be interpreted in more than one way, for example in terms of its commitment of resources, or its location in relation to British culture. However, we suggest the main factor as a lack of *ideological* commitment to the funeral. CNN was much more interested in the funeral as *performance*, with numerous comments on the extent to which it had been rehearsed, on the 'military precision' of it all, and on how the British Royal Family now 'do' this kind of thing rather well, even if this had not always been the case in the past, a comment which would shock those who regard Britain's historical mastery of ceremony as absolute.

Finally, evidence from another empirical approach. Robert Turnock's British Film Institute study *Interpreting Diana* (Turnock, 2000) involved the circulation of a qualitative questionnaire to 450 respondents, mailed two and a half days after the funeral, of which 278 were returned, which, though its author is careful to downplay their representativeness, comprise an interesting body of responses to place beside Billig's earlier empirical study. After discussing whether or not those 40% of the respondents who on hearing of the Princess's death reported 'feelings of shock, disbelief and distress' were experiencing 'grief' (33) – Turnock is sceptical – he considers how respondents accounted for this, some being unable to do so, others listing factors such as how their own family might cope in such a situation, or how the Princes might cope (34). Dwelling on the implications of the fact that 'previous knowledge and experience of {Diana} had been mediated' (53) Turnock speculates about the extent to which 'people are perhaps becoming more dependent on media images, characters and depictions to provide the resources to help establish identities and trust'.

In this perspective we might understand the reactions as a magnified form of the distress which seems to occur when television characters are killed off. Given what we noted above about the uniquely mediated nature of Diana, an extreme effect of this kind would not be unlikely.

Seventy per cent of the BFI respondents did not participate in 'any public or private displays of grief for the Princess of Wales', a figure which according to Turnock's comments on the sample (a 3:2 ration of women to men; probable higher than average

TV viewing because of self-selection; further probability of higher TV viewing because of older age range) is probably substantially lower than a representative figure; in other words on this basis we would expect quite a lot fewer than thirty per cent of the population as a whole to have participated in 'displays of grief'. Add this to a feeling on the part of many of the BFI respondents that media coverage was 'too much', 'overkill', 'increasingly unbearable' (60–61) or even 'dangerous', with comparisons of how TV raised comparisons with the manipulation of Stalin and Hitler (83), and other evidence besides of distantiation in the sample from some of the claims made about 'the nation' by the BBC (and ITN and other British reports) and we still find ourselves concluding that the overseas reports were more reliable.

We return to the significance of these clearly very discrepant televisual accounts – and their relationship to 'the thinking of the public square' – at a later stage.

3.   The Gnawing Absence of Reality:
Fables of The Royal Boudoir In The British Media

Royalty as a phenomenon of production, as well as consumption

Previous chapters have established that there are a variety of reasons to explain why royal and monarchical media accounts assume their typical forms and contents. A number of interests coalesce around the production of royal narratives in the UK, principal among them:

- the interests of media proprietors, managers and editors. While needing to negotiate a certain space for narrative tensions – which may include performing 'criticism' of the institution of monarchy – they cannot conceivably allow the undermining of the institution, nor its cast, in any serious manner. Royalty is an irreplaceably valuable media topic and commodity. These media interest groupings are also generally conservative;

- the interests of any conceivable British government – for all conceivable British governments are relatively conservative – whose concern will be to balance upon that narrow strip of ideological territory on which British government and opposition parties cluster. Loyalty to the monarchy is a strong symbol of 'common sense' values in Britain, traditionally a Tory virtue which must be mimicked, currently, for example, by New Labour, even (intermittently) by Scottish nationalists;

- the interests of those socio-economic groups in Britain who most clearly benefit from a widespread consensus that British society is in a state of natural development from its historical matrix, and that it is not in need of – or even that it is significantly threatened by – any radical alteration in course (this in turn ensures conservative government policy);

- specifically, the interests of the Royal Family, the landed aristocracy, the mercantile elite of the City of London, new elites, and indeed any of the social groups enjoying spectacularly higher incomes and vastly more beneficial terms of existence than is normal. Britain is in the new century now more unequal than at any time since the Industrial Revolution. New elites – such as the sportocracy and media elites – tend to cultivate, and be cultivated by, existing elites, in alliances offering mutual support for their disproportionate enjoyment of material benefit.

But can the rest of the British public in some sense be fooled by this obvious stratagem of distraction and ideological reinforcement – royalty as 'circuses'?

One response is to suggest that this presents too inactive a model of the audience. In fact we later propose a modification of this account, exploring a more active conception of what the public may be doing when involving itself imaginatively with royal families.

But another kind of answer to this is that in a society which is quite widely (mis)recognized as 'post-political' it is particularly easy to consume ideology when under the impression that one is merely consuming; though of course ideology has always worked best when least detectable in the atmosphere.

It is true that some trends in our media-saturated society have led commentators to deduce that consumption has in some sense partially replaced the ideological and the political elements in our lives; and that additionally these dimensions have been greatly complicated by fractures and reforgings in collective forms. But it is nevertheless hardly more than a statement of the obvious to insist that in a culture increasingly definable as a media culture, there is also great potential for ideological saturation, however realized. This is true despite all that has been noted above about fractures, resistances, apathies, privatisms, breakdowns in representative forms, and other phenomena which seem to indicate limits to ideological functioning.

If we examine specific ideological questions (say, in societies in Western Europe) such as the understanding of Islam; or evaluations of feminism; or, for that matter, mutual European ideologies of neighbouring nation-states, we will encounter yet-powerful ideologies still exerting dominance over large majorities, and, moreover, across demographic divides.

The interests of media producers and retailers are placed first in our list because they are probably decisive. It may be true that the phenomenon of monarchy in the media is primarily economic and secondarily political – as well as cultural and psychological. However, we might say that the phenomenon manifests itself in a circuit of production and reception in which eventually it seems to have acquired economic and political importance *because* it is originally of cultural and psychological importance.

That is to say, even if royal media production is driven most strongly by economic benefit to the media industry, and political (or psychological) gratification to its proprietors or custodians, it is also true that exposure to royal events and personalities finally manifests itself as an imagined psychological need, conditioned by cultural reality: or indeed as a cultural reality, conditioned by psychological need, depending on one's philosophical inclination. Either way, it becomes immensely hard to deny the reality of a public and private need for royal narratives and imagined participation in royal lives. The embeddedness of some of the language of engagement with royalty (fairy tales, outpourings of grief) is very striking, speaking of deep structures of psychological relationship. Even the weaker emblem of 'soap opera' bespeaks at the very least an addiction.

And so – in this account – the media 'serve a need' by spending so much time on, and devoting so much space to, royal phenomena. But as we saw in previous sections, we should do better to remain very sceptical over claims by media professionals and professional politicians that there is really a strong emotional, psychological or political bond between nation and royal family. An alternative possibility is that much of the apparent energy in this relationship is produced by massive quantities of *manufacture*.

There is ceaseless and unsparing *work* by royal public relations and marketing experts, by journalists, editors and presenters, by politicians and civil servants, on constantly *reproducing* the royal phenomenon. In this perspective, the consumption of royalty, as a phenomenon of a highly consumerist society, nonetheless throws more attention back on to the production dimension of the production-consumption relay (Harvey, 1989; Crook et al., 1992) than might be evident in other comparable commodities. For example, the Spice Girls were the first manufactured female pop group ever to achieve world-scale music chart domination, and were part of a 1990s phenomenon of pop manufacture. But the manufacturing process, though clearly understood, is not especially visible in popular music. Part of our task in this book is to make more visible the manufacture of royalty, but in fact this specific phenomenon of cultural manufacture is already quite widely familiar. Allegations of gross over-production of royal news are part of the common material of 'interactive' debate between media professionals and their publics. However, this does not result in a decline in the volume of royal manufacture, since complaints about royal over-visibility are generally interpreted as evidence only of superficial irritation, and in any case as a minority plea.

Yet there are limits to the engagement with royalty and monarchy characteristic of any group of media institutions in every state, where not in terms of volume then certainly with respect to framing. And there are some clear lines of fracture which give us clues to the limits of economic functioning of royal media texts, and suggest where the importance of politics and ideology takes precedence.

For example, though there has been so much royal gossip in the media since the 1980s, there are significant limits to what is said. The next section discusses as its main focus several editions of a run of bio-documentaries focusing weekly on different royal personalities, and screened by the UK's Channel Five television during the first half of 2001, though other evidence is also considered. These programmes take the form of a narrative with voice-over strongly augmented by frequent filmed interview extracts with sources who are generally royal biographers, authors and journalists; though occasionally friends or acquaintances of the British Royal Family contribute, and there is expert commentary, from example from a fashion editor on the reshaping of Camilla Parker-Bowles for a royal role.

As will be seen this series produces some remarkable claims, for example about a series of extramarital affairs of Prince Philip, including the claim that he had a twenty year relationship with Princess Alexandra, and that the Queen was fully aware of it. Some qualified doubt is raised over Prince Andrew's paternity and it is claimed that the Archbishop of Canterbury was among many members of the establishment long aware of Charles's relationship with Camilla, mistresses being regarded as a standard aspect of the sexual life of an incumbent of the role of Prince of Wales. Yet there are very significant absences in the series, no mention being made for example in the edition on Diana of her relationship with the physician Hasnar Khan, regarded by some insiders as much more significant than her dalliance with Dodi Fayed. Though the Duke of Edinburgh is held, by at least one source in a programme on him, to have an illegitimate son (with French show business star Hélène Cordet) there is no mention of two others whose existence circulates in unsubstantiated rumours. Yet the series dares, in the edition on Prince Philip, to juxtapose photographs of Prince Andrew and a royal aide, Lord Porchester, subsequently Earl of Carnarvon, the Queen's Racing Manager since 1969, to suggest an alternative paternity for the Queen's third child.

If one further augments this novel set of perspectives on royal behaviour with other factors which have occupied relatively small quantities of space in the media-conspicuous royal consumption, for example, or persistent royal predilections for activities such as hunting and racing – it is not difficult to begin to construct a view of British royalty drastically different from the usual myth(s). There have indeed been moments, as will be seen, when the adulation even for Diana was not at all present, for example during her relationship with Dodi Fayed and very near to the time of her death, when in fact she was being constructed as an irresponsible hedonistic playgirl. But at these moments media criticism of one royal family member is – in the process, analyzed above, of 'serial realignment' – offset by praise for others, for example a sense emerging from some media accounts, at the depth of Diana's reputation, that the Princess Royal with her solid, unremitting and often unpublicized charity work was a better representative of what royalty is really about. In this way the institution and the conservative symbolic value of the Family can be protected.

Royal-speak: *langue* and *parole*

To appropriate de Saussure's terms, there seem in fact, to exist in the language of monarchy, a royal media *langue* and a royal media *parole*, themselves at least in part identifiable as such because of interests and taboos which operate beyond the media world itself.

Ferdinand de Saussure's discernment of the features of *langue* and *parole* as foundational concepts in his establishment of linguistics as a discipline was neither clear nor consistent, but has remained of great value despite that, because of its considerable suggestibility as a concept (Culler in de Saussure, 1974: xi–xxv; Hawkes, 1977: 20–24, 42–49). In de Saussure's own accounts the relationship between former and latter is characterized variously, for example distinguishing between social and individual, or psychological and physical dimensions, but in general *langue* can be seen as suggesting the abstract system which we refer to as language, the whole possible language, where *parole* refers to everyday speech acts, actual concrete usages of language. In Chomskian terminology this latter realization becomes 'performance' generated by a preceding 'competence', which concept corresponds to de Saussure's *langue*.

In our royal instance we seem faced by a capacity to produce 'speech acts' about royalty and monarchy which far exceeds the actual 'performance' of royal journalism, which is realized within limitations in the domain of *parole*. What would restrict this linguistic performance? In fact this is a bigger question than it even appears.

We have opened this chapter with some speculation about how the interests of elite groups may be associated with the maintenance of the British monarchy in a consensual environment, and the expression of these interests is part of the explanation of the presence of restriction in discussing royal matters. Beyond that, however, lie other considerations, for example of cultural style, which we investigate below. The nations whose monarchies are investigated in this study have national press and broadcasting institutions, the output of whose individual newspapers and news programmes are often marked by very different styles from those encountered in the British media, not least because of major factors such as the uniqueness of Britain's tabloid press.

When trying to understand the nature of 'what is said' in Britain – really also of course what is written – as distinct from what is offered in Europe, we have to bear in mind the existence of a variety of social and cultural differences, some of which we can only briefly acknowledge here, rather than develop. For example, British culture has seldom been at ease with abstract ideas in the way that some European cultures are, and an accompanying anti-intellectualism in British life makes it difficult from the start to raise much debate about abstract differences between monarchies and republics. The success of the British tabloid press is at once symptom and guarantor of a cultural climate hostile to ideas. There are domains of journalism and likewise journalistic styles which are little known in the British media. Though the British are by European standards major purchasers of newspapers, most newspaper sales in Britain are of tabloid papers whose journalism is largely focused on celebrity, television events, royalty, sport, scandal and highly simplified and polemical snippets of politics.

For the time being, and given the international scope of our study, let us note that there are some large differences in context which need to be borne in mind when analyzing both intra-national and international ideological features. These include:

- the relationship between specific cultures, societies, and state apparatuses, and their media institutions and outputs, including matters of finance, ownership, control;
- the relationship between, in particular, specific political cultures and their media institutions and outputs;
- the degree to which specific societies and cultures have unevenly absorbed and/or reproduced postmodern developments like globalization and consumption;
- the nature of media audiences, especially in a media environment in which more and more media output is tuned to demographically determined audiences;
- the adaptation of media organization and practice which occurs in different regions or states as a result of the previous relationships;
- discursive practice in the context of specific national or regional cultures;
- discursive practice within specific media-economic formations, such as the British tabloid press, or state television;

This schematic presentation of some relational aspects of the argument is offered here only as an indication of the overall theoretical dimensions of comparative studies of this kind, not as an agenda for detailed pursuit in the rest of this book. But while any individual study can hope to illuminate only parts of such a large theoretical structure, these parameters nonetheless suggest analytical proprieties which we try to observe. For example, in what follows in this chapter, which focuses on the British case, it is the particularity of the British social, cultural and political – and media-economic – context that is salient.

Revelation, circumspection and credibility

One of these Channel Five documentaries, *Prince Philip: Power Behind the Throne?* (transmitted 8 May 2001) seems especially committed to leading viewers beyond the established limits to the mythicizing of British royalty. Though viewers are theoretically free to doubt the assertions of participating sources in these and all other royal documentaries, programme directors cannot avoid, simply through having control of stills, historical footage, editing patterns and other devices, tending to validate or to remain neutral on the truth-claims of contributors. A motif used throughout the Philip edition of this series is to demarcate sub-episodes of the biography within the overall programme with slow motion shots of a hand hovering over a chess-board or making moves, a conjunctive device which also makes a commentary. For example, the hand at one point picks up a queen, which seems to amplify the programme's depiction – rather well balanced though it is overall – of Philip's origins as a destitute European royal on the make, aided by his calculating uncle, Louis Mountbatten.

More than one of the sources interviewed seem prone to seeing Prince Philip's behaviour over the years as essentially scandalous. Royal author Nicholas Davies sets the tone early on, talking of how 'Philip discovered, very early on, that whenever he went on shore leave, anywhere in the world, he got on extremely well with members of the opposite sex' and recounting in outline his adventures with naval friend Mike Parker, later Philip's private secretary. But Davies's contribution is validated by the programme narration – 'Meanwhile, like most sailors, Philip enjoyed his shore-leave, especially with his navy pal Mike Parker', says the narrator, while we are shown monochrome stills of Philip and Parker, then glamorous photographs of nightclub singer and movie actress Hélène Cordet. 'Another friendship during the war which was special to Philip', says the narrator (a perhaps scurrilous Spanish website investigated by the authors of this book describes Cordet as 'la Camilla Parker de Felipe'). The start of this relationship of course precedes the royal wedding in 1947.

Nicholas Davies's account raises in its very language some of the problems of evaluating media constructions of royal events:

> It has always been rumoured that Prince Philip had a child by Hélène Cordet and this child by the name of Max for some unknown reason went to live in China but no-one has ever spoken officially about it. It's been accepted unofficially that Max is his son but no-one really is worried and Hélène Cordet has never admitted that.

Statement (1) is that the claim is a 'rumour'. Statement (2) that 'no-one has ever spoken officially about it' could easily be seen as pointing us toward a conclusion that in fact Max is not Philip's child, or does not exist. But statement (3) that 'It's been accepted unofficially that Max is his son' clearly seeks to revalidate the claim while statement (4) that ' no-one really is worried' locates the rumour as a fact to which everyone is resigned. But statement (5) 'Hélène Cordet has never admitted that' seems to take us back to the beginning, to unsubstantiated rumour. Ancillary claims by the same source, for example later that 'George VI wanted Elizabeth to have *nothing* to do with Philip. George VI I'm afraid saw right through him' and that 'Philip was basically 'a ne'er-do-well' may serve merely to alert viewers to the possibility that Davies, like so many royal commentators (who seem prone to developing partisan feelings) is inclined to offer Philip the disbenefits of the doubt over most judgements.

This is analogous to a description of Charles and Diana's honeymoon in another programme in this series, on Diana (transmitted 22 May 2001). Royal author Ingrid Seward says:

> They spent a lot of time sunbathing, reading, and just being in each other's company, Diana tells a slightly different story, she said she was already in the *huge* grips of bulimia and was rushing down to the wardroom to get buckets of ice cream, and she says that Prince Charles read a lot and didn't pay enough attention to her so we've already got sort of [indistinct] ['of'] differing stories here.

Though the edition's director gives us a shot of the route below decks to illustrate the tale, it is very difficult to know how to judge this account and we do not know how Seward has been edited in the final cut. That 'they spent a lot of time sunbathing, reading, and just being in each other's company' is not, in the form it takes in the documentary, contextualized as a claim in competition with Diana's counter-claim. Instead we are left to deduce that this must have been a claim either of Charles's, or of some further observer or commentator. That only Prince Charles read, and not both of them, is a modification of the first version, but that he 'didn't pay enough attention to her' is a new feature of the narrative, neither implied nor excluded by the initial statement that 'they spent a lot of time sunbathing, reading, and just being in each other's company'.

That he 'didn't pay enough attention to her' belongs to a different level of reporting, being not a physical description of how the couple were disposed, say, on the deck or in a cabin, but rather a subjective evaluation of appropriate interpersonal behaviour. This is far too difficult for anyone to judge, perhaps even – or perhaps particularly even – for the Prince of Wales to judge, and he had the advantage of being there, albeit perhaps not wholly in spirit. When Ms Seward appears to say that there are 'differing stories here', in fact we are not sure who is the author of the story other than Diana. And we not only, in that case, have differing stories, but a mélange of different levels of truth-claim, complicated by an apparent mid-clause change of verbalization in the final sentence which renders the claim yet more indistinct.

These programmes, like many others, involve commentators quite legitimately offering mutually incompatible views of royalty. We learn that Charles's valet has reportedly said of Diana, that 'in all my years I've never seen anyone as tricky or determined as she was'. This contrasts with more sympathetic accounts. But sometimes documentaries plainly contradict themselves at a more damaging level. In the edition on Diana, Nicholas Davies says that within two or three days of Charles's proposal to Diana (6 February 1981, made public 24 February) 'she moved from there (i.e. Clarence House, where she goes the day after the proposal) to Buckingham Palace and took rooms next to Charles's rooms. I have it on the absolute first hand account that that six months of their relationship was *fantastic*. They were totally together the whole time.'

But after the programme briefly recounts the wedding, the narrator then says 'and after the wedding, came the first real opportunity for Diana to be alone with her husband'. This is curious, since according to Davies, who is a major informant of the programme and used extensively in the series, the couple have spent from around 9 February until around 29 July in adjoining suites at Buckingham Palace, 'together the whole time', although of course they have not been alone, technically, as husband and wife before 29 July; and perhaps we are meant to assume that Diana was chaperoned twenty four hours a day for six months before the wedding. Either that, or Davies is mistaken, which would have serious implications for the quality of information offered by the entire series.

Likewise, on an edition of the Channel Five series on Camilla Parker-Bowles, (broadcast on 29 May 2001) James Whitaker, Royal Correspondent of the Daily Mail, thinks that Charles and Camilla slept together two nights before the wedding with Diana. He is initially very open about issues of credibility:

> The former valet of the Prince of Wales, Stephen Barry, told me that Camilla and the Prince of Wales had slept together two nights before the wedding took place. There's no particular reason to doubt him on this, others have thrown a load of cold water on it and said no it's not true, but I don't see why Stephen should lie and certainly Diana believed that this had happened too.

On the other hand, royal biographers or reporters tend to take sides in royal disputes as we have seen. Whitaker, for example, is keen to support Diana's contention that a legendary pre-marriage 'night of lust' between her and Charles on a royal train did not take place, but his explanation of why he knows that it doesn't is not very clear:

> On that very night when Diana was meant to have been on that train I know that she wasn't (hesitation) at the, on the hours suggested because on that same night (photograph of Diana in long coat and gown, head downturned and arms folded in the glare of the flashlight) she was attending a birthday party at the Ritz Hotel in London's Piccadilly, I know she was there because I saw her there. Anyway, Diana herself called me over, during the middle of this fury, and said 'it's just not true that I was on that train, I was at the party, and I did not go on it'.

Whitaker's account is interesting in that despite his stout assertions over the events, he inadvertently qualifies the force of his own first-hand evidence of having seen Diana at the Ritz 'on the hours suggested' by his tentative language; he corrects himself, having been apparently going to say 'at the hour suggested'. That would imply that all he could really attest was that Diana had not gone to the train *at that moment*, though of course she might have gone later, so he amends his statement to 'on the hours'; though in fact he cannot know what happened later – the 'myth' claims that she left the train in the morning ('disappeared the next day', as he puts it himself) so Whitaker cannot know what she did after he saw her. And though 'Diana herself called me over', this turns out to have happened not at the Ritz at the time, but after the story broke, though at first hearing the fact that Diana has 'called him over' seems to strengthen the evidence from his sight of her at the Ritz. All he receives, then, is the sort of denial a journalist would expect, after the event. (In fact on balance the programme suggests that the woman on the train was probably Camilla. This event had occurred, or failed to occur, in early November 1980 and was reported in the *Mirror* as a secret visit by Diana.)

All of the foregoing accounts demonstrate not only the existence of limits to *parole* in articulating the nature of royal events, but difficulties for respondents too. For a particular way of speaking about royal families to operate fully as language, the utterances made must be comprehensible and acceptable within a speech community. In fact there are elements in a number of these accounts which may seem to sacrifice objectivity for partisanship (interestingly, in the instance of these royal authors and correspondents, any amplification of facts seems to be motivated more by loyalty and self-presentation as an 'insider' than by the desire to sensationalize). Let us note here – it is a matter to which we return in the conclusion of this book – that there are questions about the role of respondents, here the television audience, in determining the limits of *parole*. Not only matters such as taboos on constructing some kinds of royal account as distinct from others are involved, but also credibility.

More truth-claims are made about the British Royal Family and other royal families than about most phenomena; only a proportion of propagators of royal facts have an interest in accuracy and many of the media outlets retailing these facts are notoriously uninterested in accuracy; and only a proportion of the consumers of these facts are interested in accuracy. Royal publicity machines have become better and better at controlling public understanding, aided in Britain by the royal family's strong links with a supportive landed class which sees protecting royal family interests as part of its hereditary duty and privilege.

Establishing the veracity of claims about royal events is a particularly difficult task. There is a specialist language of veiled revelation – 'one is led to believe', 'I have been reliably informed' – some of it shared with other domains such as politics, but in the instance of royalty particularly opaque. This can be a result of commentators knowing less than they pretend, but genuine discretion is also motivated by a very particular relationship between seeker and source in the royal context, manifested by an unusual sense of privilege plainly demonstrated by those royal correspondents with real access, who – unlike treacherous royal lovers like Diana's James Hewitt, who tell all for money from the tabloids – wish to keep their relationship with the royal family healthy, because they value it as a privilege in itself. It is, sociologically, a significant fact that it is still so difficult to evaluate a large proportion of royal information in an age in which protection of privacy is for most social groups extremely difficult. Very substantial royal leaks occur, as in the 'Squidgygate' or 'Camillagate' instances, but then these have often turned out to have been placed in the media domain as part of internecine palace wars, and are therefore better seen as emblematic of royal control than journalistic intrusion.

Returning now to the documentary on Philip with which this phase of the discussion began – the general drift of Nicholas Davies's assessment of Philip, albeit balanced in the film by some very positive comment from other sources, seems substantiated by other accounts of Philip's life which are attested, as it were, by the programme's whole apparatus, and not just individual sources.

- Prince Philip may have technically committed treason by corresponding with his sisters in Germany during the war. To avoid these letters falling into Allied hands, emissaries, one of whom is Anthony Blunt, go to Germany to acquire the documents.
- Philip and private secretary Mike Parker are in the habit, after Philip's wedding, of sneaking off for wild nights in the West End under pseudonyms. They are followed assiduously by the press, who however never manage to pin anything on them.
- Philip's trip to the Melbourne Olympics of 1956 engenders a 40,000 mile world tour described by Philip as his 'personal contribution to the Commonwealth ideal'. In this instance the programme enlists our unqualified belief in misbehaviour on the part of Philip and Parker. Nicholas Davies remarks 'one does understand, that – did Mike Parker and Philip enjoy themselves? and the answer is yes, they did' while royal author and historian Andrew Davies says: 'And there we have nine months, tootling round the world on a huge great yacht, centre of the attention of the kind of people they wanted, friends, charming young ladies, the opportunities were there, why not take them'. (The programme does not mention, as other sources do, the rumour of another illegitimate child as a result of this adventure.)

Probably the most serious allegation which arises from the programme is of Philip's involvement in the Profumo affair. After colour footage of the Houses of Parliament there follows a monochrome still of Christine Keeler. 'Next' says the narrator 'the 1960s and the scandal that would bring the establishment to its knees. Profumo. Was Philip involved?'

It turns out that Philip and Stephen Ward were acquainted for years, both being in the Thursday club. Profumo affair author Douglas Thompson talks of Ward having a 'very, very strong reputation as a man who could take away all your aches and pains, and it got around, in society. They all would meet up, and drink lots of champagne, oysters were a necessity, they always had to have oysters for the libido, and it was a jolly lunch that stretched into the afternoon, and then on to parties, and Philip was very fond of these'.

Ward in 1961 was given permission to sketch eight members of the Royal Family including Philip. The narrator notes that the sketches are being exhibited in London as the Profumo scandal breaks, and Blunt is again dispatched, this time to buy the sketches. However photographs allegedly featuring Philip, Ward and two girls (shots of Blunt and Philip accompany this account in the film) supposedly find their way to Cecil King. In June 1963 there is a *Mirror* story referring to the 'foulest' aspect of the scandal being a rumour of Philip's involvement – which the *Mirror* says is unfounded.

These allegations, which the programme seems to invite us to take seriously, are accompanied by others which the programme itself invites us to regard sceptically, for example, Philip spends an evening in 1948 dancing with actress Pat Kirkwood. It is subsequently rumoured that Philip has bought Kirkwood a white Rolls-Royce to encourage her discretion over a (likewise rumoured) affair, but Kirkwood strenuously denies – well into very recent times – the development of any romance.

Some allegations are left entirely to the judgement of viewers: Nicholas Davies claims that 'He did go for film star-type people because those were the ones that attracted him – as well, let me say, as numbers of polo wives, two or three of whom have told me that they'd had their flings with Philip.' The narrator continues: 'Merle Oberon, Daphne Du Maurier and others have all been mentioned. But nothing has ever been confirmed.' This is over a slow zoom into a photograph of a smiling and inscrutable-looking Philip. The implication of this shot – chosen rather than, say, a happy family photograph at Sandringham or Balmoral – is that the lack of definite knowledge of these events may be a function of Philip's cleverness rather than his propriety.

Royal biographer Christopher Wilson says Fleet Street has been waiting for forty years 'to try and nail Prince Philip in bed with another woman.' The programme also implies emphatically that Philip and Princess Alexandra had a twenty-year relationship – Nicholas Davies says 'the Queen knew about it, of course'.

But the most daring moment in the programme, where it comes closest to defying a substantial taboo surrounding the Queen herself, is over the paternity of Prince Andrew, born in February 1960. There is no visible hook for raising the question other than a doubt raised by the highly controversial biographer Kitty Kelley, who has suggested that Andrew looks very like Lord Porchester, the Queen's racing manager since 1969, later Earl of Carnarvon. The director shows us a photograph of Lord Porchester, admittedly looking quite like Andrew, but then again perhaps selected on that basis (the authors have looked at other photographs of the Earl, for example on the House of Lords website, which do not bear this resemblance). The programme however seems to wish us to take this allegation seriously.

Nicholas Davies, whose manner when talking about Philip is fluent and confident, says, speaking very slowly and carefully with pauses and self-corrections:

> There have from time to time been suggestions that not only was Prince Philip 'putting it about' but that Elizabeth got involved with one or two *amours*. I've looked into these and there are possibilities that Elizabeth had – how can I put it – very close friendships with two or three men in her life. But never to the degree of having an affair.

However the narrator, over footage of royal family shots and also the Houses of Parliament, stirs the pot not a little:

> To add to the intrigue is the unusually long embargo placed on cabinet records relating to the royal family in 1959. Macmillan felt the contents sensitive enough not to release the papers for a hundred years as opposed to the usual thirty. In 2059 Philip will be one hundred and thirty-eight and Andrew, ninety-nine.

This can only be interpreted as an intended reinforcement of the sense of major scandal and raises questions about the absence of other versions of these events elsewhere in the media (there are scattered and not especially authoritative websites with fragments of comment on some of these allegations but there is, in fact, remarkably little alternative information, or even allegation of scandal, on British royal matters on the Web, which might lead to further forms of speculation).

What is notable about these 'revelations' – other than how little of substance has ever been discovered about Prince Philip by the media – is how they form a quite completely alternative version of his character from that which the media generally settle for. In fact, this programme itself balances its outrageous moments by including contributions from commentators who are very complimentary, like Christopher Wilson, about Philip's 'modernization' of the Royal Family. Even the iconography of the programme is well balanced. In addition to the nightclub shots of Hélène Cordet and a publicity still of Pat Kirkwood, featuring the legs which, we are informed, were sometimes referred to as the 'eighth wonder of the world', are stern and responsible shots of Philip in uniform looking very much like a mainstay of the Family and the Nation. The documentary both plays the game and departs from its rules at the same time. The seldom-uttered *parole* of scandal, in fact of a monarchy of medieval licence and extraordinary self-indulgence – Philip after the Coronation consoles himself with two aircraft of the Queen's Flight, two Westland helicopters, four Rolls Royces, all funded by the treasury for official engagements, and additionally buys seven polo ponies, eight family horses, a catamaran and four yachts – is closed down considerably by the *parole* of quotidian British subjecthood which accompanies it.

But this retrieval from the normally unperformed *langue* of royal accounts nonetheless suggests the possibility of constructing a really drastically different version of royalty.

Transformation

In this section, we can observe 'one way of speaking', about Prince Charles's 'mistress' Camilla Parker-Bowles, becoming another way of speaking, about Camilla Parker-Bowles the worthy candidate for entry into the Royal Family. The programme on Camilla (transmitted 29 May 2001) like others in this series consolidates a new stage of advance in the development of 'alternative' revelations about royal behaviour. As we have seen, a previous programme even goes so far as to speculate about whether or not the Queen herself has had extramarital affairs, a very unusual realm for British television to enter.

Prince Charles's biographer Anthony Holden takes the view that Charles probably thought it reasonable to have a mistress – 'this had happened in several previous generations of his family' and he feels that it was 'probably the basis on which he married Diana', and that this was the position of 'his parents, the Archbishop of Canterbury, the British Establishment, many of whom knew about his affair with Camilla and did not expect him to give it up'.

This is really not the *parole* of the British media, yet it is unlikely that this knowledge is especially restricted, given the social interaction of elite metropolitan groups. There is a language (in fact more than one) which is spoken to the public as part of the royal narrative and another retained by journalists, editors and other circles in which knowledge is present, this less restricted *parole* being publicly unspeakable because of how these collective interests (press, broadcasting, courtiers, government) wish royalty to be understood.

Mail Royal Correspondent James Whitaker talks this other more restricted language, in pretendedly offended terms, when commenting on the Camilla tape: 'there was clear evidence of the love that Charles and Camilla had for one another when Charles was still married to Princess Diana' – he places accents on the last two terms, *'Princess Diana'*. Whitaker is perfectly well aware of royal marital double-dealings, he is after all a royal correspondent, but here he is role-playing. Likewise, when discussing the Queen's more recent attitude to Camilla:

> The Queen is a deeply religious, moral person and she views Camilla as an adultress who had an affair when she was married to one of her Guards officers Andrew Parker-Bowles, was having an affair with her son, she doesn't accept her at all.

Well, in the light of previous revelations about the Family – unless they are all to be disbelieved – we may conclude that the Queen may or may not accept Camilla Parker-Bowles, but that she is unlikely to have been shocked by her affair with her son, since she is certain to have known about it.

The documentary is a revealing passage of television on Camilla, not only because of what it reports more or less reliably about a deliberate process whereby Camilla was increasingly marketed to the British nation by royal interests, allied to substantial media interests; but revealing too as a television programme whose own purpose is to establish within the paradigm of royalty a figure who has had a tenuous connection with it.

As the memory of Diana's funeral receded, the media began to realign themselves around figures of the long-term future – especially William, some of whose construction is examined below – and mid-term figures, among whom Camilla becomes ever more certainly a player. This edition of the Channel Five series thereby produces a reflexive effect of both helping establish Camilla as a potentially mainstream figure while also revealing how this process has been accomplished by palace and media interests.

The section of this film which deals with the media transformation of Camilla between 1992 and the death of Diana in 1997 begins with a still of a beleaguered Camilla in a tight composition, a head and shoulders, left-facing profile shot with Camilla to the right of the frame, and in the foreground a man shielding her, presumably, from other photographers, with a copy of the *Times* ('Smith makes last-ditch bid to avert defeat', clearly reads the headline, providing a sort of comment, for historical consumption, by way of gloomy, assonant reference to the doomed Labour leader). The photograph subdivides, by means of a central vertical, Camilla from her gallant protector, isolating her symbolically in her half of the frame and signalling that there is nowhere for her to hide from media interest; for though the message of the photograph is that she is being shielded from photographers, she has been caught nonetheless. She looks saddened, deeply pensive and resigned.

The narrator starts: 'But the one left out in the cold to fend off the press was Camilla Parker-Bowles'. Her biographer Christopher Wilson summarizes the unhappy state of the affair: 'She was harassed in every way possible by the British press, her property was invaded and she was treated appallingly'. Two more photographs are shown over this commentary, one in which she looks very distraught, trying to hold a headscarf over her forehead with one hand, clutching a bag and a newspaper with a headline (about her and Charles) in the other, head down, presumably blocked from escaping by reporters and photographers, mouth open and teeth exposed in what looks like a cry of despair. In a second photograph she looks despondently thoughtful, photographed in her car, partly concealed by a headscarf, and visibly exhausted. Wilson continues:

> She was called ugly, dowdy, terrible jokes were being made about her, cartoons in the paper, trying to make out that she was a woman of easy virtue, and she had to endure this public humiliation without any kind of support from anybody whatsoever.

It is very revealing to look at these photographs of Camilla and then inspect the photographs of Diana which follow directly in this documentary, for they are so different as to suggest two quite distinct kinds of relationships between the two sets of photographs and the real world. Where those of Camilla are revelatory and painful, documenting personal and social agony, the shots of Diana which follow, taken, for this Channel Five documentary, from the front page of a contemporary broadsheet, are redolent of a sort of media-awareness which seems to belong to an altogether different process of 'mediation' from the one Camilla Parker-Bowles is embroiled in; shots which reveal nothing at all about Diana except how she wishes to be photographed (in what was a short television interview which took three days to shoot). A triptych of full-face shots of Diana, in their turn stills from the Panorama interview, show her respectively doe-eyed and self-pitying, with a mournful upward glance; in the second, bravely determined and strong. A third shot is more open, rather less self-conscious in expression, but at best a fashion shot in which she is impersonating light-heartedness.

There is pain in at least two of these shots but it is pain which has been harnessed by someone who has become expert in an iconography of pain. As in Baudrillard's third phase image, this is a sign which threatens to obliterate its object. The contrast between Camilla's helplessness in front of the camera and Diana's sovereignty over the medium is remarkable when juxtaposed.

In January 1996 the terms of the divorce were settled. 'From that time Camilla Parker-Bowles became a visible fixture in the Prince's life' the narrator tells us: however, 'her public image was a problem'.

In fact up until this point it hasn't been all that much of a problem for the media, since along with the Duchess of York and Prince Edward, Camilla could be used by the British media to attract readerships or audiences by running the sort of hostile stories and unpleasant jokes about these royal peripherals which the British public appears to like.

But 'the problem' by 1996 is that since Camilla is going to be a fixture, the media may find more economic leverage in liking her than disliking her. Therefore they may not be resistant to royal publicity-machine initiatives remarketing Camilla as a likeable country-loving woman who will make a suitable consort (of some sort) for the future king.

But Charles requires to spend some of his time in urban settings so Camilla will have to pass muster in the cities too. The documentary turns to Hilary Alexander, Fashion Editor of the *Daily Telegraph*, to explain the technical dimensions of the challenge.

Alexander, in pince-nez, pearls, and with an impressively large black chiffon rose pinned to the neck of her rose-pink top, is seated beside a computer monitor which displays as she speaks a series of images of Camilla which illustrate her argument:

> Most of the photographs of Camilla that were published in the press were (sort of) snatched, you know, kind of paparazzi shots, and she was hiding, or she was drawn, she was worried, she probably was feeling psychologically battered on all sides and you can understand people would see this and think oh, you know, she just looks like some horrible old bat.

The narrator continues, 'Her image began to change in the mid-1990s when she swapped her county look for something more sophisticated'.

If there is a broad cultural convention which dictates that urban life is more 'sophisticated' than rural life, coverage of royalty seldom challenges it. As can be seen elsewhere in this book, when Diana died the English media spoke of the Royal Family as being in some sense out of the country when they were only in it, at Balmoral, though admittedly in remote Scotland. In the documentary under discussion, royal biographer Penny Junor notes that in 1984 Charles and Camilla resumed their relationship, in Junor's account on the initiative of concerned friends of Charles: 'Camilla by this time was a very unhappy woman living in Wiltshire', explains Junor without further explanation of cause and effect, over a photograph of Camilla in her Wiltshire garden, admittedly looking cheerless, though whether or not as a direct result of living in Wiltshire is difficult to deduce from the image itself.

The first new image of Camilla we see has her looking confident in the back of a limousine, bejewelled and in a black dress. Alexander explains:

> Her hair is much softer, it's sort of slightly blown-dried, it looks as if it's got a lot of texture, it looks kind of touchable and pretty, and just a little bit fluffy and nice, whereas before it seemed to be either quite tightly curled or it was always crammed under a riding hat and you couldn't really see that much of it.

This is presented in terms of a transformation. But presumably Camilla's hair hasn't really changed its texture, and it seems likely that the old Camilla had, on the odd occasion, taken her riding hat off. But of course nobody had photographed her for the press then, so what we are now encountering is a modest mythic echo of Diana's transformation from shy child nurse to global superstar, as well as that confusion between media image and real world object which holds that Camilla Parker-Bowles was a woman with a riding hat.

This transformation likewise involves visible charity work, a royal prerequisite. We view next an attractive publicity-orientated photograph of Camilla taken in 1996. She has become patron of an osteoporosis charity. The photograph shows her looking relaxed, elegant and happy. 'This was a new view of Camilla to a lot of people', says a friend. But the new Camilla is put on hold because of Diana's death, as Penny Junor points out:

There had been a subtle campaign to make Camilla more acceptable to the British public, from probably about the mid-1990s, which was severely set back when Diana died, for all sorts of reasons, I think Charles and Camilla were both seen as the villains at that point and it would have been completely tasteless and wrong and impossible to have entertained any thought of bringing Camilla out again.

There are now low-level shots from outside St James's Palace of parading guardsmen, brisk and very businesslike, sending message of military precision as well as of a post-funeral return to business: the narrator resumes 'When, a year later, Prince Charles's publicity machine at St James's Palace swung back into action, it appeared to have developed a much more sophisticated approach.' Anthony Holden points out how royal 'events' are often in fact phenomena of marketing or public relations: 'A lot of the stories that are deliberately leaked in ways that the public perhaps don't always realize, William had tea with Camilla yesterday, they got along famously' – shot of *Sun* full front page, Camilla meets Wills headline – 'that is using the children. Those events are orchestrated by the St James's Palace machine and if it were natural I would think great, terrific, you know, we hope they'll get on together, specially if she's going to be the woman in their father's life.

Another leaked story is that William has planned a surprise fiftieth birthday party for Charles; and has invited Camilla. The stills accompanying this information are of Camilla now looking positively regal, earrings and necklace sparkling in the light from the flashguns, in the back seat of a chauffeured car. The message is that if Camilla is now acceptable to the sons of Diana there should be no cause for a rejection of her close presence in the Royal Family from elsewhere.

The footage we see moves steadily away thematically from the hunted Camilla of the early 1990s toward standard royalty footage, shots of Camilla formally dressed in black, receiving a bouquet on a crowded pavement, getting into a black limousine, all the while being filmed and photographed: biographer Christopher Wilson opines that 'the public want to be able to see Camilla Parker-Bowles out in the open, they want to see her talking to people, meeting people, interacting with people, just in the way that Diana used to do. They want to get to know Camilla Parker-Bowles.'

They are not going to get much choice. The narrative informs us, accompanied by shots of Camilla in the country on horseback, that she is still most comfortable out riding – 'it's a county set image in keeping with other members of the Royal Family, and she's beginning to adapt and smile for the cameras'. There are suggestions in this formulation that she is now a member of the Royal Family ('other members') but also by implication that she may be more similar to them than Diana was, because though of course Diana was the daughter of an earl, she was not closely associated with the country pursuits of the other royals.

A further expert summary from fashion editor Hilary Alexander is preceded by a happy, confident, even radiant head and shoulders close-up of Camilla in riding costume and hat. Alexander approves of the new images of Camilla now being produced: 'People have had a chance to see photographs of her which show her looking happy and attractive'. However as a fashion expert she seems torn between her sense of how far it is plausible to commend Camilla's photogenic qualities and her desire to be generous: 'I mean obviously a lot of the time the pictures we see of her are on a horse...'

A news extract follows in which Charles and Camilla are leaving the Ritz hotel in slow motion to a barrage of flashguns and screams of delight from spectators. 'It's the picture royal watchers have waited for, Charles and Camilla in public as a couple for the first time. They were met by an explosion of flashguns as they left the Ritz Hotel in London moments before midnight', begins a reporter with a strong Scottish accent.

By a curious accident of editing, the preceding Scottish accent reinforces the sense that Alexander's continuing expert summary of Camilla's fashion style – Alexander is now facing the computer monitor – parallels the television form of post-match micro-analysis of passes and shots in football, so often conducted in Scottish accents. Part of her expert analysis runs across slow motion shots of the couple getting into their limousine, so Alexander's already evident air of expertise is further enhanced. We are now watching a Charles and Camilla match analysis. The commentary underlines the process of Camilla's continuing transformation. Alexander:

> It was the first chance we really had, officially, to do a photograph of them together. She was wearing Tomasz Starzewski, beautifully tailored black evening coat, *fabulous* choker, and she looked, you know, quite relaxed. I think she's certainly responding to the camera more, by accepting the fact, whether she really loves it or not, that the camera *is* going to be there, and it's much better if you flash a quick smile, stop for a few seconds, give everyone the shot they want, and then move on.

Camilla's biographer Christopher Wilson, does not agree: 'She can in no way compete with Diana in the fashion stakes...She has to wear some smart clothes when she's turning out at the Ritz Hotel, but the designer clothes which are being chosen are tragic and wrong'. But the programme editor's laudable wish to include balance in the argument is undermined by the fact that Wilson's protest is conducted in a straight-to-interviewer indoor location shot without any accompanying footage or stills, so there are no examples of 'tragic' or 'wrong' outfits: compared to Alexander's computer monitor post-match analysis style there is no contest.

A consultation with the relevant Vogue designer biography informs us that Camilla was probably right to dress herself at this stage in Tomasz Starzewski, indeed precisely right. Between 1989 and 1999 Starzewski 'remained one of Britain's more traditional designers', adopting as his central tenet the supply of 'glamour, pure glamour' (www.vogue.co.uk), these characteristics of glamour anchored by tradition being precisely what, one presumes, Camilla needs at this moment in her transformation.

Alexander, however, also has reservations about Camilla's new image: as soon as Wilson finishes we cut back to footage shots, Charles and Camilla exiting from a green Rolls-Royce. Alexander continues: 'That pink dress with the long sleeves I did feel was sort of a slight mistake, it's a wee bit mumsy...', and the sequence with Camilla in the mumsy pink dress turns out to be a much-screened extract, enlivened by the emblematic moment when she leaves the green Rolls-Royce – and turns the wrong way, walking toward the front of the car while Charles heads off in the proper direction. Camilla as she corrects herself lengthens her stride and pace to catch up, directed discreetly by a man holding the Rolls-Royce door, and by Charles: she still has some way to go, that seemed to say. It was shown in news broadcasts, apparently with the intention of depicting Camilla as still in the process of learning how to become royal.

But finally the documentary's editing is itself now hastening Camilla's transformation. The mumsy pink sequence is edited tightly against another Alexander analysis, in nearer close-up, pointing at the monitor enthusiastically, head turned away from the camera in concentration, at a close-up of Camilla, now in blue, in the back of yet some other limousine, with Charles.

> I think she looks very confident there. I *love* the way the little sort of button hole, look, on Prince Charles, matches the dress. It's nice, isn't it.

She pays this last tribute staring appreciatively at it. It's as though Charles and Camilla are already married. And Camilla's biographer immediately thereafter does indeed speculate on marriage, though the Queen is next pictured looking pensive and alert. 'But what does Her Majesty the Queen make of all this? Is she ready to welcome Camilla into the Royal Family?' The voice-over is reminding us, with 'Her Majesty', that Camilla is still just a countrywoman who is well outside the official royal circle.

In the end the Queen meets Camilla at a party at Highgrove but the *Mail*'s Whitaker, who is the chief representative of propriety in this documentary series, insists that the Queen has thereafter kept her distance. The programme concludes that while Camilla's role in Charles's life is assured, her public role is uncertain: but the footage which accompanies the speculation, of hundreds of flashguns exploding as a regal-looking Camilla accompanies Charles at a public function, suggests how the matter may be resolved.

PART TWO
EUROPEAN MONARCHIES AND THE MEDIA

4. The UK, Spain and Beyond:
Monarchy and Modernity

Royalty and Media Narrative

In his 'Introduction to the Structural Analysis of Narratives', French semiologist Roland Barthes observed that:

> the narratives of the world are numberless. Narrative is first and foremost a prodigious variety of genres, themselves distributed amongst different substances – as though any material were fit to receive man's stories. Able to be carried by articulated language, spoken or written, fixed or moving images, gestures, and the ordered mixture of all these substances; narrative is present in myth, legend, fable, tale, novella, epic, history, tragedy, drama, comedy, mime, painting... stainglass windows, cinema, comics, news item, conversation. Moreover, under this almost infinite diversity of forms, narrative is present in every age, in every place, in every society; it begins with the very history of mankind and there nowhere is nor has been a people without narrative. All classes, all human groups, have their narratives, enjoyment of which is very often shared by men with different, even opposing, cultural backgrounds. Caring nothing for division between good and bad literature, narrative is international, transhistorical, transcultural; it is simply there, like life itself (Barthes, 1987: 79).

Any study of the complex role(s) of monarchy in contemporary European societies will quickly come to the conclusion that, whatever the actual realities of monarchic existence and powers might be, the primary – in the sense of most consumed – presence of monarchy in these societies is in the form of narrative, indeed at times of a vast array of narratives. And these narratives, of course, must and do change over time. Indeed, a narratological analysis of recent key moments in the history of British monarchy provides compelling evidence of Lyotard's claim (1984) that, in the age of postmodernity, certain 'grand narratives' of yore are vulnerable to fragmentation into a series of *petits récits* as the social and political structures which once maintained their hegemonic position come under increasing pressure. In this chapter we concentrate on coverage in Continental Europe of the announcement of the separation in 1992 of Prince Charles and the then Princess Diana though, for reasons which will quickly become apparent, we will concentrate on coverage of this story in Spain.

The 'story' breaks

The separation of Charles and Diana was announced on 9 December 1992 during an EU summit being held in Edinburgh and hosted by the then British Prime Minister, John Major. Though the trials and tribulations of the British monarchy had no possible relation with the official business of the EU, John Major took time out of this meeting to announce this separation in tones reminiscent of those which might accompany a royal death, despite the fact that the strained relations between the husband and wife in question had been widely known for some considerable time in advance. Coverage of this event in the European media – in particular the written media – was intense: of the over forty newspapers we consulted only one – the highbrow German weekly newspaper *Die Zeit* – paid the announcement no attention at all. Many newspapers provided coverage stretching over several pages, while some Sunday editions had special sections dedicated to the British royal family in general.

A first distinction which can be drawn is the difference in tone between television and newspaper coverage. In general television coverage was respectful, at times quite lugubrious. The press, on the other hand, allowed itself a much wider range of responses, mixing more or less unadorned statements of what had happened with at times caustic or even gleeful comment with highly visible doses of schadenfreude.

As an initial example, we might look at the sarcastic response of the French daily *Le Figaro* (10 December 1992). We should remember in this respect that this announcement also took place against the background of the American invasion of Somalia with high-level coverage throughout Europe of the turmoil then engulfing that country. Referring to the separation *Le Figaro* pointed out: 'The dreadful evils of the day, the famines, crimes, pollution, corruption, all are forgotten, everything is giving way to a piece of news which is taking on world-wide apocalyptic proportions: Charles and Diana are separating'. Some idea of the dominant tone of the Spanish press in covering the event can be gained if we compare *Le Figaro* with the commentary of the weekly magazine *Cambio 16* (21 December 1992):

> Relegating at a single stroke all the wars, plagues and famines of the world to the realm of indifference, the tremendous piece of news exploded like a bomb: 'Charles and Diana are getting separated'. It was the day of the invasion of Somalia by the marines; from India, the religious war between Hindus and Muslims was spreading to Pakistan and England itself; Eastern Europe was in flames from Sarajevo to Tadjikistan, and in Western Europe, bogged down in the tangle of Maastricht, the unemployment queues were getting longer; Africa was coming apart with tribal wars, AIDS and famine; from Latin America came the thunder of coups d'état, the bombs of the drugs mafia and guerrilla attacks. And the world press in unison, from the Financial Times to Hola, chorused the terrible news: 'Charles and Diana are getting separated'.

While the point being made is substantially the same, it is immediately apparent that the Spanish magazine has, so to speak, got its teeth into the idea in a way which the French newspaper has not: in particular, the level of sarcasm is much higher. This is symptomatic of Spanish coverage of the event as a whole, and is a point to which we shall return on several occasions below.

Press v. television

State-owned Spanish Television took the announcement of the separation of Charles and Diana very seriously indeed. As in a number of other countries, normal programming was interrupted for a news flash bringing this grievous news to the Spanish nation, and subsequent programmes were cancelled as British royalty 'specials' were shown. Its first channel (La Primera) dedicated much of its *Informe Semanal* – a weekly current affairs programme – to this topic. It was introduced by a female presenter dressed in black against a black background and employing a hushed and almost tearful mode of address. It carried a lengthy special report on the history of the royal marriage and a detailed blow-by-blow description of Queen Elisabeth's 'annus horribilis'. The report concluded with the words that 'everyone, absolutely everyone, has come out a loser'.

The lugubrious tone of these and other official reactions caused considerable irritation in the Spanish press (as the quote already given illustrates): the press did not take anything like such a doom-laden view of events, which it indeed saw as out of place (Spain, incidentally, like other southern European countries has no tabloid press: all the newspapers quoted hereafter belong to the 'quality' sector). As the conservative – and indeed in the Spanish context historically pro-monarchist – Madrid daily *Abc* (11 December 1992) put it, referring to the leading government and opposition figures in Spain at the time (the Zarzuela is the official residence of the Spanish king):

> Only a country which has little respect for itself can give rise to a storm of debate like that caused here by the separation of the Prince and Princess of Wales. If you believe some commentators, the day after John Major's announcement Pons, González, Aznar and Anguita should have gone to the Zarzuela and said to the King: 'Sir, thanks for the services rendered, but we have to proclaim the Third Republic. Lady Di has separated from her husband.'
>
> When Spain was a respectable, and therefore a respected power, a crisis in the English royal family would have concerned only the Spanish royal family, for reasons of family relationships. National public opinion would have noisily celebrated the institutional disarray of Perfidious Albion and its expected loss of political power.

It is immediately clear that the *Abc* journalist is saying a great deal more about Spain here than he is about the UK, but the general tone of Spanish press reporting on the royal separation was as a rule up-beat and elated: it was, by and large, enjoying the discomfiture of the British royal family, and the glory which, it argued, was reflected on its own royal family as a result.

The British Royals
From Dynasty to Dallas: telling the (British) royal story
As mentioned earlier, talking of royals anywhere in Europe – indeed, we might surmise,

anywhere at all – means getting involved in a series of stories some of which have been running for a very long time. There is nothing unconscious about this: newspapers, magazines and television stations throughout Europe constantly make explicit reference to narrative categories in their coverage of royalty, and also make use of the distinctions between narrative genres to indicate changes in direction in one or other of the narratives being developed.

As was the case with every aspect of media coverage of the 1992 separation, the longest exposition – indeed, deconstruction – of this theme was to found in Spain, again in the pages of the *Cambio 16* (10 August 1992). Having begun with a reference to the Nicaraguan poet Rubén Darío's widely known poem on a fairytale princess, '¿qué tendrá la princesa?' (what's wrong with the princess?) it goes on to describe the genre of 'monarchic-sentimental drama' – a genre invented by a group of Spanish writers – as it might apply to the British royals:

> But the monarchic-sentimental drama would never achieve as much success as in England, where monarchs have always kept people talking. Henry VIII beheaded his wives, George IV hated Caroline, his wife (a bit scatterbrained, true, but that hardly warranted his leaving the poor woman in the street during the coronation, as he did); they compared Edward, that prince and fairy, with *Jack the Ripper* and Edward VII [*sic*], a good man, abdicated to marry a divorcee.

The rogues reign while the good abdicate. Over and above the obvious sarcasm which suffuses comments such as these, what they make clear is that the Spanish press is refusing to accept the narrative categories emanating from the British royal house itself, and will use its own narrative definitions in a construction of British royalty to meet its own specific needs.

The historical narrative

Coverage of royalty operates through a number of simultaneous narratives on different levels. The 'outermost' layer (so to speak) of this narrative system is a historical narrative linking current monarchs with the past – in the case of the British monarchy with the ancient past – and at the same time manipulating elements such as the formation of peoples, nationhood, tradition, national psyche and so on.

Elements of this historical narrative which appeared in coverage of the Charles and Diana story throughout Europe were references to the Treason Act of 1352, numerous references to Anne Boleyn, Mary Queen of Scots, King Henry the Eighth, and above all Queen Victoria. European reproductions of this narrative were often ironic. The German weekly magazine *Der Spiegel*, for example, amused both itself and its readers by printing an article on Prince Charles in which the latter was constantly referred to using the German version of the 'royal we' – a grammatical structure where the singular noun for 'Highness' (Hoheit) is followed by a plural verb. This highly anachronistic structure was sufficient on its own to relay at least one view of the British historical narrative in the Federal Republic of Germany. A cartoon in the likewise German weekly magazine *Stern* showed the princes Charles and Andrew (both suffering marital problems at the time) sitting beneath a portrait of Henry VIII. As they commiserate with each other Henry opines 'You wimps'.

Where Spanish involvement in this super-narrative differs from that in the other European countries covered is in its consistently aggressive tone frequently involving references to historical conflicts between Spain and England. The clearest example of this is to be found again in *Abc* (11 December 1992) and takes the form of a Spanish revenge for what are seen as ancient and recent English insults (Churruca was an Admiral of the Spanish Armada):

> The English Crown is so closely linked to the greatness of that country that, remembering the Armada, Trafalgar, and Catherine of Aragon, the sunken galleons, the sack of Cadiz by Drake's pirates and, of course, Gibraltar, the spirit of Churruca would be jumping for joy in the heaven of dead seamen. This recently separated couple who had the nerve to spend their honeymoon in Gibraltar is now receiving its just punishment for its imperialist perversity. Let's see if they learn their lesson.

More importantly, however, Spanish newspapers and magazines in general refuse to accept the validity of the English historical narrative, presenting it as a sham which disguises an empty present. 'Henry VIII was a real king, whereas prince Charles is simply a symbol of royalty. In those days the essence of royalty was power, and not, as it is now, tradition', suggested *Cambio 16* (21 December 1992). The British monarchy 'has more of a past than a present' wrote the weekly magazine *Tribuna* (14 December 1992), adding that what was required was 'a change in the legitimation of the monarchy such that the references to the past are changed for a justification preferably of a functional or operational kind, bringing with it the need for a democratisation which would mean... bringing up to date its value systems'. As will be pointed out later, we are again dealing here as much with references to Spain as we are with references to Great Britain.

The fairy tale
The dominant European form of narrative in relation to Charles and Diana in 1992 was, beyond any shadow of a doubt, that of the fairy tale. When the fairy tale was working, wrote *Cambio 16* in Spain (21 December) 'millions of people throughout the world discovered the existence of things made in Britain which they thought had been extinct since the collapse of the empire: war planes, polo horses, Scotland [*sic*!], Covent Garden, Van Dyck'. The dominant motif, was, however, that the fairy tale was now over.

The level of saturation achieved by references to this narrative genre is difficult to illustrate satisfactorily, but some idea of the scale of this phenomenon can be gained from a simple statistic: in the over forty different European publications covered by this study, more than sixty references to 'fairy tales' were found. However, the statistic on its own does not give a clear idea of the prominence of such references. On one occasion – in the Norwegian daily tabloid *VG* of 10 December 1992 (and *VG* is Norway's best-selling newspaper) – the entire front page was given over to a photograph taken from the royal wedding of 1981, with the single headline 'The end of the fairy tale'. A similar front-page headline was to be found in *Cambio 16* (21

December 1992), which had earlier written (11 December 1992) 'With the eyes of 750 million people throughout the world fixed on the bride, the former nursery-school teacher, with her schoolgirl look, was playing the leading role in a fairy tale... Now, with the separation of the Prince and Princess of Wales the fairy tale is vanishing', while the Flemish daily *Het Volk* (10 December) carried as the front-page headline of one of its sections 'The fairy tale is over'.

This narrative was accompanied by many references to Cinderella and to authors such as Hans Christian Andersen and the Brothers Grimm, and was often connected to notions of anachronism and modernity. In Germany the weekly *Das Neue* (12 December) wrote: 'What a cruel end to the erstwhile fairy-tale couple Diana and Charles!... However, it remains the case that it was she who thoroughly restored the dusty and antiquated royal house', while the Dutch popular daily *De Telegraaf* – in an article entitled 'Diana: a princess who once again can be a woman' – mused (10 December 1992):

> The end result of it all is that Princess Diana is no longer a fairy-tale princess but a modern young woman. Many women who are trapped in unhappy marriages will recognize them-selves in her and identify with her... She can again conquer the world as a princess who has clearly emancipated herself and has taken the reins of her own life in her own hands. She is no longer the unhappy Cinderella-like princess who alone in her castle had to carry on sad hour-long conversations to tell her friends how she actually felt.
>
> The Diana of the nineties yesterday made her entry as a princess who wanted once more to become a woman.

The sheer dominance of references to this genre shows that it is no sense coincidental. A number of European newspapers pointed to its official source: the idea was re-launched (the royal fairy-tale narrative having in fact been around for a very long time) by the Archbishop of Canterbury during the royal wedding itself – an event which provided 'some fairy-tale recession glamour' (Williamson, 1985: 83) and 'a unifying balm for the nation' (Brunt, 1992: 289) – which was seen on television by the largest world-wide TV audience prior to the Gulf War. *Cambio 16* (21 December 1992) was one of the publications to pick up on this point: the wedding, it wrote, was 'a "fairy tale", as the Archbishop of Canterbury defined it... nothing similar had ever been seen anywhere other than in fairy tales'. Indeed, as many sources also stressed, the entire 1981 wedding had been staged with the fairy-tale narrative – in particular Cinderella – in mind.

The fairy-tale narrative, in almost all its European manifestations, was used as a vehicle to indirectly criticize the anachronistic nature of the British monarchy and its lack of contact with reality. As the daily *Il Messagero* put it in Italy (10 December): 'And now the ugly fairy tale is falling apart... in the ancient Scottish castles the ghosts of the royal family think that it would have been better to do what they did to Ann Boleyn and Mary Stuart.' What happened, in fact, was that an English discourse was appropriated by the press of other European countries and turned inside out. It was effectively used against those who launched it as part of a quite different agenda.

Again, however, Spanish publications developed the notion of the fairy tale more than in any other country, using it as a vehicle for multiple attacks on the British monarchy.

Thus *Cambio 16* (21 December 1992) suggested that 'the "fairy tale" was the basis of the entire story: because it was its symbolic justification. And once the fairy tale had finished, the story finished'. *El Mundo* (13 December 1992), in a heavily sarcastic article, stressed the gap between the official fairy-tale narrative and the real life of a British princess, suggesting a lack of human warmth. Discussing the disappearance of 'princess' as a job as opposed to a role in a story, it suggested that this was due to one factor in particular:

> Above all because some of those who have tried to be one [a princess] didn't have the necessary CV and went into the tale as Alice went into Wonderland or as if they owned the place, thinking, perhaps with the best of intentions, that all that stuff about the magic wand, the tiara, the ermine, castles and jesters would smooth out any conjugal tiffs.
>
> But her implacable mother-in-law, whom Diana is about to bring down without losing her angelic look, took it upon herself to point out that no, that being in line for the throne is a job which is as slavish and self-sacrificing as being an enclosed nun... And that, just as in the fairy tales, you have to be prepared for the most charming prince proving to be a frog and turning into a toad.

In a slightly earlier edition, the same newspaper expressly mentioned the 'fairy tale in reverse', using a level of language which – for the Spanish press at least – is surprising in its colloquiality:

> What has happened in Great Britain is a fairy tale in reverse, but the wisdom, astuteness and age of this old monarchy should cause it to rush to turn the story round the other way again, and look for another fairy (there are heaps of fairies in the European dynastic branches, in the family trees or the trees of Hyde Park or in Shakespeare's comedies). Even a fairy from Soho, from Portobello Road or from heavy porn will do, and she would probably be better at getting breakfast ready in time than the princess with the boobs.

Figure 1. In their Cinderella cartoon in Diario 16 (10 December 1992) Gallego y Rey present the Diana story as a fairy tale gone wrong

While the suggestion that 'Charles, the erstwhile dream prince, had turned into an ugly frog' (*Der Spiegel*, Germany, 23 November 1992) and references to 'a fairy tale in reverse' (*L'Unità*, Italy, 10 December 1992) could be found elsewhere in the European press, nowhere was the idea of the anti-fairy-tale developed as much as it was in Spain, nor with such obvious aggression, nor with such an obvious sense of enjoyment.

The soap opera

Since royalty and narrative appear to be indissoluble, the vacuum left by the collapse of one narrative form must be replaced by another. The genre most often chosen by European newspapers as the successor to the fairy tale is the soap opera, with seventeen references in the titles analysed. While both the soap opera and the fairy tale have tended to operate simultaneously in the UK – ' "The Royals" is the longest-running soap opera in Britain', wrote Rosalind Coward in 1984 (1984: 163) – in Europe the emergence of one was seen as the sign of the death of the other. The link between the end of the fairy tale and the transfer to soap opera was made by a number of European publications. Thus the Italian daily *La Repubblica* wrote on 10 December 1992:

> And so the beautiful fairy tale ends in collapse... The reality of the situation confirms the substance of that confused and uncontrolled and even a little legendary magma of rumours and revelations which have placed the British royal house, and above all Charles and Diana, at the centre of a soap opera [in English] in which reality, today, is greater than fantasy.

The same link was also made explicitly by *El Mundo* (10 December 1992):

> So they didn't live happily ever after. After eleven years the bubble of the fairy tale was burst, pricked by the spinning wheel, and with its loss of air it looks more like a soap opera.

Reference to this narrative genre could be found in the French, Italian, German and Norwegian presses – with suggested titles ranging from 'Buckingham-Dallas' (*VSD*, France, 17 December) through 'Palace-Dallas' (*Der Spiegel*, Germany, 23 November) to 'Dallas on Thames' (*Le Point*, France, 12 December) – but it was again in the Spanish press that they dominated: almost one half of the total references to soap opera come from Spain. Thus the dailies *El Mundo* (10 December 1992) and *Diario 16* (10 December 1992) and the weeklies *Interviú* (21 December 1992), *Tiempo* (28 December 1992) and *Tribuna* (4 January 1993) all refer to the story as a 'culebrón', a pejorative term widely used in Spain to dismiss the soap-opera genre as culturally worthless. It is also only in the Spanish press that we are given any idea of who the cast of such a soap opera might be. This is provided by *El Mundo* (10 December 1992):

> However, the soap opera is only just starting. Now all the secondary characters who have some part to play in the business will march past. Evidence will be given on behalf of the groom by Camilla – the prince's friend – Camilla's husband, the confidantes of Camilla's

husband and so on. Some extravagant majordomo will sell a few confessions to the gutter press and everyone will have a great time consuming morbid curiosity and melancholy.

Evidence will be given on behalf of the bride by her friends, her hairdressers and maybe some rock singer elevated to the princess's dreams. As for the family, not a chance.

Soap opera is a narrative genre enjoying low prestige. The soap opera is, therefore, a counter-discourse to the official English fairy-tale narrative, and is again chosen specifically to provide a negative and even condescending view of the British Royal family.

The Spanish Royals
The historical narrative
It will have been clear in the foregoing that the Spanish media were in no sense talking only of the British royals. Nineteen ninety-two was an important year for Spain. It had hosted the Seville Expo with great success, it had held large-scale celebrations of the quincentenary of the Discovery of the New World in 1492 – an ideal opportunity for much re-writing of history – and it had been the centre of world attention when the Olympic Games had been held in Barcelona in the summer of that same year. King Juan Carlos had been a major presence at all these events, but in particular in Barcelona where viewers around the world were able to see him in his shirt sleeves warmly embracing every Spanish athlete who won a medal.

A more sustained analysis of the presentation of the Spanish Royal Family in the Spanish media immediately reveals that the latter's treatment of the British royals is in fact part of a much larger project both of writing the contemporary history of the Spanish royal family, and of rewriting the history of twentieth-century Spain. Spanish royal history is presented at this point as different in many crucial ways from the British one, being shorter, more compact, more tightly controlled, still intact, and based on a different set of premises. The most obvious difference is the absence of the historical super-narrative. The decision to avoid the historical super-narrative would appear to be a conscious (though, as Chapter 5 will show, not necessarily an irreversible) one. Thus, while *Tribuna* (14 December 1992) wrote that 'the Spanish monarchy does not have the same [historical] justification as the British one', *Tiempo* (25 January 1993) wrote: 'this monarchy has nothing to do with those of the past, due to its purely parliamentary and constitutional character'.

Implicit in this refusal of the historical narrative was criticism of the antiquated and wasteful British monarchy. For example, the British court came in for a great deal of criticism in the Spanish press due to its sheer size and running costs. Contrasted with this, an insistent theme in the Spanish press's coverage of Juan Carlos was what it called his 'allergy to setting up a court' (*Tiempo*, 22 February 1993), which is also contrasted with the situation in Britain: 'There is no court in Spain, as opposed to what happens in Britain – where the court gives rise to very many costs for the public purse', wrote *Tribuna* (14 December 1992). An extravagant court was seen as something belonging to the past. *Tiempo* (25 January 1993) again made this clear:

In the past... there might have been as many as 2,000 people in the Royal Palace at any time of the day: counsellors, diplomats, nobles, bishops, dames, minor nobleman, bureaucrats, butlers, servants, rogues, nabobs, jesters, postulants, merchants, supplicants, windbags... Nowadays, the King's entourage is more humble. Today the King has a modest palace, a simple routine and a very small retinue of servants.

Indeed, the Spanish royal historical narrative at that time was confined to the late twentieth century. Juan Carlos's story was not yet the continuation of a thousand-year story: it was a story of contemporary Spain, its most frequently quoted dates being 1975 (the death of Franco), 1978 (the approval of the Constitution), 1981 (the failed coup d'état led by a group of Civil Guards) and 1992 itself for the reasons given above. We will return to the historical narrative – and more recent attempts to extend it – in the following chapter.

This truncated Spanish historical narrative responded to what were at the time clearly articulated and widely accepted political needs. The symbolic political function of the Spanish royal family was not yet to provide continuity with the past, but specifically to legitimise a break with the past, in concrete terms with the Franco regime. In general terms the Spanish media were not at all dewy-eyed about this: it was widely accepted as part of the legitimising function of the Spanish Royal Family. Thus *Cambio 16* (21 December 1992) approvingly quoted a British academic who suggested that:

> What most attracts the attention of British observers [to the Spanish Royal Family] is the fact that the King and Queen of Spain seem to have a clear idea of the role they are playing, which enables them to give the impression that the monarchy is an important and useful institution for the country. Of course, it has a great deal to do with the exceptional circumstances which surrounded the arrival of King Juan Carlos as Head of State, as well as the role of 'pilot of change' he fulfilled during the first months of his reign, the most critical point of which was the night of 23 February 1981.

Tiempo (21 January 1993) also makes the question of legitimation clear by contrasting the highly irregular nature of Juan Carlos's accession to the throne with his actions in opposing the attempted coup in 1981: 'Juan Carlos I, who came into History on the sly, gained for ever the right to reign as a result of his actions that February evening when, dressed as a general of the army, he stopped the military coup'. Juan Carlos was then – and in important though somewhat modified senses continues to be – a symbol of historical rupture and renewal, a discourse within which the super-narrative of the distant past had at that time no part to play.

The 'monarchic-sentimental drama'

In the early nineteen nineties the royal love-story narrative in Spain revolved mostly around the heir to the throne, prince Felipe, particularly in connection with his relationship with his then unofficial fiancée, Isabel Sartorius, though the infantas Cristina and Elena also figured. However, this narrative is not remotely as well developed as those relating to Charles and Diana: there are no fairy tales, no soap operas, no vaudevilles and no sentimental novels. This is expressly contrasted with the situation in Britain.

The general press view of the Spanish royals is that they do their job professionally, and therefore leave little room for intrusive and uncontrolled reporting. As *Diario 16* (10 December 1992) puts it:

> But in any case, you can't help thinking of the immense good fortune we have had with our Royal Family, and in particular with our two Infantas, and it is right that we should reflect on the enormous advantage of professionalism as against those little amateurs who are swarming around out there in the big wide world.

In fact, the soap-opera narrative is expressly rejected in relation to the Spanish royal family. Thus *Tiempo* (11 January 1993) congratulated prince Felipe on the 'serenity of his relationship with Isabel Sartorius, which everyone has contrasted with the ridiculous soap-opera of his cousins, the prince and princess of Wales'.

Anachronism and Modernity
The Dago's revenge
A constant theme in European reporting on the separation of Charles and Diana is the clash between anachronism and modernity. In a sense this also represents the end of the historical narrative, in much the same way as the soap opera is the end of the fairy tale. In this counter-narrative, Diana is the representative of modernity, while Charles and the Royal Family in general represent fossilisation and decay. Their failure is seen as their inability to cope with the 'contagious virus of modernity' (*Diario 16*, 10 December 1992[1]) which Diana brought with her. As *France-Soir* put it (10 December 1992), it was 'traditional culture versus punk', while in Germany the *Frankfurter Allgemeine Zeitung* described it as 'Old nobility against young capital city society' (14 December 1992). Belgium's *La Dernière Heure* (10 December) took the view that 'The English court is starchy and rigid in its traditions which are unbearable and out of touch', while in France *Le Figaro* of 10 December described Diana as finally being 'free to listen to the rock music she prefers to the classical music which her husband adores, free no longer to go to the polo matches played by Charles, free to go out to the "disco" and not come back till dawn, free to give herself over entirely to the pleasures of fashion and haute couture'. This view was even projected back to the moment of the wedding, with *La Repubblica* writing in Italy (10 December 1992):

> Some, after so much time, remember and appreciate the fact that the princess, on her wedding day, perhaps in a youthful burst of independence, refused the centuries-old formula of the Anglican church... which contains the obligation to 'total obedience' by the woman to her husband and limited herself to accepting the less anachronistic formula of 'respect' and 'affection'.

Le Monde (11 December 1992), for its part, speculated at some length on the issue of tradition versus modernity:

In France, and in other countries in general, there is often a tendency to see the British monarchy as merely the surviving remnant of an outdated system of government, kept alive by a pronounced taste for tradition together with considerations relating to tourism. Such an approach underestimates the role of the monarchy in the institutions of Great Britain and the profound influence it exercises on the mentality of the British... The customs and ceremonial which surround the royal family have changed little over the centuries, which gives the British Crown such a traditional appearance, without equivalent among European monarchies.

This latest crisis suffered by the Windsor family in fact reveals a crisis of identity, no doubt that of tradition coming face to face with modernism, and the difficulty of adapting one to the other.

This is one of the most insistent themes in European coverage of the separation (and European sympathies were clearly with Diana), but the notion of being rooted in the past is at times extended to cover the British people as a whole. Thus the Italian daily *La Stampa* (10 December) wrote:

Often, when they are looking for a solution, these islanders search among the certainties of the past rather than the among the unknowns of the future: and the entire English past, for more than a millennium, except for Cromwell's brief republic in the seventeenth century, has flown by alongside a throne. But that throne was mysterious, enchanted, that's how the subjects wanted it. Now, queen, princes and princesses are all naked, as in Andersen's fairy tale.

A common twist to the story is that the British monarchy, rooted in the past, was simply overwhelmed by the technological advances of the modern age (and above all by the intrusive activities of the tabloids – a major talking point throughout the European media). As *La Repubblica* in Italy put it (10 December 1992):

On a grey December afternoon of what Queen Elisabeth called her 'annus horribilis' the contradiction between the constitutional role of the British monarchy, which has always had an almost sacred aspect in the eyes of its subjects, and the role of the mass media in the society of instant communication, of live TV broadcasts and mobile telephones, exploded dramatically. During the reign of Queen Victoria, the great constitutionalist Walter Bagehot said of the monarchy: 'Mystery is its life. We must not allow the light of day to take away its magic'.

While the weekly *L'Express* added in France (24 December):

Question: has a curse struck the Windsors?... With its carriages, its hunts, its castles and its obsession with a petty bourgeois model of family life, the royal family thought it could prolong the era of Queen Victoria indefinitely. The XXI century has caught up with it brutally today, with its string of divorces, its scandal sheets, its mobile telephones which are easy to tap and money which can loosen the tongues of servants believed to be the most faithful.

In Germany, *Der Spiegel*'s view (23 November), linking this topic with that of the decline of the British Empire, was that:

> The Windsors compensated their subjects for a world which had become a small and often wretched lot. However, even the Lord above is powerless against the ability to listen into cordless telephone conversations, fast telephoto lenses, and the passion for gossip of retired servants... the decline of the second Elizabethan age has long since begun.

As part of this discourse of anachronism, Britain's inability to accept the end of Empire was mentioned in several countries. Thus in France the weekly magazine *L'Express* wrote on 24 December of 'The growing gap between an institution which lives as it did during the time of the empire and a society which is changing rapidly', adding:

> But there's the rest, all the rest, this extraordinary gap between the pomp of an institution which is still operating as it did during the time of the empire, when the palace ruled over a quarter of the planet, and the reality of the current power of the kingdom... Brooks Baker and all the ethnographers who are experts on Buckingham Palace stress the blindness of the court, the obstinate refusal of Her Majesty to move in the world as it is.

In Germany *Der Spiegel*, writing before the royal break-up on 23 November 1992, described how 'The British empire collapsed, its once mighty industries are rusting, slums proliferate in the cities, the state is heavily indebted abroad, its place in Europe is uncertain... but such problems have been unable to damage the House of Windsor'. In Norway the daily tabloid *VG* wrote on 11 December:

> It is the British royal family's special role in modern British history which makes the event something more than a personal tragedy or constitutional curiosity. The monarchy symbolises more than any other institution British national identity.
>
> Their role as a symbol of national unity and continuity was all the more valued in the period of uncertainty which followed the war. While the sun went down over the British empire it shone all the more brightly on the British monarchy.
>
> The more insecure the British are over their future, the more the pay homage to this symbol of their national identity.

However, the Spanish press would develop this idea with an enthusiasm and a glee seldom found elsewhere, and linked it to broader issues of Britain's place in contemporary Europe. According to *La Vanguardia* (10 December 1992):

> [Elizabeth II] is witnessing simultaneously the decline of her country and the disintegration of her family... Great Britain is today an island stripped of its overseas possessions and leaning against Europe with the worry of not knowing whether to join it unreservedly or to insist on retaining some vestige of its 'splendid isolation'... [royalty] does not go with the reality of the times and the national situation.

Linked to this were constant references to Britain's antiquated class-system. Thus *Der Spiegel*, profiling the British monarchy a few weeks before the announcement of the separation, wrote (23 November) of the "old boys network', Eton and Harrow, Oxbridge-cast', adding:

> class barriers are higher here, privileges are passed on from generation to generation more easily than anywhere else in Europe: one percent of the population owns 17 percent of the private wealth; two thirds of this wealth – a unique situation in the western world – was inherited... Only in Britain can the feudal rites, and the luxurious games of the aristocracy be admired, as though nothing had happened, no French or industrial revolution, no World Wars.

Contrasts with what is presented as the situation of the Spanish monarchy are an insistent feature of this dialectic (*Tribuna*, 14 December 1992):

> Rooted on the rock of an empire which is sinking, her Gracious Majesty's crown still sticks up like the ridge of a reef which has been submerged by the high tide of a long process of decolonisation. Other younger and apparently less granitic monarchies, among them the Spanish monarchy, are based on a vigour which the British Crown would dearly love to have.
>
> What is actually happening? What are the reasons for the difficulties the British Royal House is going through. Simply, its anachronism.
>
> Sheltered behind legal antiques, the inhabitants of Buckingham Palace had succeeded in living with their backs to the inevitable changes which were taking place in society, as if the world had stopped for them.
>
> First of all, the characteristic which most describes the current Spanish Monarchy is what is mainly lacking in its London counterpart: modernity. The fact that our monarchy was restored only seventeen years ago has forced the Spanish Crown to be written down within the context of a Constitution as up-to-date as that of 1978.

The tone of these commentaries would become astonishingly personal at times: 'The British royal family has horribleness built in. The richest of the rich, the most stupid of the stupid, the most irresponsible of the irresponsible', wrote *Tribuna* (14 December 1992).

Compared with this, positive evaluations of the Spanish monarchy are to be found everywhere in the Spanish press. 'The impeccable attitude of the Spanish royal family cannot and does not seem comparable to that of the British royal family either', wrote *Tribuna* (14 December 1992), adding: 'It's not true what they say about comparisons being invidious: they're invidious for those who come out worse. And, frankly, our lot are much better'.

And when *Tiempo* (11 January 1993) published the results of a survey in which 600 Spaniards had voted Juan Carlos as 'the most loved Spaniard of the year', it wrote:

> King Juan Carlos has no need to say, as his cousin Queen Elizabeth II did recently, that this has been an 'annus horribilis'. On the contrary, 1992 has been one of the most fruitful and happy years on a public level for the monarch. The photo of the Royal Family all together

at the inaugurations of the Seville Expo or the Barcelona Olympics went all around the world and made the King Spain's best ambassador.

The references to Expo 92 and the Olympics are crucial to an understanding of this discourse. Spain is now presented as a successful modern country with a successful modern monarchy which is universally praised and admired. In short, what is happening in the Spanish press, to a degree not found elsewhere, is that Spanish newspapers of varying quality, political colour and geographical reach are taking advantage of the situation to score points over the British monarchy, and by extension over Britain itself. Britain emerges from this comparison as backward, anachronistic, repressive and out of touch, while Spain is presented as modern, dynamic, democratic and European.

This really is the Dago's revenge, and the revenge element explains a great deal of the glee with which the Charles and Diana story is tackled in the Spanish press. Here is Spain getting its own back. A well-established northern-European discourse dismissing Mediterranean countries as underdeveloped and backward (O'Donnell, 1994) – a discourse which, at least as Spaniards perceive it, is closely associated with Britain, this perception being linked no doubt to the phenomenon of mass British tourism in Spain – has been enthusiastically stood on its head.

The Rediscovery of History

An interesting feature of Spanish coverage of the 1992 separation was the emergence of signs of a tentative attempt to renew the Spanish historical super-narrative. For example, the relationship between crown prince Felipe and Isabel Sartorius led to a controversy of sorts (admittedly a relatively minor one), duly reflected in the Spanish media, over the continuing validity of the Pragmática sobre Matrimonios Desiguales (Law on Unequal Marriages) drawn up by Carlos III in 1776.

But a much more obvious, and much more publicly orchestrated attempt was made following the death of don Juan, count of Barcelona, who died on 1 April of the following year. The father of Juan Carlos, and passed over for succession to the throne by Franco, he was 'the king who never reigned', being described by *Tiempo* (22 March 1993) as 'the missing link' with 'the historic monarchy, that of Alfonso XIII and the previous monarchs who are in the Monastery of El Escorial'. Although don Juan never ascended the Spanish throne, Juan Carlos decided to bury his father in the Panteón de los Reyes at El Escorial, the official burial place of Spanish kings, thus symbolically restoring the continuity of the Spanish crown.

Although this decision was interpreted by *Tiempo* (29 March 1993) as an attempt by the king to write 'his own version of recent history', official support for this initiative was extremely strong. The Government, meeting in extraordinary session on the day of don Juan's death, issued a decree allowing the funeral in El Escorial to take place with full royal honours, a decision which, according to the Catalan-language weekly magazine *El Temps* (12 April 1993) met with 'much unanimity and little controversy'. The bishop officiating at don Juan's funeral, monseñor Estepa, spoke of 'the exemplary figure Juan de Borbón represented for the history of Spain', while the reactions of

Pasqual Maragall, mayor of Barcelona, were reported in the Catalan daily *Avui* (4 April 1993) as follows:

> The mayor of Barcelona, Pasqual Maragall, stressed the fact that... he [don Juan] made the historical continuity of the institution of the monarchy possible, as well as contributing decisively to the restoration of democracy in Spain.

While *Tiempo* (12 April 1993) spoke of his 'leading role in the construction of modern Spain', *Cambio 16* (12 April 1993) wrote: 'Today his figure eclipses that of his opponent over decades: General Franco... he was, in any case, the last victim of the Spanish Civil War'.

These events show, however tentatively, that Juan Carlos's role (both assigned and assumed) in legitimising the modernity of Spain was already enjoying considerable success in 1992. In a process which would gain momentum as the nineties proceeded and achieve a kind of consolidation in the new millennium, the Spanish Civil War and the Franco dictatorship were already becoming things that Spaniards read about in history books and special supplements of Sunday magazines. Now that Francoism could be constructed as a historical exception, a wrong turning on the road to modernity which had now been put right, the rediscovery of historical continuity had become a possibility again. 'The Monarchy is carrying through a process of restoration which is no longer just constitutional, but is deeply rooted in the people', wrote *Tiempo* (29 March 1993), while *Tribuna* (14 December 1992) asked: 'What has Juan Carlos done if it is not to re-establish in the collective memory the permanent contact between Crown and people?'

1   *Diario 16* is a daily newspaper published by the group which also produces the weekly magazine *Cambio 16* quoted earlier.

5. Spain – Two Weddings and a 'Friendship': *From the Modern to the Postmodern*

The Myth of Monarchy In Spain

All societies inherit, reproduce and generate their own myths, and no analysis of media coverage of Spain's two royal weddings of the nineteen-nineties – or indeed the later controversy regarding crown prince Felipe's friendship with Norwegian model Eva Sannum in early 2001 – is possible without some preliminary remarks on the myth of monarchy in that country. The concept of myth itself is, of course, to some extent a controversial one. Writing in the sixties, Kermode was able to state confidently that myth was a 'degenerate' form of fiction whose fictionality has been forgotten – 'Fictions can degenerate into myths whenever they are not consciously held to be fictive' (2000: 39) – a definition to which he returned recently in an epilogue written for a re-edition of his book (2000: 187). At what we might call the other end of the spectrum, post-modern theorist Gianni Vattimo argued towards the end of the eighties that there is now only myth: all narrative is myth – 'Demythologisation has itself come to be seen as a myth' (1992: 39) – likewise an idea he restated recently in a new essay written for a re-edition of *The Transparent Society* (2000). Our own view is a development of the theory advanced by Barthes (1966): in other words, we see myth as a discursive strategy which works to naturalise the contingent, to make the historical seem a-historical: as Barthes himself put it, 'We reach here the very principle of myth: it transforms history into nature' (1972: 147).

It is seldom possible to track the emergence of a myth with any accuracy: myths enter the public domain in slow and often diffuse ways. In the case of Spanish monarchy, however, an exact date can be given if not for the emergence of this myth, then at the very least for its consolidation: this was 23 February 1981 when a group of Civil Guards stormed the Spanish parliament, took the MPs hostage, and called for a general military insurrection throughout the country in order to re-install a military dictatorship. This coup failed. It failed for highly complex reasons relating to intricate relationships of power at all levels and in all quarters of Spanish society. This is not, however, the analysis which either dominated then or has survived till now. In contemporary Spanish political mythology this coup failed because King Juan Carlos appeared on television and reaffirmed his continuing allegiance to the democratic order. This myth is in fact now so all-pervasive that no event relating to the monarchy can take place without its making a forceful reappearance. These events have included both royal weddings of the nineteen-nineties, the twenty-fifth anniversary of Franco's death and of Juan Carlos's coronation in 2000 (*El País* published a special 32-page supplement to celebrate this event, while the weekly magazine *Cambio 16* dedicated its entire issue to it), and the twentieth anniversary of the 1981 coup in February 2001.

93

Below are some quotes relating to the coup itself and other dates in between. Early reactions saw the king working in concert with other social forces:

> It was the King, in fact, who once again emerged as the key to the situation, with the support of the Spanish people, not at all prepared to allow a minute section of the Armed Forces to impose a military coup which would destroy the still weak bases of the free and democratic political system which Spaniards have given themselves. (*La Vanguardia*, 24 February 1981)

Slowly but surely, however, all other actors would fade into the background, and only the king would remain as the saviour of the day:

> We live, thank god, in liberty... What would have become of that liberty, in a Spain without peace, had it not been for the calm and decisive actions of king Juan Carlos on 23 February 1981. (*La Vanguardia*, 10 September 1989)
>
> The active role of the monarchy in the Spanish transition [to democracy], as a force for the moderation of tension and a symbol of unity, is considered throughout the western world as the firmest basis for the future of the institution. (*Tribuna*, 14 December 1992)
>
> Juan Carlos I, who came into History on the sly, won for ever the right to reign after his actions on that February evening when, dressed as commander-in-chief of the Armed Forces, he stopped the military coup. (*Tiempo*, 25 January 1993)
>
> He is rightly given credit for having eased through a peaceful transition from dictatorship to a democracy which, though having its faults, provides the most dignified framework for co-existence which Spain has enjoyed in its recent history. He is credited with the firm decision to maintain constitutional legality on the night of 23 February. (*El Mundo*, 19 March 1995)

In the expanded form of this myth, Juan Carlos becomes the guarantor not only of democracy, but also of the on-going stability of the country. For example, two editorials in *La Vanguardia* on the occasion of the 1995 wedding contained the following statements:

> In the midst of the political storms our country is experiencing, the monarchy is viewed as a secure value and a guarantee of institutional stability. Almost twenty years have passed since that day when the King became the Head of State. Most citizens know that the institution of the monarchy has been able to harmonise the opposing interests of Spaniards in the service of a Constitution approved by referendum. Beyond legitimate party struggles, and the crises which Spain is experiencing both politically and socially, the royal family led by King Juan Carlos is a reference point which it is in no-one's interest to forget. (*La Vanguardia*, 18 March 1995)
>
> On those occasions [the change of regime in 1975 and the coup of February 1981] the role of the Crown – Juan Carlos is not just King, he is a King with all the symbolic weight that that has acquired over the centuries – was and remains decisive for the stability of the country. (*La Vanguardia*, 19 March 1995)

While *El Mundo* wrote on the twentieth anniversary of his accession to the throne:

> On that night [23 February 1981] it became clear that the Crown was a key element in the safeguarding of our system of liberties... It was precisely he who did more than anyone that ill-fated day to neutralise the ambiguities of others before solemnly addressing the country. (*El Mundo*, 22 November 1995)

Within the terms of this myth, Juan Carlos is presented above all as a professional King who is useful to his people:

> As the Prince of Asturias [the crown prince] has said on several occasions, everybody has to prove his fitness for his job on a day-to-day basis, earning it with his effort. This is the example his father is giving him, gaining the appreciation of the citizens, not only on the great decisive occasions, but also in the hard, stressful – and also no doubt often unattractive – daily grind. (*El Mundo*, 22 November 1995).

And so it continues, as these quotes from 2000 and 2001 will show:

> ... 23 February legitimised him in the eyes of Spaniards more than all the pedigree of the dynastic line. (*El Mundo*, 22 November 2000)
> And he was in his place, defending democracy when he needed to, on the dramatic night of 23 February 1981. (*El País*, 22 November 2000)
> ... people forget that the essential mission of the king is to defend compliance with the Constitution, as he showed by his actions... when faced with the coup on 23 February, actions which consolidated his popularity and prestige among all Spaniards. (*El País*, 22 November 2000)
> When circumstances are difficult, he appeared in the front line as a symbol of national unity and Head of the Armed Forces. He represented the panacea to an interminable night, like the night of 23 February 1981 and, after his television appearance, the people slept peacefully. (*Cambio 16*, 27 November 2000)
> ... the role of the monarch was decisive in stifling the rebellion. Don Juan Carlos's television message allowed Spaniards to go to their beds that night safe in the knowledge that the coup had failed. (*El Mundo*, 23 February 2001)

These are only a few examples of a myth whose constant and exuberant renewal is now a fundamental part of the Spanish political landscape.

The Royal Wedding of March 1995
Spain – One, Great and Free
The wedding of the infanta doña Elena de Borbón y Grecia to don Jaime Marichalar took place on Sunday 18 March 1995 against a background of increasing political tensions in Spain. The socialist party, PSOE, in power uninterruptedly since 1982, was showing increasing signs of political fatigue, and was under constant attack from newspapers such as *El Mundo*. Accusations of corruption against the government were reaching a

peak – mainly in relation to the financing of the clandestine anti-terrorist group GAL and the embezzlement of funds by and subsequent disappearance of the head of the Civil Guard Luís Roldán – and the international conflict with Canada over access to fishing waters was in full swing. This last conflict was viewed as particularly irritating in political circles in Spain due to the obvious lack of support from some of its EU partners, most notably the UK. On the economic front, Spain was grappling with intractable unemployment and a spiralling budget deficit.

Media interest in the royal wedding was intense, and indeed started some time before the wedding actually took place. Two thousand four hundred and twenty-six journalists were accredited to cover the event itself, and as many television cameras – one hundred and fifty in all – were deployed as at the Barcelona Olympics. Live television coverage was provided by the public service broadcaster Televisión Española (TVE) through its first channel, La Primera (and also worldwide via its international satellite channel), under the guidance of Pilar Miró, former head of TVE and filmmaker in her own right. The images provided by TVE were also relayed to all the other terrestrial broadcasters in Spain with the exceptions of the second public service channel, La Dos, the subscription channel Canal Plus, the Basque channels of Euskal Telebista, and the second Catalan channel Canal 33. There was thus little choice available to Spanish television viewers that day. The assumption that this lack of choice would be broadly acceptable to the viewing public is in itself, of course, worthy of interest. The audience peaked at around 11.5 million viewers during the ceremony, just over one quarter of the population. The particular version of this televisual event (images plus commentary) we will concentrate on below is that offered by La Primera itself.

Television coverage

Leaving aside for the moment the complex and highly detailed technical preparations for this broadcast – for example, holes were drilled in the ancient masonry of Seville Cathedral to allow aerial shots of the bride and groom to be taken – the televisual experience of the viewer was a complex amalgam of three dominant discourses:

– the visual discourse of the images themselves
– the religious discourse of the liturgy, readings and sermon
– the commentary provided by the male and female commentators, Carmen Enríquez and Manuel Lombao, which can itself be further subdivided as outlined below

There were other elements of interest – most notably the use of music – but we will concentrate mainly on the three areas outlined above.

The visual discourse

Apart from the predictable shots of the infanta and groom at various points in the ceremony, of other members of the royal family, and of the various celebrants, two elements of the visual discourse stand out:

– Televising of the royal wedding was characterised by an unproblematic (indeed to some extent celebratory) coverage of members of other royal families from around the world. Particularly before the ceremony proper began, there were numerous shots of visiting members of thirty-eight royal households. This was heavily reinforced by the verbal commentary, which treated all with equal respect even if they came from countries which are small and only nominally independent (Monaco, Liechtenstein), or countries from which the royal families have been in one way or another removed (Greece, Romania, Bulgaria: indeed, this group was the largest of those represented), or indeed countries whose record on civil and human rights is not entirely unblemished. Royalty and monarchy were casually presented as essential values beyond historical change and political boundaries.

—   A number of moments in the ceremony were given over to music. Without exception these were used by Pilar Miró to bring particular elements of the architecture of Seville Cathedral to the attention of the viewer. The most striking example of this took place during the singing of the Agnus Dei. In a single, uninterrupted shot which lasted no less than two minutes and fifty seconds, the camera slowly moved its way up one side of the reredos, along the top and back down the other side. Throughout this entire shot the whole of the screen was filled with the most lavish and intricate gold-plated baroque designs. Verbal commentary a few moments later listed the numerous artists and sculptors who had worked on this particular piece of architecture, pointing out their links with previous Spanish monarchs. The sheer opulence of this display was not only stunning in itself but also astonishing in a city which was an unemployment black spot in a country with one of the highest rates of unemployment in Europe.

These two elements of the visual discourse perform a similar function along two different axes, linking Spain's monarchy synchronically with other monarchies of the world, and diachronically with other monarchies of Spain's imperial past. This diachronic link was also stressed by the verbal commentary: 'In this way the cathedral adds another page to its long history of important events, of its connections with the monarchy, of its ties with the monarchy... this link, this powerful link between the Kings and Queens of Spain and Seville'. There was also much comment on Seville's new shield whose central design graphically represents the phrase 'it has never deserted me' ('no me ha dejado'), apparently celebrating Seville's undying loyalty to Spanish monarchs throughout the ages.

The religious discourse

The religious discourse was essentially predictable in its content. Its most striking element was, however, in its delivery. Although the royal wedding took place in Seville, capital of Andalusia, there was not a single Andalusian accent – highly characteristic within Spanish dialectology – to be heard. With not a single exception, all of the celebrants spoke High Castilian of the most thoroughbred and orotund kind.

Andalusian accents were to be heard when, after the wedding ceremony itself, the infanta moved on to the Iglesia del Salvador to lay her wedding bouquet on the tomb of her great-grandparents. These accents were provided by a choir all of whose female members wore flamenco-style dresses, and whose male members – guitarists – also wore the traditional black flamenco garb. These accents were therefore part of a discourse of exoticism well removed from the central stage of this event.

Whether intentional or not, the delivery of the religious discourse subordinated Seville and Andalusia to Castile and Castilian, and placed the source of the event solidly in Madrid. Andalusian specificities were recognised only to the extent to which they could be contained within that pattern of dominance. What is being reproduced is a discourse of the essential oneness of Spain. As the commentators suggested: 'Doña Elena is responding to the affection shown to her by the Sevillians and by all Spaniards... and we are sure that all those who are watching this wedding on TVE wish her the greatest happiness', or again, 'the King and queen are waving in response to the affections of the Sevillians, and of all the people of Spain', or yet again 'Seville is in a way the heart of the whole of Spain, on a day like today, but usually as well'. This discourse was also reinforced in other ways. A drawing in *El Mundo* of 19 March showed the King holding the bride and groom in his hand. His obverse shadow behind him depicted him holding Spain in his hand.

The verbal commentary
The commentary provided by TVE's two-person team was characterised by constant changes of style and emphasis. The most striking of these can be summarised as follows:

- An official discourse, consisting mostly of information which was obviously being read, relating to visiting dignitaries; lists of artists, architects, writers etc. connected in some way with the history of Seville Cathedral; lists of previous Spanish monarchs and their connections with the city; information concerning the music being played, its composers and performers and so on. In moments such as these the style of the commentators is relatively formal, they speak in properly formed sentences, they correct each other in the case of factual errors, and their language is generally conservative.
- A conversational discourse, relating almost uniquely to members of the royal family, and to a lesser extent to those who had gathered outside the cathedral to witness at least part of the event in person. At these moments the style of the commentators is highly informal. Their sentences are rambling and often unfinished, often grammatically incomplete, they interrupt each other, they laugh and joke, they address the viewers directly, they even allow themselves the use of some frankly informal lexical items, as when a fountain in Seville is given its local name of 'fuente de los meones' ('fountain of the pissers').
- Despite the opulence of the occasion and the lushness of the decor, this discourse insistently stresses the ordinariness of it all. This is a constantly returning *leitmotiv*. A few examples should suffice to give a flavour of what's involved:
- Commenting on the fact that little was known in advance about the bride's dress: 'We think this is natural since all brides want to make an impact, cause a surprise, and that no-one should know anything about the dress they're going to wear on that day which is so important for them'.
- Summing up the ceremony: 'Also their Majesties the King and Queen... on many occasions you can see the joy on their faces, the emotion, naturally the state of mind of any parent, in this case august parents, but which any parent feels in a situation, at a moment, in a ceremony such as the one we have just experienced'.

- The wedding is presented as just a normal, simple family wedding: 'We must also say that the cathedral has been adorned with flowers, but in a very simple way, always in accordance with the instructions of Queen Sofía who, right up to the last moment, has supervised down to the smallest detail of her eldest daughter's wedding'. The infanta is presented as someone all Spaniards know well on an almost personal level. There are many references to 'typical gestures', even 'classical' gestures by the bride, to her 'spontaneity', to her sensitivity: 'You have to remember that the infanta is a very sensitive person, she is a person who gets emotional in those peak moments, those key moments'.
- Despite their obvious wealth, the newly-weds even somehow become representatives of their own generation with all its problems. Talking of a particular square in Seville, the commentators point out: 'It has been chosen by young people, it is the young people's place, the place of that generation the newly-weds also belong to... they know that they are of their generation, and they have the worries, the fears, the joys, the sadnesses which people their age have, and the concerns that people their age have'. There is a long section outlining the infanta's concern over youth unemployment, and talking of her encouragement to young people not to become demoralised, and not to give up hope.
- Through this conversational discourse Spain is constructed as a profoundly democratic and egalitarian society, a point to which we shall return in greater detail below.

The complex and overlapping discourses of the televisual event as experienced by the viewers of TVE at least can be summed up as follows: Spain is constructed as a country which is unified, despite a number of very obvious internal tensions (see below); it is constructed as a country still in touch through its monarchy with a magnificent past stretching into the present; and it is constructed as a country where all are citizens alike, enjoying the same freedoms whatever their rank or status. In short, Spain is constructed as 'One, great and free' ('Una, grande y libre'). The three adjectives given above are, of course, one of the fundamental slogans of Francoism, and adorned all Spanish coins minted during the Franco dictatorship. This slogan is actively being re-signified. As we argued earlier in relation to Spanish coverage of the announcement of the separation of Charles and Diana, one of the political functions of the Spanish monarchy is the elimination of Francoism from the collective memory. This function is being vigorously pursued in coverage of this wedding.

Press coverage
Press coverage was also extremely heavy, particularly in women's magazines such as *¡Hola!* and *Lecturas* – who were just as interested in the fashions as anything else – but also in the generalist press, all of whose Sunday editions contained lengthy special supplements on the event. According to *El País* of 20 March 1995, coverage in the national dailies amounted to almost 400 photographs and 159 pages of text... not counting the women's magazines, the so-called 'prensa del corazón' (literally, 'press of the heart').

Following a pattern which we had already ascertained in relation to Spanish coverage of the separation of the Prince and Princess and Wales in 1992, it was once again the case that the press response was more complex and multifaceted than that offered by television. While television covered the royal event with seriousness and respect, the press in general allowed itself a mixture of respectful reporting, serious analysis of its more general political ramifications, and at times quite caustic commentary on the contrast between a country in economic and political crisis and a wedding of this level of opulence and magnificence. On a number of occasions this took the form of cartoons. Thus *La Vanguardia* of 18 March carried a cartoon showing Felipe González sitting facing a night sky in which the moon has the face of Luis Roldán. The trawler Estai – at the centre of the fishing row with Canada – is beginning to move over the moon. However, approaching a little further from the right, the royal carriage is about to blank out both. Felipe comments: 'There's nothing like an eclipse (the term 'eclipse' had been much used in the press prior to the event).

El Mundo of the same day also shows Prime Minister Felipe González addressing Juan Carlos: 'Now that we've started, Your Majesty, why not marry princess Cristina next week, and then the prince the week after that, and then the palace housekeeper the week after that, and then the chamberlain...?' Behind his back he holds a newspaper whose headline is 'The royal wedding eclipses the political situation'. In the same edition of this (generally anti-PSOE) newspaper Francisco Umbral wrote that Seville/Spain was no longer 'a concentration camp for the unemployed, but the oldest Empire in the west', adding with reference to the monarchs attributed with the foundation of the Spanish state in the fifteenth century: 'When Spain cannot impose itself through the macroeconomics of a certain González, it imposes itself through the

Figure 2. Idigoras y Pachi's cartoon in El Mundo *(18 March 1995).*

macromonarchy which comes from Ferdinand and Isabel'. There was even scorn at the obvious attempts to link the current Spanish monarchy with previous monarchies of Spain's periods of greatness. As Baltasar Porcel wrote in *La Vanguardia* (18 March 1995): 'However, I refuse to simply swallow, story after story, the sensational media mountain... with its magnificent complement of genealogical digressions as the essential and most important part of the wedding of the infanta Elena and Jaime Marichalar', a view which did not, however, stop most newspapers – including this issue of *La Vanguardia* – from reproducing this particular discourse in a very uncritical fashion: family trees tracing the ancestry of both bride and groom, describing them as 'two lines which go back to the Middle Ages'.

The general thrust of the contrast between government and monarchy was, however, one which very much favoured the monarchy at the expense of the politicians. A few examples will make this point clear:

> The wedding is taking place when the country is going through one of the most difficult periods politically since the death of Franco. The atmosphere of corruption is obvious.
>
> Popular satisfaction and curiosity [with the monarchy] derive from a subconscious dignity and usefulness which benefits us all. Because, moreover, the Crown has earned its prestige, its influence with its hard, instinctive, open work, just as any other unique and creative person or institution of our time can do. (*La Vanguardia*, 18 March 1995)

This reproduces a discourse which was clearly dominant in 1992 when contrasts were being made between the Spanish and the British monarchies: the Spanish monarchy is presented as a job, and its members gain respect for doing the job well. An edition of *El Mundo* from November of the same year featured a cartoon of the King and Queen in the royal sitting-room. He muses: 'Twenty years as King. Not bad with the unemployment we have in Spain!'. This discourse continues in force.

And while the Government is presented as being completely out of touch with society at large, the monarchy – and in particular the King – is presented as having stayed closely in touch, not with his *subjects*, but with his *fellow-citizens*:

> But a second union took place between the Spanish Royal Crown and the great majority of the citizenry. This union has been made periodically since King Juan Carlos became Head of State twenty years ago... Twenty years later the King's family has grown along with the new rights of Spaniards, the practice of democratic normality and the undoubted social progress which have marked the twenty years of his reign. (*La Vanguardia*, 19 March 1995)

While, in the case of the British monarchy, the best its members can expect is to be linked with a vocabulary and discourse of 'good works' (patronising charitable institutions, visiting the sick and the elderly, championing worthy causes), the current Spanish monarchy has been absorbed into a discourse of democratisation, modernisation, the expansion of political and civil rights – a discourse whose link with the lived experience of many Spaniards continues to be highly problematic.

The Royal Wedding of October 1997
Centre and Periphery

Spain's second royal wedding of the nineties took place on 4 October 1997 between the royal family's second oldest daughter, Cristina, and the professional basketball player Iñaki Urdangarin. As the infanta had been working in Barcelona for five years prior to this date – she worked in the Cultural Foundation of the Catalan bank La Caixa – and the groom (although Basque by birth) had not only lived in Catalonia as a child, but was at that time playing professionally for the handball team of Barcelona Football Club (he had also represented Spain at the Olympics), Barcelona was no doubt to some extent the 'natural' choice for the wedding.

From a purely technical point of view, coverage of the Barcelona royal wedding was to a large extent Seville mark II. Pilar Miró was once again invited to be in charge of the televising of the event for Spanish Television (tragically, she died very shortly after), and the investment in terms of technology and personnel was again on a massive scale: 127 cameras in all, 47 of them inside the cathedral itself, almost 4000 journalists accredited to cover the event.

As Antonio Burgos pointed out in *El Mundo* (5 October 1997), referring to the archbishop of Barcelona who would officiate at the ceremony: 'Doña Cristina was not married by monsignor Carles. Doña Cristina, like Doña Elena, was married by Pilar Miró, media high priestess who has invented a new liturgic rite'. In what represented something of an advance on the situation two years before, TVE's images were taken by virtually all other television stations, both private (including this time the subscription channel Canal Plus) and regional (with versions in Catalan, Basque and Galician) throughout Spain, meaning that once more there was very little choice available to viewers that day (these images were also distributed to over 90 countries worldwide).

Claims that '80% of Spaniards' or '22 million viewers' watched the event proved somewhat misleading, since this turned out to be the cumulative total of all those who had tuned in at some point for at least one minute. The actual audience for the marriage ceremony was 10–11 million, similar to the national audience for an important international football match.

Our coverage is once again that provided by TVE, the most watched station on the day (5.6 million viewers for the ceremony itself). The general feel of the coverage – the mix of formal and informal styles, of official 'read' information and spontaneous comments – was very much in line with what had gone before, but there were, none the less, differences. Within a Spanish context a wedding in Barcelona is a very different phenomenon from a wedding in Seville: as an article in *El Mundo* pointed out (4 October 1997): 'Barcelona is not Seville and the wedding of the future Duke and Duchess of Palma de Mallorca cannot be compared to that of the Duke and Duchess of Lugo which took place in the capital of Andalusia on 18 March 1995'. And other things had changed in the intervening two years as well: there had, for example, been a change of government and, on a somewhat different level, there was also the small matter of Diana's funeral in between.

The political background

The most striking difference between Catalonia and Andalusia is their respective historical relationship with the rest of Spain. While Andalusia became part of the Kingdom of Castile – which would be the nucleus of the emerging Spanish state – with the fall of Moorish Granada to the Catholic Monarchs Ferdinand and Isabel in 1492, Catalonia, which supported Carlos de Austria during the Spanish War of Succession in the early eighteenth century, did not lose its local autonomy until the signing of the Decretos de Nueva Planta following the military defeat of the Carlists in 1714 (the King who inflicted this defeat was Felipe V, a member of the Bourbon family to which the current king, Juan Carlos, also belongs). Catalonia has always had its own language, Catalan, its own culture, and in the early part of the twentieth century it developed its own institutions under the Second Republic (1930–36), a period when it set up its own Parliament – the Generalitat – which was in fact dominated by the republican party Esquerra Republica de Catalunya (ERC).

Catalonia was also one of the earliest regions in Spain to industrialise, the nineteenth-century Catalan bourgeoisie being the first industrial bourgeoisie in Spain. This group of people have had – and continue to have – a complex and frequently contradictory relationship with central power in Madrid, often manoeuvring for increased devolved power, but almost invariably backing Madrid in moments of heightened working-class agitation: though there were of course exceptions, by and large they supported both the military coup of General Primo de Rivera in 1923 and Franco's uprising in 1936. Franco did little to repay their support after the Civil War, not only abolishing the Generalitat but also banning the Catalan language from public use – in education, the media and so on – for most of his almost forty-year dictatorship. Thus while the Franco regime appropriated many symbols of Andalusia – flamenco, castanets, mantillas – as symbols of Spain producing a strong symbolic association between region and centre, the relationship between Catalonia and the centre, both during the Franco regime and after, has often been tense and hostile.

With the return of democracy in 1977 significant changes were to take place in the relationship between Catalonia and the centre. The constitution of 1978 recognised Catalan as one of the four official languages of Spain (the others being Castilian, Basque and Galician), the Generalitat was reconstituted in the same year following the Statute of Autonomy, and language legislation in 1983 began the process of re-establishing Catalan as the language of Catalonia, particularly in the public sphere. The increasing autonomy achieved by Catalonia (along with other regions such as the Basque Country) was not always welcomed by all sectors in Madrid, the language legislation in particular being a constant sore point throughout much of the eighties and nineties. In fact, the language question was one of the dominant issues of the 1992 Olympic Games, with fierce arguments in the Spanish media as to whether the Games were Spanish or Catalan, and what their official language could be. The question of the 'symbols of Catalan identity' and 'difference' from the rest of Spain has been a highly controversial one since the return of democracy. All of this was very much in the air in the run-up to the royal wedding. For example, writing in *La Vanguardia* on 3 October, Antonio Burgos, ironising on the term 'hecho diferencial' ('differential fact') much used at the time by Catalonia to emphasise the reality of its difference from the rest of Spain, suggested: 'You have a royal wedding in Seville and it's something that concerns the whole of Spain. You have a royal wedding in Catalonia and it immediately becomes a differential fact'. On 6 October the same author (Andalusian by birth) wrote in the Andalusian edition of *El Mundo*: 'Barcelona and Catalonia play the role they want to play in Spain, and make the wedding into a differential fact. Seville and Andalusia play the role assigned to them by Spain and make the wedding into a fact of central Spain, in spite of the autonomous regions'.

Changes in the composition of central government had also led to significant changes in Catalonia's involvement in the governance of the Spanish state. When the Socialist party PSOE failed to win an outright majority in the 1993 elections, they sought to secure their position by reaching agreements with both the Basque Nationalist Party PNV and the moderate Catalan nationalist party CiU, the party of the Catalan president Jordi Pujol. In return for their support, the regions (all regions, not just Catalonia and the Basque Country) were given a number of concessions, for example direct control over a larger share of their own taxes, something which also drew considerable hostility even from other (poorer) regions who felt that their share of the national cake would thereby decrease. From 1993 to 1996, while this agreement lasted, the conservative press in Madrid frequently attacked Catalonia, its President and its language policy as a way of attacking the Socialists still in power, causing something of a siege mentality to develop in Catalonia itself.

The 1996 elections saw the end of the Socialists' long administration, and the emergence of the right-wing Popular Party, PP, as the main party in Spain. It too, however, was short of an overall majority. Having spent three years criticising the pact between the Socialists and the nationalists, it now also entered into a very similar agreement with PNV, CiU and some other smaller regional parties. Catalonia thus continued to remain crucial to the central governance of Spain, but its ties with a now conservative government spared it much of the hostility and aggression it had faced during its agreement with PSOE. While the first royal wedding was before this period of change, the second was after it.

The event

Relations between Catalonia and Madrid – indeed on occasions with the monarchy itself – had been troubled for much of the eighties and nineties, particularly in connection with the Olympic Games. For example, the King had been whistled at by the crowd when he arrived late for the official opening of the Olympic Stadium in Barcelona in 1989 (Cardús, 1995: 165–196), and the question of the symbology of the Olympics themselves – both linguistic and visual – had been the subject of heated and at times quite vitriolic debate: the idea of images of the streets of Barcelona lined with Catalan rather than Spanish flags being beamed around the world was something which many conservative sectors in Madrid had found extremely difficult to swallow. The announcement of a royal wedding in Barcelona gave rise, therefore, to fears that similar tensions would re-emerge. There was even some desultory debate early on as to whether 'I do' would be said in Castilian ('sí, quiero') or Catalan ('sí, vull'), and whether nationalist feeling in Catalonia would result either in disruption of the event, at worst, or a lack of enthusiasm at best.

A certain level of protest was in fact recorded, and not all in Catalonia. Thus the leader of the Basque National Party, Xabier Arzalluz, declined his invitation to the wedding, as did the leader of the left-wing party Izquierda Unida, Julio Anguita. Students in Barcelona marched the day before the wedding protesting, not about the wedding itself, but at what they saw as the 'invasion' of their city by security forces (there were no fewer than 4500 police lining the route on the day). The small independence party PI – a breakaway from the historical ERC – not only hung enormous Catalan flags with anti-monarchy slogans from the Sagrada Familia cathedral (one of them proclaimed 'Bourbons, out of Catalonia'), but also organised a special barbecue on the wedding day where they cooked a typical Catalan sausage called a 'butifarra': the joke was lost on no-one who could speak Catalan, since a 'butifarra', as well as being a sausage, is the term used to describe the obscene gesture consisting of bending the forearm energetically upwards in the direction of the person being insulted while clasping the upper arm with the other hand (in fact the Catalan novelist Vázquez Montalbán had explained this detail to Spanish readers in an article in *El País* on 29 September). But it was all very low key.

As an article in *El Mundo* (4 October 1997) put it: 'The political class in Catalonia has closed ranks around the Royal Family. Apparently there are no longer any problems of protocol like during the Olympic Games'. In fact not even the question of which flag would adorn the streets came up: gone were the Catalan colours of 1992, and in their place came miles of royal blue – the background colour of the royal flag itself – adorned with the new shield of the city of Barcelona and the word 'congratulations' in three languages: Catalan, Castilian and Basque. And then there was television's ability to simply ignore what it did not like. A small anti-royalty demonstration organised by MP Pilar Rahola on the balcony of the headquarters of the PI as the procession passed was neither shown nor mentioned (though it did elicit some comment in the press). In the midst of all this good will, there was even a (in some ways rather astonishing) reconciliation with history as the bride and groom made their way to the cathedral in an open-top Rolls Royce formerly used... by Franco!

Television coverage of the wedding

TVE fielded a three-person studio team for coverage of the event, aided by numerous on-the-spot reporters. The studio team consisted of Ana Blanco – well known to Spanish viewers throughout Spain since she often fronts the main evening news bulletin – Javier Algarra, a Catalan (who was, therefore, despite commenting only in Castilian, able to give the various buildings in Barcelona their proper Catalan names . pronounced correctly in Catalan), and royal 'expert' Carmen Enríquez who had also commented on the previous wedding. Much of what they had to say followed the same lines as 1995. Thus there were numerous unquestioning references to the various royals attending – representing a total of forty royal families – several of whom were given the title of 'king' or 'queen' even if they were no longer reigning (King Simeon of Bulgaria, King Michael of Romania etc), there was much explanation of the history of the main buildings involved (the cathedral, the palaces and so on), exegesis of the music used and paintings filmed.

The differences between coverage of this ceremony and its predecessor in 1995 could be summarised as follows:

– There were no references to Barcelona being in any way the 'heart of Spain'. The idea that the 'whole of Spain' was in some sense present was of course mooted on occasions, with comments such as:

It's from this point on that they will be greeted by the people of Barcelona and of all the cities of Spain and the whole world who are in the streets, because it would be wrong to say that there are only Barcelona people here, people from all over have turned up,
    The people of Barcelona, of the whole of Catalonia and of the whole of Spain have come to Barcelona to pay their respects to the young couple.

Despite this, Barcelona's specificity as the capital of Catalonia was respected in several, if somewhat understated ways. Thus the Archbishop of Barcelona Ricard Maria Carles was able to say a few words in Catalan at the beginning of his sermon in the cathedral, and when he addressed the newly-weds in the Basílica de la Mercè where the bride went to leave her bouquet, he spoke only – and at considerable length – in Catalan (translated into Castilian for TVE's viewers by Javier Algarra). The 'oneness of Spain' was constructed in other ways, but ones which took account more openly (if somewhat stereotypically) of its status as a plurinational state: in the trilingual 'congratulations', in hymns being sung in both Catalan and Basque during the ceremony, in the newly-weds witnessing the Catalan dance 'sardana' on entering the Basílica de la Mercè, the erection of two typically Catalan human towers on leaving, and later witnessing the Basque dance 'aurresku' on arriving at the Palace of Pedralbes. However, despite the specificity of things Catalan being respected, the event was seen by TVE's commentators as 'a magnificent opportunity to strengthen the links between Barcelona and the highest institution of the state'.

– Relatively fewer references to the 'ordinariness' of it all. These were not entirely absent. For example in a 'special' on Cristina broadcast before the ceremony she was shown as a young girl enjoying an 'education without any type of privilege', while the groom was later described as showing 'the nerves any groom would have on the day of his wedding', but they were – at least compared with Seville, relatively few and far between. There may have been less need for this given the groom's obvious status as a commoner (much commented on in the press).

– The much higher political content of the sermon. This was in fact quite striking as the archbishop urged the bride and groom to work for 'the defence of the poor, the struggle for decency' and condemned 'the unjust distribution of wealth' which resulted in people 'living beneath the poverty threshold'. He also informed the infanta that she had 'inherited from her parents... the ability to be in tune with the people' and spoke of her father's role as 'guarantor of democracy in our democratic state at difficult times'. In speaking in this way Ricard Maria Carles was continuing what is now a long-standing tradition of political interventions by Catalan bishops in favour of the disadvantaged and the dispossessed.

– The much more obvious tourist pitch. The section of TVE's coverage broadcast worldwide was introduced with shots of many of Gaudí's works throughout Barcelona (the Parc Güell, the Sagrada Família and so on), and later in the day viewers were treated to aerial views of the port, the Tibidabo and the Olympic venues on the Montjuich. We were informed that the three motifs of the day were to be the Gothic, the Modernist and the Sea, and no opportunity was missed to make reference to parts of the city which might come under one of these headings (even the bride's dress was described as 'inspired by the Gothic and Modernist styles'). There was considerable comment in the press about how much 'Barcelona' hoped to make from the event (perhaps connecting with a widespread stereotype in Spain which depicts Catalans as both entrepreneurial and tight-fisted). As the Andalusian daily *Córdoba* put it (5 October 1997): 'Barcelona promoted itself as much or more than during the Olympics... Barcelona once again offered the best image, the palpable proof of its maturity, its Europeanness'.

But again there was the constant mixing of the historical and the modern. Though the bride and groom were referred to as a 'modern couple' (Cristina was described as 'an independent woman with a strong sense of responsibility'), she was accompanied to the cathedral by horsemen 'wearing armour in the old style as in the times of Alfonso XIII' and was addressed by the archbishop of Barcelona using the royal 'you' (ie: in the plural). There were many references to the World Fair held in the city in 1929, and even the bride's dress was based on that worn by Queen Victoria Eugenia, the wife of Alfonso XIII. There was even one – only one – fleeting reference to the Civil War. The almost forty-year long Franco regime continues to be well-nigh unnamable. Even his Rolls Royce will be referred to in future as the one in which the infanta went to her wedding: as the columnist in *Antena 3 Noticias* put it on 5 October, 'The two youngsters were even up to the memory of Franco who, careful how you go, still glows in the origins of this Juan Carlist monarchy'.

Though not mentioned at all on television, it would be wrong to leave coverage of this wedding without mentioning the funeral of Lady Diana, which had been a media event of some importance in Spain. 'Goodbye to the funeral, here comes the wedding', wrote Carmen Rigalt in *El Mundo* of 4 October. And broadly speaking this wedding was seen in the press as a positive Spanish reply to that funeral, a restatement of modern Spanish royal values in the face of a decadent British monarchy under threat from below. For example, an article in *Antena 3 Noticias* on 5 October noted how 'The spirit of Diana passed through here, and people are delighted with the popular appeal of those royal personages who have it', while columnist Antonio Burgos opined in *El Mundo* of the same day that the wedding had been so successful that the couple would go on to 'play in the European Cup of Royal Weddings, the Champions Cup of Boosts to the Monarchy after the bombshell at the House of Windsor'. 'Diana's funeral', he went on, 'has passed like a whirlwind through the Monarchies of Europe' and 'Without Diana's funeral, it is impossible to understand the critical and public success of this wedding'. Royal families have learned, he concluded, 'that their peoples do not forgive when royal personages do not do their duty, become cold and lose their sense of where the winds of the popular will are blowing'.

History in the Remaking

The two Spanish royal weddings of the nineties continue the twin strands of the rewriting of history which was already apparent in Spanish media coverage of the separation of Charles and Diana in 1992. In the Seville wedding re-establishing the links with Spain's long monarchic past was the dominant tone, while in Barcelona the effacing of the Franco monarchy was more to the fore. This (political) strategy is by no means limited to the coverage of royal events, but the royal family is a key element in its elaboration. As Carlos González argues (1994, 8):

> The political 'transition' towards a liberal democracy, in the form in which it developed in Spain, necessarily involved a process of 'invention' of a liberal democratic tradition in our political culture. This meant the creation of a set of symbols among which the Monarchy would acquire the status of an 'exemplary' institution.

And so it continues. On the twenty-fifth anniversary of the death of Franco in November 2000 *El País* produced a special supplement entitled 'That Remote Dictatorship', while *Cambio 16*'s reversible issue of the same week (27 November 2000) – half on the king, the other half (turning the magazine upside down) on Franco – described the latter as 'Undone, completely undone'. In his recent study of the Transition (from dictatorship to democracy) in the late seventies, Salvador Cardús talks of an 'erasure and reinvention of the collective memory... in which the media participated with particular enthusiasm... they took over the function of creating of constructing a national mythology' (2000: 24–5). As we hope to have shown, some twenty-five years later this process of 'Disremembering the dictatorship' (Resina, 2000) was still a dynamic one, its enduring energy suggesting doggedly high levels of vigilance by those concerned about the emergence of alternative points of view.

A Royal Friendship – 2000–1
A Model for the Future?

With the weddings of the two infantas over, considerable media interest – indeed, impatience – now focussed on the future plans of the one remaining unmarried royal, the thirtysomething crown prince Felipe. His first publicly acknowledged girlfriend had been Isabel Sartorius, the daughter of a minor Spanish aristocrat, their relationship lasting from 1989 to 1991. Despite her now long-distant rejection, the mythically youthful figure of Isabel Sartorius (not, of course, the real 36-year-old single mother now living in Madrid) made a substantial comeback in the media in the early months of 2001, particularly in the weekly magazines, where pictures of her in a somewhat melancholic pose appeared with some regularity. The reason is not hard to find: they were part of truly colossal outpouring of discourse in relation to the news of prince Felipe's friendship with willowy Norwegian model Eva Sannum. Though this friendship came to an end in 2001, we wish to dedicate the remainder of this chapter to an analysis of one of the most debated subjects of the that year in Spain... though it was not, of course, the only one, others including BSE, the arrival of foot-and-mouth disease, and by far the most discussed topic of all, the finally fruitless attempt by the ruling PP and the leading opposition party PSOE to join forces to defeat the Basque National Party in the autonomous elections held in the Basque Country in May.

A controversy (slowly) emerges

¡Hola!, Spain's most widely read celebrity magazine – and inspiration for both the British *Hello!* and the French *Oh la!* – was the first publication to break, or more correctly to re-introduce, the story of Felipe and Eva. The couple had in fact first met in 1997 in Norway at a party held by prince Haakon, and their relationship grew while Eva was working for the 'Magic' modelling agency in Madrid in the same year: indeed, a photograph of them dining together with friends in a Madrid restaurant in 1997 was not only given considerable publicity at the time (Apezarena, 2000: 450), but was also one of the most consistently reproduced in the weekly magazines in the early months of 2001. After a few months in the Spanish capital, however, Eva went back to Oslo – apparently to avoid the increasingly intrusive attentions of Spanish journalists – and, though the couple were occasionally seen here and there in different locations, all went quiet regarding their relationship until December 2000 when *¡Hola!* published two issues in a row on their 'friendship'. The first of these appeared on 7 December, and featured a photograph of Eva (along with four other photographs of other people, one the same size and three smaller) on the front cover, together with a five-page article inside showing her in various formal and informal poses, these accompanied by a separate photograph of the prince. In typical *¡Hola!* style, the article is dominated almost entirely by photographs at the very considerable expense of text, but there is sufficient of this to inform us that she is a 'beautiful and discrete young woman who speaks six languages and loves sport' and that she is in second year of a course on Advertising in Oslo. The following week a very informal photograph of the couple on holiday in India during the spring of 2000 dominated the front cover of the next issue of *¡Hola!*. Inside, a five-page article gave some details of the holiday, repeated much of what had been said the week before, mentioned other royal 'love matches' in The Netherlands, Denmark, Belgium, Sweden and Norway, and finished with the view that 'marriages based on love are real and are likely to last forever whether the groom is a prince or a beggar'.

In our 'media-savvy' age, of course, the element of stage-management in a carefully controlled leak of this kind – particularly given that *¡Hola!* is often referred to as the 'unofficial journal' of the royal family – is plain for all to see. Even so, reactions were muted, with the 'serious' press apparently unwilling to follow *¡Hola!*'s lead. *La Vanguardia* of 8 December 2000 (*¡Hola!* is often available before its official publication date) commented on both pieces, reproducing much of the information with little change, but employed a spoiling tactic by adding (with reference to the official residence of the Spanish royals) that 'Although *¡Hola!* enjoys great credibility due to the sobriety of its reports... the facts have shown that this magazine does not have a direct line to the Zarzuela, which communicates only through official statements'. On 10 December *El Mundo* suggested that *¡Hola!*'s 'insistence seemed to many to be strategic', and saw the whole thing as a 'plan drawn up to prepare (or at least sound out) Spanish public opinion', though a somewhat longer article in the same issue advised the prince against marrying someone 'whose boobs were known to all and sundry'.

This initial burst of activity was followed by a lull of some months (excluding *¡Hola!*'s coverage of the couple's skiing holiday with the prince's sisters and their husbands in Saint Moritz in February) until the weekly *Tiempo* published a four-page article on 5 March 2001 not on Eva (though a picture of her did indeed appear), but on Isabel Sartorius, described in the title as 'the longed-for "princess"'. It ended by quoting an unidentified source 'close to the king' as taking the view that Isabel would have been much more suitable as queen than either Eva Sannum or Gigi Howard (the prince's immediately previous girlfriend) as she was an 'exquisitely educated aristocrat'. Over the next two months or so *Tiempo* would achieve a certain protagonism in this field. Its issue of 26 March dedicated its entire front page to the couple, with the heading 'Twelve decisive months for Eva Sannum'. Inside a six-page article gave exhaustive information on the new royal girlfriend and her family background, and explained the prince's strategy of taking a year to gradually introduce her to the Spanish people in order to both gauge their reactions and see how she stood up to the inevitable public scrutiny. An associated article (published in the same pages) took an extremely relaxed view regarding who the prince married, adding 'A society which rejects mediaeval marriages of convenience should not, at this point in time, be the target of the monarchically correct'.

In its following edition (2 April 2001) *Tiempo* congratulated itself on the impact its earlier article had caused, explaining how it had been taken up not only by other newspapers and magazines, but also on radio and television. The snowball was in motion. It gathered more speed with the announcement that Socialist MP José Bono was proposing the repeal of the Salic Law so that in future the crown would pass to the reigning monarch's first child regardless of the latter's sex (both Felipe's sisters are older than him). *Tiempo*'s three-page article on this topic (9 April 2001) quoted article 57.1 of the Spanish constitution enshrining the prior claim of male children, and contrasted it with the situation in other countries.

However, real critical mass would not be achieved until the end of that month. *Tiempo*'s edition of 23 April had as its front-page headline 'The monarchs cannot control the princes: rebellion in the palace' and carried photographs of Felipe and Eva, Willem-Alexander of the Netherlands and his fiancée Máxima Zorreguieta, Haakon of Norway and his fiancée Mette-Marit Tjessem Høiby, and 'turbo prince' Frederik of Denmark. Inside, a six-page article recounted the 'problems' faced by the reigning monarchs in these countries, also bringing in the Sophie Rhys-Jones 'sheik affair' and Camilla Parker-Bowles. The dominant note of this article – and one which would surface insistently as this controversy gathered pace – was that monarchs no longer enjoyed the privileged lives of yore: on the contrary being a monarch was one of the toughest jobs around, demanding enormous personal sacrifices from those on whose shoulders it fell. Thus 'historian and genealogist' Ricardo Mateos was quoted as saying:

> any prince without a throne has a better life than one with a crown... These live in demo-

cratic countries where the citizens call them to account... the crown has become a burden, and this requires compensations such as marriage for love, which gives them a more satisfying private life.

Thus a group of the most wealthy and privileged people in Europe becomes constructed as the victims of history, and even of democracy.

In the same issue as this article appeared, *Tiempo* also published an interview with José Luis de Vilallonga on the second volume of his memoirs *Otros mundos, otra vida*. Vilallonga is much better known in Spain as the biographer of King Juan Carlos – his (to put it mildly) rather indulgent biography entitled *El Rey* , a book which he referred to in this interview as 'our book' (ie. the King's and his), having appeared in 1993 – and he was therefore asked his opinion on the prince's choice of girlfriend. 'The important thing', he answered, 'is that he should marry someone who is prepared for a very difficult job. But this young lady suddenly turning up from Norway... You know, it's given me a bit of a fright'. But this was not Vilallonga's only engagement with the issue. On 20 April the very conservative and traditionally monarchical Madrid daily *Abc* published a lengthy article by the same author entitled 'A Prince's Duties' in which the latter responded to an article in the same newspaper published on 3 April urging the prince to pay no attention to those 'dynastic bluebottles' who were suggesting that he should subordinate his feelings to 'dynastic interests'. Without mentioning Eva Sannum at all, in his reply Vilallonga expressed the hope that 'when the prince gets married, he will marry, not necessarily a princess with royal blood, no-one is asking that of him, but a woman prepared by her upbringing, her character and her education to carry out the very difficult job of Queen of Spain'. His final point was the following:

> I would view as a grave error a marriage which put us on a par with the British and I would perhaps begin to calculate the chances of a Republic which would save me from having to bow before the wrong kind of queen.

With its hectoring tone, its sneering references to 'the common people' with their lack of understanding of complex affairs of state and its deliberate exaggerations (there are references to 'the Nordic countries where nothing ever happens, perhaps because of the cold') this article is obviously provocative in its intent. In this it was enormously successful. Over the next two to three weeks the amount written and said on this subject would reach colossal proportions, particularly from 1 May (international Labour Day) on. On Sunday 6 May *El Mundo* would in fact print a lengthy series of extracts from all the main Spanish dailies on this topic, while in its edition of 14 May *Tiempo* – again featuring Felipe and Eva on its front cover – invited fifty people to give their opinion on whether 'Eva is the right woman' (no-one asked whether Felipe was necessarily the right man). By 21 May the controversy was going strong, with *Tiempo* publishing not only a two-and-a-half-page-plus article on the topic, but also a two-page 'open letter' from José Oneto to the prince.

Romantics, Constitutionalists, Monarchists and others

Much of this tidal wave of text was, of course, simply journalists filling up column inches or airtime and thereby earning a wage. As Antonio Burgos wrote in his column in *El Mundo* on 2 May:

> I calculate that this is article number 849 written over the last couple of days about the Prince of Asturias and his possible wedding with the much talked-about Norwegian model. I calculate that Eva Sannum has been worth an average of 4.7 days wages to each columnist in Spain. The radio stations are giving off smoke, the television stations are enjoying record audiences and the magazines are having a field day.

But, as discourse is an immanent dimension of text, any tidal wave of text exists simultaneously as a tsunami of discourse. And the discursive battle-lines along which this particular controversy would be to some extent acted, and to some extent fought out, are ones with which we will become even more familiar in subsequent chapters, though some particularly Spanish variations did, of course, also emerge.

A romantic discourse. Given Eva Sannum's working-class background, the prince-and-the-pauper elements of the situation proved impossible to resist. References to Cinderella were commonplace (*Tiempo*, 26 March 2001; *La Vanguardia*, 1 May 2001) – indeed, the 'special' on Eva Sannum in *El Mundo's* website was entirely structured around this fairytale, Disney-like drawings and all – though a variation was a reference to the 'Prince and the shepherdess' (*El Mundo*, 1 May 2001) and another the 'Prince and the chorus girl' (*El Mundo*, 10 December 2000). Within the terms of this discourse all that counts is whether or not the two love each other, in which case they should get married. Though it uses a rather ancient narrative form as a structuring element, this discourse presents itself as modern, as opposing not only mediaeval 'marriages of convenience' – an argument which would also be deployed in Norway and the Netherlands (see Chapters 7 and 8) – but also those 'monarchists *enragés*' (*Época*, 30 April 2001) still defending an 'outmoded version of the monarchy' (*El Mundo*, 1 May 2001) which places 'reasons of state' before individual feelings.

A constitutional discourse. As also happened in Norway and the Netherlands, Spanish readers enjoyed a sudden improvement in their knowledge of the Spanish constitution, particularly paragraph 32 relating to abolition of the so-called 'Pragmática de Carlos III' on morganatic marriages, paragraph 57.1 relating to the Salic Law and paragraph 57.4 establishing the requirement for the prince to obtain the approval of both his father and parliament to be able to marry without losing his rights to the throne. They even learned that paragraph 64 makes the parliament responsible for any political acts of the monarch. Much debated also was the section of the constitution which states that, should the king die before his heir reaches the age of eighteen, the queen will act as regent for that period, the question asked being whether a model could ever be an acceptable regent and therefore head of state (an identical constitutional argument was put forward in both Norway and the Netherlands in relation to their 'unconventional' future queens: see below). The official argument of the constitutionalists was that 'the prince's marriage is not a subject which should be approached wielding opinion polls or to the roar of the columnists' opinions, but with the strictest adherence to the legalities' (*El Mundo*, 30 April 2001). Despite its would-be technical nature, however, it is abundantly clear that this discourse provided a vehicle for a range of judgements, political or otherwise: as Juan Esteban put it in *El Mundo* (2 May): 'on the basis of our Constitution, the Heir can get married to whomever he wants, but not to just anyone'.

The elements of this discourse relating to a possible regency were opposed both by the romantics arguing that they were overstating the political power of the monarch (*O Correo Galego*, 1 May 2001) and also by the 'modernisers', one of whom, the socialist MP Cristina Alberdi, even went so far as to advocate 'harmonisation' within the EU on this subject (*Tiempo*, 9 April 2001)

A monarchic discourse. This is in fact a discursive 'set' which can be further subdivided as follows:

A traditional monarchic discourse. This discourse defends the monarchy as the ultimate symbol both of national unity and of a certain kind of historical continuity. Its exponents can be well aware of the irrational and undemocratic nature of this symbol, but defend it none the less. For example, Gabriel Cisneros, member of the ruling PP and one of the fathers of the constitution, had this to say of the repeal of the Salic Law (*Tiempo*, 9 April 2001):

> You take the institution of monarchy as a whole, with all its historical characteristics and features, and if you accept something as, so to speak, irrational as the principle of inheritance, why introduce false elements of modernity such as women enjoying conditions of equality with men? I am clear in my mind that it is a historic legacy from the past and it works so long as it maintains those characteristics of a historic legacy.

Proponents of this discourse make frequent reference to the catastrophic results of inappropriate royal love matches in the past. Vilallonga, for example, not only brings examples from Spanish history but also talks at length of the problems caused by Princess Diana and the Duchess of York who both looked for love in marriages where it was irrelevant (*Abc*, 20 May 2001). And the fact that Eva Sannum had modelled underwear for a fashion catalogue was a much used disqualifying argument by this group, who contrasted her behaviour with that of former queens. As historian Carlos Seco Serrano put it in *Abc* (29 April 2001):

> It would be inconceivable to see on the Throne which in the last century was occupied, with absolute dignity, by María Cristina de Austria and Victoria Eugenia de Battenberg, and is occupied today in an exemplary manner by Sofía de Grecia, a young woman endorsed for her 'perfect measurements'.

There were many reference to future Spaniards having pictures of their queen in 'bra and panties' on their walls (*El Periódico*, 1 May 2001) or in the cabins of their trucks (*El Mundo*, 1 May 2001). What proponents of this discourse demanded of the prince was a sense of 'duty' and 'responsibility'. This was opposed by romantics foregrounding 'love' and by 'modernisers' foregrounding 'professionalism'.

A modernising monarchic discourse. Proponents of this discourse are well aware of the 'contradictions which an institution which is old-fashioned by nature will have to face in a world changing at a meteoric pace where only that which adapts to the new rules will prevail' (*El Mundo*, 6 May 2001). They therefore argue against the 'genetically correct' (*El Mundo*, 6 May 2001) and stress that the future of the monarchy lies in its increasing 'professionalisation', an idea which, as we saw earlier, has been around in Spain for a very considerable time. Among their 'models' are, for example, the current queens of Norway and Sweden, both 'commoners' but very professional monarchs, though as far as Eva Sannum was concerned, they were clearly further subdivided into two camps – those who did, and those who did not believe that she could meet these professional criteria. This discourse presents Felipe as having been trained for the 'job' as no other prince before him: 'he has the richest and most varied experience ever enjoyed by any heir to the Crown', wrote *El Mundo* on 6 May, while José Oneto declared in his open letter (*Tiempo*, 21 May 2001): 'We have one of the best prepared heirs in the history of Spain'. However, if we bear in mind that exactly identical claims have been made for Willem-Alexander of the Netherlands – for example, 'No heir to the throne has been more thoroughly prepared for his future task than prince Willem-Alexander' (*Volkskrant*, 31 March 2001) – we can see that this discourse is by no means limited to Spain.

From this point of view, the origin of the future queen is in itself irrelevant, so long as she is willing to learn and is up to the 'job'. As *El Periódico* put it (2 May 2001), 'Any intelligent woman can learn the job of queen, while the history of the world shows many bad queens who had the best CVs as far as lineage is concerned'. Indeed, parading examples of dreadful monarchs – both kings and queens – from the past, for all their royal blood, was a favourite tactic here. Thus Baltasar Porcel in *La Vanguardia* (5 May 2001) referred to Fernando VII, Isabel II and Alfonso XIII, all from Spanish history, while others (*El Mundo*, 9 May 2001) brought in similar figures from the history of other European countries.

It is this group, above all, which stresses the monarchy as a job, as unremitting hard work demanding constant abnegation, emphasising 'all that sacrifice, all that doing without, all those sorrows and self-discipline, all those obligations and absences' (*El Mundo*, 4 May 2001). As in the case of Norway (see page 114), this group sees itself as defending the monarchy not only against the claims of the pre-modern, but also against possible encroachments by the postmodern, against those who want a queen with 'the advertising glamour of a soft drink' (*Diario 16*, 1 May 2001). As one writer who clearly did not feel that Eva Sannum was 'up to the job' put it – referring to two very popular television programmes in Spain at the time – insisting on professionalism would prevent 'what we all feared, a model who not only was on a par with the minor celebrities who win prizes on "Tómbola", but who into the bargain had shared a flat with one of the wretched participants in "Big Brother"'. Or as Editor Pedro J. Ramírez wrote in a lengthy editorial in *El Mundo* on 6 May, referring to a number of extremely popular weekly magazines and television programmes:

at this moment in time, when televisual or magazine voyeurism is both bread and circus of the people, nothing is more dangerous than ending up as an icon of this implacable journalistic consumption. But that, which is the real biblical curse threatening the monarchies – you'll appear in Hello!, in Diez Minutos and even in Pronto and Qué me dices every week and they'll talk about you in Tómbola and Corazón, corazón – can happen to you just as easily with Eva Sannum as with a princess with Waterman ink in her veins.

It is the spouses of the British royal family who are most frequently advanced as a nightmare scenario by this group due to their abject lack of professionalism, and the prince is encouraged to avoid at all costs ending up with 'a Diana of Wales, a Fergie, or what's worse, although until a couple of months ago this would not have seemed possible, a countess of Wessex' (*El Mundo*, 9 May 2001).

However, it is worth pointing out that this modernising tendency was also opposed by the 'modern' romantics, who grouped them together with the traditionalists. As Rafael Torres wrote in *Diario 16* on 3 May:

> The intervention of some so-called 'royal journalists', gentlemen smelling of mothballs... has also proved rather picturesque... They believe themselves to be the pillars of the Crown and take it as a personal affront when Felipe fools around with a good looking girl when, in their opinion, he should marry a 'professional', in other words an old hag. And what's more, the fact that the girl appears showing her breasts in a calendar is enough to give them a heart attack

A Juancarlist discourse. This is, of course, a peculiarly Spanish variation on the monarchic discourse, has been around in Spanish political and media culture for a very long time, and is used in different ways by both traditionalists and modernisers. It takes the view that Spaniards are not in fact particularly wedded to the monarchy as an institution, but primarily to the figure of Juan Carlos in view of the role he is held to have played in the restoration and consolidation of democracy. Monarchists who take the view that Spain is a Juancarlist rather than a monarchist country believe that the continuation of the monarchy after the death of the current king is by no means assured: future monarchs will have to win the respect of the people through their 'hard work' and 'dedication' just as Juan Carlos did. This had been one of the opening arguments of José Luis de Vilallonga's earlier biography of the king (1993: 9), and is essentially also the argument in his article in *Abc* of 20 April:

> The Spanish Monarchy is based firmly on Juancarlism, but when one day the curtain falls on the good deeds of an exceptional sovereign, the Monarchy, as an Institution, will be again called into question by those nostalgic for Republics which in Spain have always ended in confusion. The heir to the Crown will then have to convince Spaniards that he possesses the qualities necessary – in other words, those of his father – to keep a firm hand on the rudder of an institution which for centuries has been able to maintain the unity of Spain.

For this group, the 'wrong choice' of a future queen will make the move from Juancarlism to devotion to a 'proper' institutionalised monarchy – whether ancient or modern – all the more difficult.

A republican discourse. This discourse has relatively little representation in the Spanish media, its main spokesperson being almost invariably Pilar Rahola, MP for the Catalan independentist party PI (whose low-key attempts at dissonance during the Barcelona royal wedding were repressed by force). Her well-known republican views did not, however, prevent her position on this issue being very close to that of what she calls the 'orthodox' monarchists (*Tiempo*, 14 May 2001):

> In any case, if they're selling us the product, at least he should marry a woman who's prepared, and who's very professional... I prefer the prince to marry a professional, from that point of view I agree with the orthodox monarchists, although for different reasons... In fact, this question amuses me only because it's going to be the downfall of the monarchy.

A similar argument was put forward in *El Mundo* of 3 May:

> I would like the prince to marry the Norwegian model because I'm a republican... The present Spanish monarchy has been useful in extraordinary circumstances. Felipe VI won't have things so easy when his time comes... And if he does what any of his subjects would do... what's the point of the Monarchy?... Señorita Sannum, welcome.

Others. The Catch-22 facing those wishing to distance themselves from such a controversy is that, unless they are able to develop a position radically outside its discursive framework, their attacks, no matter how caustic and eloquently articulated, in the end merely add to the already existing discursive mass. A good example of this is Margarita Riviere's article entitled 'The Snowball' published in *El País* on 6 May. In it she fumes about the scale of a controversy drummed up by 'a couple of antediluvians in Madrid', about the underlying male chauvinism of it all, about how it is distracting people's attention from other more important issues. Her final position is a modernising, meritocratic one – 'today real nobility is a question of talent and not inheritance' – and she pins her hopes on future generations who will be much more like 'Eva Sannum and Felipe de Borbón than we can imagine'. Refreshing views, no doubt, but ones whose expression added over 600 words to an already mountainous quantity of text. Perhaps only the Catalan-language daily *Avui* (1 May) achieved real distance by having Eva Sannum's 'vulgar family tree' discussed by two women having a fictitious conversation in a sauna. Mirth-provoking, but poor in explanatory power.

Spain in transition once more

Two things distinguish this Spanish controversy from those we analyse later in this book. The first is its extraordinarily high level of internal incoherence. Thus republican positions can at times coincide closely with orthodox monarchist views, while traditional monarchists show high levels of overlap with modernising ones: the discursive cocktail of Vilallonga's article of 20 April, for example, has many points of contact with José Oneto's modernising 'Open letter to Don Felipe de Borbón' in *Tiempo* of 21 May. Meanwhile, the romantics attack both the constitutionalists and monarchists of all hues, while clearly identifiable elements of the romantic discourse are used by a number of modernisers and at times even by some constitutionalists. It is not at all unusual to find to some extent contradictory standpoints in the same article: for example, Antonio Burgos's piece in *El Mundo* of 1 May includes traditionalist discourses defending the 'non-democratic' nature of the monarchy, modernising Juancarlist discourses stressing the monarchy as a job, and Bagehotian notions of magic and distance. The incoherence extends even to the smallest details. In his open letter in *Tiempo* José Oneto cannot decide on a level of formality and addresses the prince with both singular and plural forms. On a somewhat different level, on 14 May *Tiempo* reported that when Felipe and Eva arrived unannounced at the De Vinis restaurant in Madrid 'those who heard her speak said that Eva Sannum spoke Spanish with some ease and that her physique "is like that of so many Scandinavians who stroll around Spanish beaches in Summer"', while a week later the same magazine quoted yet another source as saying on a different occasion: 'She didn't open her mouth. When she did her Spanish left a lot to be desired and her physique is nothing to write home about'. At the same time, virtually all sides made use of Princess Diana or other British royal consorts, past or present, in defence of their views.

And then there were the rumours. Though the Chief of the Royal House wrote to *Abc* on 3 May stressing that Vilallonga's article could not be in any way interpreted as expressing the king's views, the author insisted that he had sent a copy to the king before publication, and it was reported that the editor of *Abc* had done likewise. Yet more rumours circulated suggesting adverse views by the queen regarding Eva Sannum, all in the midst of official denials and silences, and there were other rumours hinting that somehow or other the government was behind the entire controversy (*El País*, 6 May 2001). This all-pervading confusion derives essentially from the fact that the apparent subject of the debate – Eva Sannum or her suitability as queen – is not in fact the real subject of the debate. Her absolute anonymity in a number of the articles in question is acutely symptomatic of what is (or more precisely what is not) at stake.

The second and very striking difference between the Spanish situation and what happened elsewhere (in Belgium, Norway and the Netherlands, as we shall see later), and one which is by no means unconnected with the first, is the almost complete silence of the politicians: indeed, *El País* suggested on 6 May that 'The question is still taboo among a large part of the political class'. A few, mostly from PP, did offer brief statements when asked by *El País* on 6 May – but both the PSOE and IU declined to answer, and after three days no-one from CiU had come forward to respond at all – and some were also included in *Tiempo*'s fifty interviewees on 14 May, but there were no official statements from any of the parties or their spokespersons, no high-profile political interventions in the debate. Apart from the journalists and professional writers such as Vilallonga, the debate was carried almost entirely by academics: by historians, genealogists, jurists, specialists in constitutional law and so on.

Far from being about the identity of Spain's future queen, this controversy is in fact about shifting patterns of power in the Spain of the early twenty-first century. The Spanish royal project is – and has been from the outset – a fundamentally *political* project, and so it remains today. It is about the maintenance of a particular compromise which emerged from the Transition of 1975–1977, which was enormously more to the benefit of certain sections (and indeed regions) of Spanish society than it was to others. At its very simplest, it contributed to the move from a dictatorial to a democratic political regime, while leaving the economic (and social and cultural) power of the Spanish bourgeoisie largely intact, its legitimation deriving not only from Juan Carlos's permanent construction as 'guarantor of democracy' and 'king of all Spaniards', but from a level of taboo virtually unknown in other European countries. For example, the Spanish version of *Spitting Image, Los Muñegotes*, never features the Spanish royal family. And when, in his television programme *Persones humanes*, Catalan comedian Mikimito allowed himself the luxury of some very mild fun at the expense of the infanta Elena in January 1994, the subsequent royal complaint brought forth apologies from the producer, the head of the channel, the head of the corporation, and ultimately the president of Catalonia, Jordi Pujol.

But the nature of the Spanish bourgeoisie itself has changed in the intervening period, with significant fissures opening up in what at one time was (the 'regional' issue notwithstanding) a relatively cohesive group with a broadly shared project. The most significant change has, of course, been the gradual but absolutely unmistakable emergence of a globalising section, first in relation to Europe, and subsequently targeting Latin America, an offensive led, sometimes in quite spectacular fashion, by the banking, communications and energy sectors. Spain is now the leading investor in Latin America, accounting for two-thirds of direct foreign investment in the region, and has moved into sixth place in a world ranking of overall outward investment (Salmon, 2001). Here and there in the debate there was the occasional echo of these developments, as when, for example, Pedro J. Ramírez argued in *El Mundo* of 6 May that the characteristics needed by a future queen should be as follows:

> those necessary to fulfil the role of consort in a constitutional monarchy in a member-country of the European Union and active protagonist in the global village. And no one can judge that better than the person who will have to be a sovereign in a world in which the very concept of sovereignty will continue to be under constant revision.

The (belated) arrival of transnational capitalism in Spain has inevitably resulted in the equally belated emergence of cultural forms which clearly demonstrate elements of the postmodern (Labanyi, 1995), one of the most striking being the dissolution of the frontiers previously separating low and high art. Those for whom these frontiers were a structuring element of their symbolic world – the old nation-state-based bourgeoisie and its allies in both the media and academia – have responded in Spain as they have elsewhere in Europe with dismissive argumentation based on discourses of 'dumbing down' and attacks on, for example, so-called 'rubbish-TV' ('tele-basura'), but these discourses betray real unease at diminishing economic, political and cultural authority, and the ghastly possibility of the emergence of a 'rubbish monarchy'. As Antonio Burgos put in *El Mundo* (1 May):

> The Crown is for the person who works for it, and with this wedding the Prince of Asturias is looking at a sombre panorama of precarious employment, a rubbish-contract[1] with the future of the Throne of Spain.

While programmes such as *Big Brother* present relatively easy targets for counter-attack, a 'dumbed down' monarchy – one 'on a par with the English' – is a much tougher proposition altogether, particularly given the institution's 'symbolic capital' in Spain (*El Mundo*, 9 May), and this is very much how a monarchy prepared to incorporate a lingerie model has been interpreted by these groups – as the cultural expression of a shift of political and economic power from the old national elites with their particular histories and value-systems – those who, as Margarita Riviere put it in *El Pais* on 6 May, 'are fed up with the fact that after 25 years there is no court other than that determined by money' – to other elites who, so to speak, have bigger fish to fry.

And so, as threatened groups always do, they have fought back. The counter-attack came from a range of individuals with a stake in the status quo arguing against what they saw either as a return to the past or as a slide into a demeaning future, and in favour of yet another negotiated compromise which might keep at least some of their privileges intact. In much the same way as the current king has been consistently constructed in Spain as the architect of the previous transition (in some sense from the pre-modern to the modern), his son is now being constructed as the key to a new transition from the modern to the postmodern. In the meantime the politicians, whose increasingly organic relationship with big business allows them limited room to manoeuvre on this front, have kept silent, and opinion polls carried out throughout the period have consistently shown that a majority of Spaniards think the prince should marry whomever he wants, and most of the others aren't particularly bothered one way or the other.

---

1   'Rubbish-contract' ('contrato-basura') was the term used to describe the short-term contracts offering very poor conditions which became highly fashionable after a restructuring of the Spanish labour market in the second half of the nineties.

6.   Belgium – A Country Reunited?

Introduction
Saturday 4 December 1999 saw the wedding in Brussels of Prince Philippe, heir to the Belgian throne, and the highly photogenic Mathilde d'Udekem d'Acoz. The bride was the daughter of a minor Belgian aristocrat and had been brought up in the south of the country in the region bordering on Luxembourg. The engagement had been officially announced on 10 September, Mathilde was officially 'introduced' to the Belgian people three days later, and the official engagement celebration took place on 13 November attended by one thousand (carefully vetted) 'ordinary people'. The wedding itself had been preceded by an official tour of major Belgian towns beginning on 21 October – the so-called 'Joyous Entries' – a tour which in fact continued into January of the following year. All of these events – the announcement, the party, the visit to different towns and cities – were the subject of intense media coverage in both the French-language and the Dutch-language newspapers and television stations, public and private, with many programmes and articles dedicated to various aspects of the monarchy in general (its history, its personalities and so on).

It was clear from the outset that media coverage on the wedding day would be on a massive scale. As the weekly magazine *Le Vif-L'Express* (3 December) put it: 'this wedding day will be the apotheosis of an extraordinary media mobilisation which began on 10 September with the official announcement of the engagement'. And indeed on 4 December coverage of the wedding completely dominated all forms of media output for virtually the entire day. Belgium's four leading television stations – RTBF (public service) and RTL-TVi (private) for the French-speaking part of the country, and VTR (public) and VTM (private) for the Dutch-speaking part – pooled their technical resources, each being responsible for covering a different part of the events of the day. Some of these stations screened over eight hours of coverage, starting as early as eight in the morning when it was still dark and temperatures were below zero. To encourage popular participation in the event – with an eye, no doubt, on its media representation – almost 400,000 train tickets were offered free of charge (a practice, incidentally, much criticised when used for very much the same reasons by the Franco regime in Spain), though in the event only 30,000 turned up in Brussels instead of the predicted 200,000 (by contrast, 300,000 people had taken part in the White March to protest over the handling of the Dutroux affair in 1996: see below).

Media coverage continued to be intense the following day, particularly in the French-language press, with the dailies *La Dernière Heure* and *La Libre Belgique* dedicating almost the entirety of their Sunday edition to the event, while the various newspapers of the *Vers l'Avenir* group brought out fourteen-page editions covering only the wedding. On Monday 6 December *La Libre Belgique* was still dedicating fifteen pages of coverage to this event. Reaction in the Dutch-language press was somewhat more restrained. On the

Sunday only the *Nieuwsblad* brought out a special edition (sixteen pages long), though on the Monday the *Gazet van Antwerpen* had a twelve-page section dedicated entirely to the wedding. As is frequently the case with such events, it was often the same people appearing on television and writing in the newspapers.

The political background

This royal wedding came at what was widely felt to be a time of crisis for Belgium, a moment when the country had been facing difficult and distressing problems over a protracted period of time. The so-called 'Cools affair', centring on the lengthy and in the opinion of many bungled investigation into the contract assassination of Socialist Government Minister André Cools in 1990, had dragged on for most of the nineties. The second half of the decade was then dominated by the ghastly 'Dutroux affair', again a long and protracted legal case centring this time on the paedophile murders of the mid-nineties and dogged by constant accusations of incompetence, political interference and downright bungling. Other high-profile scandals included the 'Brabant murders' when various body-parts turned up in the south of the country around Mons, and the 'dioxin affair', a scandal centring on the discovery of dioxins in cans and bottles of Coke which led to their massive recall amid strong feelings of public panic. In 1998–9 there was also the Agusta-Dassault scandal involving a contract for helicopters and defence systems for Belgium's F16s, and the KB-Lux affair, centring on tax evasion via accounts in the KB-Luxembourg bank. To cap it all, there were revelations relating to an illegitimate daughter of the King's, the much commented-on Delphine.

On a somewhat different level, this was also a period of a marked level of anxiety above all in Wallonie – the French-speaking part of Belgium – regarding the future of its relationship with Dutch-speaking Flanders. The Constitution of 1993 (Leus and Veny, 1996) had ushered in, for the first time in the history of Belgium, a genuinely federal arrangement giving much greater powers to the governments of both Wallonie and Flanders (and also setting up a separate 'region' of Brussels). This sense of political division is, of course, further compounded by Belgium's status as a multilingual state, having Dutch, French and German-speaking communities and all three languages as official languages. All of this, together with the activities of the Vlaams Blok, a Flemish party arguing for secession and the setting up of an independent Flemish state (small-scale protests by pro-Flemish-independence supporters at various of the 'Joyous Entries' were suppressed by force), had caused – and was continuing to cause – noticeable levels of unease in Francophone Wallonie in particular regarding the future integrity of Belgium as a country in its current configuration. All of these anxieties would surface in highly visible ways in coverage of the royal wedding, both on television and in the press. While different, of course, in detail, from the 'problems' besetting Spain at the time of its first royal wedding in 1995, broad similarities can be seen between the general situation in the two countries at the moment of their respective royal events.

Media coverage of the wedding
Television coverage
Our television coverage of this event comes from the French-language commercial

channel RTL-TVi (as a result, the various places, buildings etc. in Brussels mentioned below are here given their French names – they all, of course, have corresponding Dutch versions), coverage which was also broadcast live on giant screens throughout Brussels on the day in question. Some additional information has also been taken from VTM's celebratory video, *Filip and Mathilde, their Youth, Love and Marriage*, based on the television reports this channel screened in Flanders over the period in question.

Live coverage on RTL-TVi was anchored with considerable bonhomie by Christophe Giltay with a five-person panel of commentators consisting of three journalists – including the Editor of the weekly magazine *Points de Vue*, a publication which, despite its title, deals only in royal stories from every corner of the globe – one historian and one royal 'expert', though these would later be joined (tellingly, surely) by a guide from the Brussels Tourist Office which was at that time holding a promotion based on the theme

Figure 3. Vadot's cartoon in Le Vif-L'Express (9 December 1999) shows the symbols of Flanders and Wallonie – a lion and a cock respectively – trying to get away from each other over a map of Belgium. However, they are held together by the royal crown. The voice bubble reads 'We are bound by links...'

'Brussels, royal city'. This studio-bound panel was aided and abetted by a very large number of on-the-spot reporters occupying key points along the route of the royal procession. The tone of the pre-wedding discussion was distinctly light-hearted and up-beat, even humorous: there was a kind of running joke over Giltay's repeated inability to pronounce correctly the name of the Polish President, and the panel even allowed itself an informal 'eye-catching hat competition' at various points during the day. However, once the scene changed to the religious wedding in the Saints-Michel-et-Gudule cathedral, the dominant discourse was one of all-pervading sentimentality with endless references to how 'moving' it all was, how 'moved' the various participants were, how 'loving looks' were exchanged by the bride and groom, how 'furtive' squeezes of the hand or 'loving smiles' could be seen, how 'tears' were being wiped away (though none seemed to be in evidence) etc., etc. There were even a few – though indeed only a few – references to the 'fairy-like' appearance of the bride, and to the wedding being like 'a fairy tale come true'.

Despite the bonhomie and the sentimentality, a number of clear political threads could be seen running through this marathon commentary: these were initially carried mostly by (as always, carefully prepared) vox pops by the outside reporters, whose prompting of their interviewees could not possibly have been more blatant, backed up where necessary by the panel, and later, when the festivities moved to the Château de Laeken, by interviews with government ministers and other members of the Belgian elite (fashion designers, opera singers, aristocrats and so on). These strands can be enumerated as follows:

This wedding has united Belgium. This was an absolutely dominant theme, with constant references to people coming from 'all corners of the country', to the 'entire population of Belgium', to a 'national consensus', and above all, and with a quite remarkable level of insistence, to 'the unity of Belgium'. One person, for example, described himself in response to suitable prompting as 'from Antwerp but Belgian first and foremost and proud of it', another as 'neither Walloon, nor Flemish, nor Bruxellois, but Belgian', while another announced that 'the majority of the population is for the union of all Belgians', referring to this majority as 'the silent majority'. Belgium was on several occasions referred to not as a country but as a 'kingdom', and there were many references to this day as a day of 'national reconciliation'. Indeed the wedding was described as a 'moment of intense communion with the Belgian population. They [the royal couple] are offering their love to the Belgian population'. This theme was not limited to the television commentary, but was also pursued by the mayor of Brussels, François-Xavier de Donnéa, in his homily during the civil wedding in the Town Hall, when he told the newly-weds: 'As a couple you are the living symbol of the future of our country, and of a modern monarchy that is loved by the people, a modern monarchy that is the guarantor of the unity of our country and carries all our hopes for the coming millennium'.

This theme was on many occasions given a linguistic turn as we were told that 'Flemings and French-speakers have come together' (indeed a number of Flemings – including Mathilde's uncle – were interviewed speaking in French), that the population had come together 'beyond the linguistic frontiers', and much was made of the trilingual nature of the wedding ceremonies, with readings in French, Dutch and German (the exchange of vows in Dutch was subtitled in French to avoid being rendered inaudible by a spoken translation). After the religious wedding in the cathedral, this whole theme was summed up by a member of the panel as follows:

> This is a wedding in which I see a certain number of signs, signs first of all as regards Belgium. There has been a lot of talk about the unity of Belgium, but even so at the same time I've observed that the different facets, the different components of this modern-day Belgium have been highlighted. It's a federal Belgium and that could be seen in particular in terms of the readings, the languages used, and all that, moreover, also of course at a deeper level, the whole wedding was marked by the immense social and human concerns of both the prince and the princess.

This wedding marks the beginning of a new and positive phase for Belgium. Coverage of the event was marked by constant references to it as a 'historic event' on a 'historic day' (it was even referred to on a few occasions as the 'wedding of the century'). It was described as 'a significant opportunity for the future of Belgium', and the country was described as 'small in size but large in terms of the emotions it can cause on a historic day like the one we are living this morning'. At the Château de Laeken the Finance Minister Didier Reynders was asked the following very pointed question:

> Some people are saying that this wedding is in inverted commas a blessing for the govern-ment since it gives Belgians the opportunity to forget... their real problems and to dream a little?

('It's good to dream a little', he began in response, before moving his answer firmly over to the charms of the bride.) Only once was this discourse challenged in any way. As the guests streamed into the Château de Laeken, journalist at *Le Soir* Christian Laporte suggested:

> However, I think we shouldn't get carried away, the population shouldn't lose sight of the fact that there is an elected parliament in this country and that the king exercises above all a power of influence so we have to get things into perspective. It's all very nice, but things aren't going to get any better, unfortunately, moreover on Monday morning the problems will come back.

The Royal Family is extremely advantageous for Belgian capitalism. No-one, of course, used the term 'capitalism', preferring instead currently dominant inclusive euphemisms such as 'the economy' or 'business', but the message was none the less quite clear. Mathilde herself was described as 'a terrific asset on the economic level' and the wedding was described as having 'economic fallout which it is difficult to express in numbers'. Much was made of the Belgian designer of Mathilde's dress, and how he would henceforth be well known in London, Paris, or certain cities in Italy and Germany; it was stressed that the limousine in which the princess travelled had had its original metal roof replaced by a glass one installed by a Belgian manufacturer; and a topic returned to on several occasions was Philippe's role as Honorary President of the Belgian Office for Overseas Trade, and how much his efforts on this front were appreciated by Belgian businessmen in the winning of contracts (a 'special' on the Prince shown in the early afternoon dedicated a considerable amount of time to this topic). Mention was even made of the fact that at official events such as this, as well as the traditional champagne, Belgian beer was also now available to participants at the suggestion of the King, and that this was a practice which had spread to Belgian embassies abroad, much to the delight of those attending functions there. To cap it all, it was pointed out that the Belgian monarchy cost a lot less than the German presidency.

The Royal Family is a key element of Belgian politics in general. Royalty and the 'world of politics' were repeatedly presented as being inseparable, the great advantage of a royal family being that it was 'above party politics' and therefore provided a mechanism via which differences could be reconciled: 'the role of the monarchy, the advantage of a royal institution is that it pacifies oppositions in a country, that it encourages this kind of dialogue, something which is sometimes less easy in certain republics'. As far as royalty and political institutions are concerned, we were informed that 'in Belgium, one does not go without the other'. The Belgian monarchy was described as a 'monarchy by contract, it's the citizens who chose it' (a broadly correct, if somewhat generous interpretation, since the German-born and naturalised Briton Léopold I was indeed chosen by the Belgian parliament as their monarch on 21 July 1831), and we were reminded that Belgian monarchs 'swear loyalty to the constitution' (and indeed the 'special' on Prince Philippe screened in the early afternoon showed his father swearing allegiance to the constitution on becoming king, and the prince doing likewise on taking up his seat as ex-officio senator in the upper chamber).

The official title of the Belgian King, it was pointed out, is not 'King of Belgium' but 'King of the Belgians' ('Roi des Belges') and 'the only sovereign is the nation', and, as representatives of what was called 'official Belgium' – members of parliament, senators, councillors etc. – arrived at the Château de Laeken in the evening, this theme was summed up by historian Christian Cannuyer as follows:

> The royal family exists only to the extent that it is recognised by official Belgium which is itself the representative of the nation. So there is no royal family without the agreement of the nation as this is expressed through its national representatives.

The royal family links Belgium with other countries on an international scale. A great deal of attention was paid to the various royal guests from other countries attending the wedding, and their links with the Belgian royal family. They were described as a group of relatives and friends getting together to celebrate a family event. While it was pointed out that 'the English are interested only in one royal family – their own' (comment was made on how little importance was being given to this wedding in the British media), the Belgian royals were constantly described as part of the 'European Gotha' or even the 'international Gotha'. This extensive network of family relationships allowed Christian Cannuyer to assure viewers that the Belgian royal family wasn't just Belgian, but was a 'European royal family'.

With its openness and closeness to the population, the Belgian Royal Family is a model for the third millennium. This theme was returned to on many occasions, with many references to the 'relaxed' and 'open' style of the Belgian court, and statements such as 'this is what princes have to be like for the third millennium'. It was perhaps the dominant theme of coverage of the festivities in the Château de Laeken, with astonishment being expressed again and again at the ease with which the cameras were allowed to wander freely among so many distinguished guests. The great point of reference for this topic was the British Royal Family, which was seen as struggling to keep up with the Belgian model, as these three quotes from different parts of the coverage will show:

> It's no secret that Prince Charles would like to move the British monarchy more in the direction of a monarchy based on closeness and equality, but also not just a so to speak spectacular epiphenomenon but an institution which is genuinely in dialogue with the nation and which suggests to it, without imposing on it, certain ways of seeing things... In one sense he's come to have a look at the Belgian model.

Do you remember the astonished look on Queen Elizabeth's face during the funeral of King Baudoin? She couldn't get over what she was seeing, and I think that also had a profound effect on her.

In Belgium protocol is insignificant compared with certain other royalties. In England [*sic*] the protocol is unbelievable. It would never be as easy as this to be in the presence of Queen Elizabeth.

The royal family is really just like the rest of us. This narrative, stressing the 'equality between all citizens' in Belgium, was pursued with special vigour during the two ceremonies, in the town hall and in the cathedral, during both of which the ceremony was described as being 'just like any wedding, of course', as the following quotes will make clear:

> Prince Philippe really looks very moved as any fiancé who is about to say 'yes' would be.
>
> This is the normal procedure to be applied to any Belgian citizen getting married in any commune.
>
> They [the King and Queen] came over as very protective, as any parents would be in similar circumstances.
>
> They're two young newly-weds, like two young newly-weds in any commune in Belgium.
>
> [The King] gave a little wave, quite simple, as any parent would do in this kind of...

The wedding was described as a 'family wedding' and the wedding photograph as a 'family photograph just as in any ordinary wedding'.

Beyond these, there were, of course, a number of other minor narratives present. There was, for example, a historical narrative. It was much understated, and rarely went further back than the establishment of the Belgian state in 1830, but it was none the less there and touched on the lives of Belgium's monarchs to date – old black-and-white footage of Albert and Paola's 'Joyous Entries' in 1959 and even older footage of Albert and Elizabeth's in 1909 were screened – and issues such as the 'question royale' and the abdication of 1950 (Noterman,1998: 57). None the less, it was all very much subordinated to the 'modern' narrative, to the story of this 'rather new Belgium' being witnessed (a much-hailed symbol of which was the bride's dress, described variously – despite its five-metre-long train – as combining 'tradition with a desire for modernism', as combining 'classicism and modernity', as being 'simultaneously sober and modern, just like the Princess herself'). Indeed, the monarchy was summed up as 'combining the permanence of very old traditions and the promises of all of modernity'. The dominance of the modern narrative, however, was not seen as incompatible with the presence of pages during the wedding, or of lackeys in imperial garb in the Château de Laeken, while mediaeval costume had been much in evidence during most of the Joyous Entries.

Press coverage

We analysed press coverage from the daily *La Libre Belgique* and the weekly *Le Vif-*

L'Express from the French-language press, and from the daily *Gazet van Antwerpen* and the weekly *Zondag Nieuws* from the Dutch-language press (in quotes from the Dutch-language press, proper names are given their Dutch form). Our general conclusion on the basis of this admittedly somewhat limited sample is that while, as a rule, there is no simple and clear-cut contrast in the way in which the event was treated by the French-language press as opposed to the Dutch-language press, differences in the range of responses possible in the two communities did seem to exist. Thus while we found relatively uncritical coverage in the press on both sides, and rather more critical analysis also on both, there appeared to be room for a greater level of undisguised hostility in the Flemish press[1] (perhaps a wider sample would have led us to modify this view a little, since there is a well-known republican tendency also in Wallonie, particularly, for example, in Liège which celebrates Bastille Day every year).

Positive reporting of the event was very much the norm on both sides. Thus *La Libre Belgique* (6 December) covered much the same ground as that covered by RTL-TVi, stressing the joyousness of it all, the love of the bride and the groom, the ordinariness of the ceremony, the sense of unity they had forged, the boost to Belgium's image abroad, entitling some of its articles 'Love was invited too', 'Mathilde and Philippe? A perfectly normal couple', 'A real political consensus' and 'A celebration followed throughout the world' (many of these articles took the form of interviews with various people involved either in the event or in its media coverage). The bride's dress was even described as 'like something from Snow White', and everything was surrounded by photographs of the radiant couple.

The Dutch-language weekly *Zondag Nieuws* published just before the wedding (30 November) dedicated – despite carrying a picture of Mathilde on its front cover – relatively little space to the event. It offered only five pages of interviews with various personalities (politicians, academics, newsreaders and so on) under the title 'Belgium spruces itself up for the fairytale wedding'. Despite this the tone was generally positive and optimistic, with the various interviewees in their different ways pooh-poohing the notion of Flemish independence and the Vlaams Blok, playing down the rumours of Albert's illegitimate daughter, comparing the wedding favourably with its overly ostentatious British counterparts of the eighties, praising Mathilde's ease with the media and ending with Prime Minister Guy Verhofstadt assuring readers that it would be 'a great day for Belgium'.

Of the various publications we were able to consult, *Le Vif-L'Express* (3 December) offered by far the greatest amount of analytical coverage of the wedding, and indeed of the Belgian monarchy in general: twenty pages of articles by a wide range of authors and including the results of a survey carried out for the magazine by the MAS company (Marketing, Analysis & Synthesis). Much of what was on offer followed the dominant trends already outlined above. Thus the opening editorial contained the following views:

> If one day she [Mathilde] becomes queen, she will find the confirmation of what she can guess already: the king reigns, but he does not govern. The powers which the Constitution pretends to give him are virtually non-existent in reality.
>
> Because the royal family is appreciated by the majority. Because it in no way impedes

the exercise of democratic political power where the citizen freely chooses his governments.

But above all because it [the royal family] fulfils an indispensable role of listening,
encouraging, stimulating, showing compassion.

And similar broadly supportive statements could be found across almost the whole
range of articles on offer:

She [Mathilde] will accompany Philippe on his economic missions abroad as Honorary
President of the Office for Overseas Trade. I bet you the princess's smile will motivate the
journalists of the countries visited even more to bring up the question of trade with
Belgium

In Belgium the king is never as useful as during period of crisis – governmental or
'social'. At times such as these the palace plays a considerably more important role than in
many other European monarchies.

It is precisely this 'closeness' which helps to make the king the 'symbol of the nation'.

However, even in the midst of all this quantitatively very dominant euphoria, there was
still an occasional but unmissable sense of unease in all the publications consulted. At
times this could be seen in the questions asked in the course of press interviews. Thus
Herman De Croo, President of the Chamber, was asked the following question in *Zondag
Nieuws*:

Foreign newspapers are saying that Mathilde can save Belgium from all those dioxin and
paedophilia scandals. Isn't it odd that a country's image stands or falls with a wedding?

While Francis Balace was asked a rather similar, if less direct, question in *La Libre
Belgique*:

People say that the royal wedding had made the Belgians 'think positive' a bit more, have
a better self-image. Will this last, or is just a flash in the pan like Baudoin's funeral?

and *Le Vif-L'Express* asked its readers this rhetorical question:

Is it because it is riven by profound cleavages, both linguistic and philosophical, that
Belgium needs to come together again in these moments of 'communion'?

The lengthy breakdown of the MAS survey in *Le Vif-L'Express* (which, in general terms,
showed a majority of the country as a whole in favour of the monarchy with a small
majority of Flemings considering it to be 'out of date') contained the following comment:

The committee of enquiry into the dioxin affair is meeting in the midst of general indiffer-
ence? The Dutroux enquiry is controversial? The nurses, teachers and nursery nurses are in

the streets? Who cares, the wedding of Philippe and Mathilde acts as a distraction which, for a while, covers over glaring problems.

While a long article on the king's functions as Head of State had this to say:

> This is how our particular monarchy is most often 'sold': the survival of the country, threatened by Flemish aspirations towards increasingly greater autonomy, now only depends, people are wont to say, on 'the national debt and the king, the last of the Belgians'. But this is the greatest idiocy in the department of received ideas: the message of union distilled by the monarchy does not of course mask – or at least never for very long – the conflicts of interest or the political, linguistic or ideological controversies which regularly shake our country. No more than it will prevent the disintegration of the federal state, even the partition of Belgium, if the Flemish movement keeps up its offensives.

A similar distancing point was made by Guy Duplat in an editorial in *La Dernière Heure*:

> Let's not confuse the new princess with Alice in Wonderland. Belgium has not become, with a wave of a magic wand, a country of worldly delights. We are still wrestling with our linguistic, political, economic and social problems, which are hidden only as long as the royal celebration lasts.

An article on 'Mathildemania' in *Le Vif-L'Express* even echoed complaints about the nature of the television coverage:

> On the television news futile sections on the wedding have sometimes taken the place of national or international current affairs topics where much more is at stake... A large part of the information corresponds in fact to what the Palace wants to be reported.

However, the most critical tone of all was to be found – at least within the limits of our sample – in the *Gazet van Antwerpen* (6 December). This newspaper was expansive in its coverage – twelve pages – but its approach to the event was very mixed. Sandwiched between two full-page colour photos – the first a montage, the second the 'official' family wedding photograph – and articles entitled 'A warm ray of sunshine through the heart of all Belgians' or 'Wedding mass full of tender moments', there were others stressing the smallness of the crowd, the poor view that most of them had as a result of the security arrangements, and criticising the issue of free rail tickets. There were also two openly rather hostile articles, one entitled 'A country of royalists, so long as the weather is nice' and another entitled 'Television showed a royal episode of Big Brother'. In the first of these Roger Van Houtte developed the idea put forward by Flemish writer Walter Van Den Brock that the Belgian monarchy was 'well subsidised folk theatre', arguing that on closer inspection it was not really so folksy after all. He went on to challenge the much vaunted 'closeness' of it all:

> On the contrary: the ceremonies were all convention and tradition and on Saturday the

ordinary man didn't once get anywhere near the receptions. But it is precisely this arch-conservative stateliness which brings about a real fairytale atmosphere which some cherish so much.

And while *La Libre Belgique* had been happy to reproduce the Snow White fairytale, he deliberately mocked it, going on to ironise the small size of the crowd.

> And when some of the spectators insistently demanded a kiss, there followed something which even Snow White[2] would have found acceptable. The spectators on the Grote Markt had expected a better performance.
>   But the biggest disappointment was the crowd. It wasn't in Brussels but at home in front of the TV. Eighty percent of this country is monarchist, but just so long as it doesn't rain, it's not too windy or too cold.

The crowd, he pointed out, was no bigger than for a large football match. The second article was dedicated mostly to the 'close-up' camerawork which dominated so much of the television coverage of the event:

HET EERSTE ONTWAKEN NAAST HAAR MOOIE PRINS

Figure 4. Canary Pete's cartoon in the Gazet van Antwerpen, 6 December 1999

You could almost touch the whole clique, who we usually just know from books, on the television screen. It was just like a royal episode of the Dutch programme Big Brother.

The author lamented the absence of 'microphones under the table' to hear the dinner chat of the 'great of the earth', but finished – making explicit reference to Belgium's best-known sexologist Goedele Liekens – expressing his relief that there had been no pictures of the wedding night. This article was accompanied by a cartoon entitled 'Waking up for the first time beside her Prince Charming'. It showed a horrified Mathilde waking to find that Prince Philippe had turned into a frog.

Belgium in transition

Analysing media coverage of the royal wedding in Belgium in December 1999, it is difficult to avoid concluding that it was essentially part of a much larger process of negotiation of important transitions in Belgian society, of which this event was merely a punctual, if of course important, manifestation. In fact the notion of transition – of a move from the old to the new – was quite explicit in much of the coverage. Thus the reception for visiting royals in the Astoria Hotel in Brussels the evening before was explained on RTL-TVi in the following terms:

> I think this also has to be seen from the point of view of the new policy now being developed by the Belgian monarchy, a policy of promoting Belgium in all its aspects and the fact that this is taking place in the marvellous setting of the Astoria contributes... it's one of the aims of Prince Philippe as Honorary President of Overseas Trade. It's also one of the aims of his father of course.

While the new closeness between monarchy and people was seen very clearly on the same channel as a break with the past:

> The Belgians, the Belgian population could never have imagined that one day they would be able to see their royal family like this, and that they would be able to realise that they're human beings and that they live... even if it's an institution which we respect, it's someone who's part of the family, for some people Prince Philippe is just like their son, their brother, the older cousin who's getting married today, so the whole Belgian population is invited to this great wedding.

Statements such as these are not, of course, just about the royal family or its relationship with the Belgian 'people'. They are about the relationship between the Belgian elite (it was no coincidence that they figured so largely in the reception at Laeken) and Belgian society at large mediated through the institution of the monarchy. Indeed, media coverage of the wedding is best seen as part of a hegemonic strategy aiming at a recovery of legitimation for the way Belgian society is managed as a whole: the 'usefulness' of the king and the royal family – a theme returned to again and again in the press in particular – was presented as their usefulness to the nation, but was in fact their usefulness to the elite.

There can be no doubt whatsoever that the nineties were a period of significant loss of prestige for those in positions of power – not just political – in Belgian society. The various scandals mentioned earlier left few areas of established power untouched: official politics, the legal system, the police, big business. The increasing federalisation of the country only served to exacerbate this loss of legitimacy from the Walloon point of view, since sectors of the Flemish media have always made it clear that, at least as far as they were concerned, outrages such as the Cools affair or the Dutroux affair were essentially Walloon problems. Towards the end of the nineties there was a quite palpable sense, if not of outright crisis, then, at the very least, of alarm. In fact the term 'crisis' was used again and again in all the newspapers consulted, with the wedding presented as a kind of antidote. As *Le Vif-L'Express* put it:

> Another coincidence: the wedding takes place at just the right time to dissipate those fin-de-siècle fears in a Belgium which has lost its way, still traumatised by the deaths and the unexplained disappearances (the Brabant killings, André Cools, Elisabeth Brichet) and by nauseating political-financial scandals (Agusta-Dassault, KB-Lux).

A quite common tactic was to restate the crisis not in terms of political legitimacy – or as a more general crisis of 'leadership' – but in terms of disunity, disintegration, or – particularly from a Walloon perspective – unreasonable demands for autonomy from the Flemish side. For example, one of the articles of *Le Vif-L'Express* contained the following statement:

> It seems that in certain political milieux or circles close to the palace the feeling is gaining ground that we've gone far enough as regards the federalism of the state, that we have to keep a link – such as the king – between the Francophones and the Flemings.

(The contrast between 'francophones' and 'flamands' – rather than between 'francophones' and 'néerlandophones' or 'wallons' and 'flamands' – is of course very telling here in terms of 'creation of collective identity', a topic specifically raised by *Le Vif-L'Express*.) This allowed the crisis to be reformulated as one of a loss of national cohesion, a crisis which an event such as a royal wedding is tailor-made to address. The horizontal unity of Belgium – an inescapable leitmotiv of this coverage – thus came to stand in for its (loss of) vertical unity, and the discourse of national reconciliation across linguistic boundaries became a placeholder for the reconciliation of ordinary Belgians with their leaders. The dominant lexeme of this new relationship was closeness ('proximité'), one of the most widely used words in both press and television coverage.

A strategy of greater (mediated) closeness has, of course, its own risks, and the debate over the extent to which greater media-personalisation is compatible with the 'mystique' required by the institution of monarchy in order to safeguard its symbolic operation is neither new nor in any way confined to Belgium. For example Brit Marie Hovland writes about a similar debate currently taking place in the Scandinavian countries: 'But can this close-up become too near? Is it the case that if the monarch becomes too everyday and too popular this demystifies and undermines the monarchy?' (2000: 57), and a lengthy article in *Le Vif-L'Express*, entitled 'The royal presence' was also dedicated to this topic and to the 'dangers' involved:

> On the one hand, by becoming media personalities, stars, the members of the royal family lose part of their symbolic specificity and conform to a standard: the functions of identification and collective inebriation which this second group of signs or modern-day divinities fulfils are not compatible with those assumed by the royal family in Belgium.

From this point of view, it is no exaggeration to say that media coverage of the wedding was haunted by Lady Diana and in a more general sense by the British monarchy as a whole, seen as an institution which had not managed this transition successfully. Diana was mentioned on a number of occasions during RTL-TVi's coverage, and her presence, physical or ghostly, was to be found in every newspaper read: in fact, an article in *La Libre Belgique* was specifically entitled 'Beware of the ghost of Diana'. Thus 'Mathildemania' was contrasted (favourably) with Dianamania, and there was considerable speculation as to whether Mathilde would end up 'eclipsing' her husband as Diana had, as in *Le Vif-L'Express*: 'Could she already be overshadowing her partner even before she is married? Like, a little while ago, a certain Lady Di...' But it was mostly the contrasts which were stressed. Thus in *Zondag Nieuws* royalty-watcher Jan Van den Berghe (the magazine called him specifically a 'royalty-watcher', using the English term) was invited to respond to the following question: 'In England the late Lady Diana didn't survive the strict protocol and the harsh schooling. Will Mathilde do better?' His answer began 'We are in a completely different situation here', and he pointed out that the 'strict protocol of Laken had disappeared with Boudewijn' (he also argued against Diana as a 'revolutionary', describing her as 'part of the Establishment'). In a sense this wedding was an attempt to lay the ghost of Diana – and all that she might represent for royalty in general and the Belgian royalty in particular – to rest.

The cost of this campaign was considerable. Estimates put the cost of the wedding at 39 million Belgian Francs (around a million pounds), and the cost of all-day-long television coverage on four channels must have been substantial. While most journalists (and many academics) were enthusiastic supporters of this mission for the recovery of lost prestige and leadership, others were, of course, much less reluctant to be recruited to a cause which they believed to be a superficial attempt to paper over the cracks. They made their voices heard, needless to say – and their small-scale cacophony came as a welcome relief amidst the symphony of applause – but they were largely drowned out on the day of the wedding itself. As for ordinary Belgians, they were represented only by the cameras (over which they had no control) and by the 30,000-strong 'football' crowd taking advantage of the free rail tickets to Brussels. Large numbers of them, however, preferred to use their free rail tickets to have a day out in other parts of the country instead.

Belgium – A Country Reunited?

1   A Spanish-language website (http//www.nuestraboda.com/noticias/bodareal.html), basing its information on a Reuters report, quotes the Flemish newspaper *Morgen* as announcing on its front page that the wedding had caused 'shame, emptiness and dissatisfaction'. Though we cannot confirm this, our general familiarity with *Morgen* gives us no grounds to disbelieve it.

2   The text in fact refers to 'a Sanne Snow White'. Sanne is a Flemish singer who was involved in a production of Snow White. However, she was taken aback by the overenthusiastic kiss the actor playing the prince gave her and the prince was subsequently forced to tone it down to a peck on the cheek.

7.   Norway – A Different Land?

Introduction

Norway has the newest royal family in Europe, being currently less than one hundred years old (only the Spanish royals could make a technical claim to being more recent due to their 'restoration' in 1975 but – as we have already argued – moves are already afoot there to re-establish their link with their ancestral past). Following a referendum in 1905, the Norwegian parliament ended its union with Sweden which had lasted since 1814 (though this decision is routinely referred to in the Norwegian media today as a decision taken by the 'people', the limited voting rights at the time meant that less then 370,000 people actually took part). A second referendum was then held to determine whether the new state should be a monarchy or a republic, with 80% voting for a monarchy. As a result, an invitation was extended to the then Danish prince Carl and his English wife Maud to become the new Norwegian monarchs, an invitation which they accepted. Carl subsequently changed his name to Haakon VII, thereby symbolically linking himself with earlier Norwegian monarchs, the previous Haakon having reigned in the XIV century. Since 1905 Norway has known only two further monarchs, King Olav and the current King Harald. It goes without saying that a monarchy which is not yet one hundred years old is a very different social, political and cultural phenomenon from one which is five hundred or a thousand years old.

The reproduction of the Norwegian monarchy – in purely physical terms – has not always been straightforward. King Olav's marriage to his Swedish cousin Märtha in 1929 was considered a sensitive issue in many quarters given that it was only twenty-four years since the dissolution of the union between Sweden and Norway (a union in which Sweden had been very much the senior partner), and the engagement was in fact originally kept secret. In the sixties Olav's son Harald was the subject of even greater controversy when, much to his parents' consternation, he declared his intention to marry a commoner, Sonja Haraldsen, a businessman's daughter whose father's premises were in one of Oslo's main streets (Storgata). Despite initial resistance from the King and his consort, and after considerable public debate, the wedding took place on 18 March 1968. However, this was small beer compared with Harald's own son, the present crown prince Haakon, who on 25 August 2001 married Mette-Marit Tjessem Høiby, a single working mother from Kristiansand in the south of Norway, the father of whose three-year-old child had earlier been imprisoned for a variety of offences including possession of cocaine and drunk-driving. Haakon's somewhat 'unconventional' lifestyle – his love of pop music, for example, and of the Quart Festival in Kristiansand in particular (where he met his future wife), as well as his views on the future of the monarchy – were of course already well known in Norway at the time: in fact they had been detailed in a book entitled *Haakon – a Portrait of the Crown Prince as a Young Man* by Fredrik Wandrup which was much quoted during the ensuing controversy, a controversy which dominated much of the early comment on the future queen.

Newspaper coverage of the relationship

The news of the relationship was first broken by the Kristiansand newspaper *Fædrelandsvennen* on 29 December 1999, this report being followed up shortly afterwards by further information in Norway's most sensationalist magazine, the weekly *Se og Hør*. As speculation mounted and the relationship quickly became Norway's most notorious open secret – being openly discussed on the front page of a number of newspapers – the prince finally arranged an interview with one of the country's most experienced television journalists, Terje Svabø, to put the record straight. The interview was filmed in the garden at Skaugum palace and went out on the main public service channel NRK on Sunday 14 May 2000. In it the prince confirmed his relationship with Mette-Marit, and acknowledged that she had in the past been part of the Oslo house scene, a scene well known for its – in a phrase which would immediately pass into journalism speak, if not into common speech – 'overenthusiastic partying' and drug-taking. This interview was the subject of quite massive media interest, and was the first chapter in an ongoing story whose subsequent main dates (prior to the wedding itself) have been:

3 September 2000	the prince buys a luxury mansion in a wealthy part of Oslo (costing around half a million pounds) for the young couple to move into together
16 October 2000	the palace confirms its approval of the relationship
1 December 2000	the official engagement is announced
10 December 2000	Mette-Marit attends the Nobel peace prize ceremony in Oslo
7 April 2001	Mette-Marit attends her first event abroad in Luxembourg

It would be quite wrong to suggest that this topic has dominated media coverage in Norway over the period in question. On the contrary, there have been long periods of more or less complete silence with quite sustained coverage of other issues: Norway's relationship with the EU (a much debated topic), the privatisation of state companies such as Telenor and Statoil and the consequences of this for small investors, fuel prices (a particularly volatile subject), proposals for how best to use the oil revenues, the split in the populist right-wing Progressive Party, preparations for the autumn 2001 general election, and so on. However, at the key moments listed above coverage was astonishingly intense. For example, on 2 December 2000 the tabloid *Dagbladet* carried an editorial which left the reader in no doubt as to its republican convictions – 'We believe that Norway should withdraw from the ranks of the monarchies... nowadays it is only the people through their votes who should decide who will be the head of state' – but it none the less dedicated no less than fifteen pages to coverage of the official announcement of the engagement.

The analysis below is based on coverage provided by the two national Oslo-based tabloids *VG* and *Dabgladet*,[1] the national Oslo-based broadsheet *Aftenposten*, and the two Bergen-based regional broadsheets *Bergens Tidende* and *BA* (Norway has a particularly strong regional press). Coverage has been dominated by a number of discourses, which might be listed as follows:

A historical discourse. The relative brevity of the Norwegian monarchy did not prevent the emergence of a well-developed historical discourse. This included not only the history of the three monarchs so far – with ancient photographs and old anecdotes being dusted down, such as the one involving prince Olav travelling incognito to Stockholm to meet his future bride using the name Olav Håkonsson – but also complex family trees not only tracing Haakon's lineage back to Jean Baptiste Bernadotte, who became King Carl III Johan of Norway (Carl XIV of Sweden) in 1810 (and showing Haakon's close relationships with many other European royals), but also tracing Mette-Marit's descendants back to end of the sixteenth century and even claiming that she too had traces of blue blood. Much was made of the fact that the engagement ring she received had also been given by both King Olav and King Harald to their respective fiancées. This particular discourse also involved occasional (mostly facetious) references to Norwegian kings from the Old Norse period, such as Magnus Barefoot or Harald the Fair.

A quite highly developed legal discourse. This was particularly evident in the early stages of the 'story'. Norwegian readers of both broadsheets and tabloids, both national and regional, were no doubt bemused to learn that paragraph 36 of the Norwegian constitution does not allow the crown prince to marry without the king's express permission (they were probably even more bemused to see the text quoted in its original old-fashioned Danish – including capital letters on nouns – a throwback to Norway's complex language situation when the constitution was drawn up). The debate was further complicated by the fact that references to the king in the Norwegian constitution are sometimes taken to mean the king in person, and at other times are taken to mean the king in his role as head of the government, in which case the reference is usually interpreted as referring to the government rather than the king himself. Jurists and experts of all kind were called in to offer opinions on this matter, and there was considerable debate as to whether the king was either legally or morally obliged to seek the prime minister's advice on this issue. There was also some debate on the status of Mette-Marit's son Marius, and whether he could ever become a prince (apparently possible within the terms of paragraph 23 of the constitution).

A religious discourse. Again this was particularly noticeable in the early stages, but tended to fade into the background once the official engagement was announced, a date and a location for the wedding was decided, and the identity of the bishop who would marry the couple was confirmed. The terms of this debate, in which a considerable number of both churchmen and politicians (notably from the Christian Democratic Party) became involved, were whether 'living together' was acceptable at all, and in particular whether it was acceptable for the future king of Norway. Despite stiff opposition from a number of those whose views were sought, opinion polls carried in all the papers showed that most Norwegians – in particular the younger generations – saw nothing wrong with the situation whatsoever. In a somewhat surprising move, Norwegian anti-abortion campaigners also proposed Mette-Marit as a model for young single mothers as a result of her decision to keep the child she had had in her earlier relationship. The final verdict of the Norwegian national dailies was that, in general terms, the Norwegian church eventually rose to the challenge posed by Mette-Marit, and – particularly when bishop Gunnar Stålsett (who officiated at the wedding) told Mette-Marit that she was starting 'a new chapter with a clean sheet' – had taken a considerable step forward in modernising itself as a result.

A romantic discourse. As in the case of the Belgian wedding and the Spanish 'friendship', there was a strong romantic discourse, though it emerged mostly as a reply to the legal and religious discourses which dominated early coverage of the story. It occasionally took the form of front-page headlines (virtually the only text on the entire page) proclaiming 'Most important of all was love' (*Dagbladet*, 2 December 2000) or describing Mette-Marit as the 'Happy girl who won Haakon's heart' (*VG*, 2 December 2000), and involved implicit and sometimes explicit attacks on some of the churchmen involved in the debate, at times accusing them of hypocrisy. It also featured many references to the 'fairytale romance' and the forthcoming 'fairytale wedding' involving the 'fairytale princess', and Haakon was described as a 'modern-day knight who defends his lady' (*Dagbladet*, 15 May 2000). There were also a number of explicit allusions to Cinderella: indeed, a cartoon in *Aftenposten* on 2 December 2000 showed Mette-Marit as Cinderella trying on a shoe offered by prince Haakon in front of a television camera operated by a regal lion. By the time of the wedding itself the Cinderella reference would achieve a remarkable level of dominance. Thus *BA*'s front-

Figure 5. Inge Grødum's cartoon in Aftenposten, 2 December 2000

page photograph (26 August 2001) of 'the kiss' (an identical photograph adorned the front page of *VG* of the same day) carried the single headline 'The Cinderella kiss' while its report was titled 'A fairytale from real life'.

This discourse did develop a kind of political edge as readers were reminded that any interference in Haakon's choice of partner would mean that his 'most elementary human rights are being broken' – this in an editorial argued by Northern Norway's most important newspaper *Nordlys* (14 May 2000), which also carried the headline 'Set Haakon free, abolish the monarchy'. *VG* (17 October 2000) also pursued the human-rights theme, stating that it's a 'human right to choose your own partner', and that 'the time is past when forced marriages were common in Norway'.

A fashion discourse. From the word go considerable interest was shown in how Mette-Marit would dress in her new role. Designers from Norway and abroad came up with a range of ideas – one Norwegian designer proposed a wedding dress based on the Folgafonna glacier lavishly illustrated in the *Bergens Tidende* of 2 December 2000 – there was discussion as to whether dark or light colours were more suitable, there were even articles on the fact that she had turned up to more than one event wearing the same dress. On a number of occasions she was encouraged to 'think Norwegian' rather than looking abroad for designs. Much attention was paid to her shopping trips to Paris and New York. Linking with the religious discourse was a debate as to whether she should get married in white. This discourse was able to make use of the fact that Mette-Marit had earlier worked selling clothes in the Galleri Albert in Kristiansand.

A rather remarkable PR discourse. What distinguishes coverage of this royal story most from any other we have analysed is the omnipresence of a highly developed PR discourse. Almost every event was scrutinised from this angle, with countless experts asked for (and very keen to offer) their views. Thus the prince's interview with Terje Svabø was seen as having been 'handled' very well, while both the palace's confirmation of their approval of the relationship and the official announcement of the engagement were generally agreed to have been 'PR disasters'. 'The party ended in chaos' was *Dagbladet*'s front-page headline on 17 October 2000, going on to describe the event as 'embarrassing and amateurish', while a PR 'expert' put it as follows in *VG* of the same day: 'If this had been a stock-exchange quoted company the shares would have taken a hammering. The management would have had a major problem'. Mette-Marit's 'performance' at the official announcement of the engagement, on the other hand, elicited headlines such as 'PR-firms impressed by Mette-Marit' (*Dagbladet*, 2 December 2001). Even the impact of the relationship abroad was seen in PR terms: as Pette Ødberg put it in *Dagbladet* on 3 September 2000: 'The announcement that he's going to live with Mette-Marit Tjessem Høiby is having a tremendous PR effect for the Norwegian export industry. People are making a huge fuss about Norway'. A long article in *VG* on 14 April 2001 entitled 'This is how a princess is made' contained a PR-company's advice on what she should say and do, and how she should dress. The same issue suggested she should even change her name. As the wedding drew near, the general consensus – summed up by Hans Geelmuyden in an article in *Bergens Tidende* entitled 'The royal Norwegian image' (11 August 2001) – was that after a shaky start the Palace had got its act together and was now dealing with its own image management – including Mette-Marit's – in a professional way.

A political discourse concerning the modernisation of the Norwegian monarchy. This was the most sustained of all the debates surrounding the relationship and the plans for the forthcoming wedding. The Bagehotian concepts of 'magic' and 'distance' were wheeled out regularly and assessed regarding their desirability (or indeed possibility) when faced with the need for 'closeness to the people' among modern-day royals. 'Haakon's relationships and lifestyle are breaking new ground within the monarchy', opined *VG* on 3 September 2000. On 17 October *Dagbladet* expressed the view that 'It's a brave attempt to combine the modern with the monarchic', adding 'In any case, it's wear and tear in the monarchic system itself which is coming to the surface... The question is can it ever catch up with social developments without making itself superfluous'. *Bergens Tidende* (11 December 2000) took the view that 'It's more to the point to take the view that Haakon's closeness to the people is a condition for the continued existence and legitimacy of the monarchy among the people', adding 'Many among today's up-and-coming generation have had problems relating to the monarchy. The royals have been stiff, remote, ornamental figures'. Mette-Marit was encouraged to model herself on other socially-committed royals such as Queen Silvia of Sweden or Princess Diana.

The 'royal question' was added additional spice towards the end of March with revelations concerning the boyfriend of Haakon's younger sister, Princess Märtha Louise. Long known in Norway for her enthusiasm for horses, travelling abroad and little else, she went through a kind of 'makeover' at Christmas 2000 when she appeared on television reading Norwegian fairytales on a children's programme. This was widely interpreted in the press as a 'conscious strategy' aimed at diverting attention from Haakon and Mette-Marit in the run-up to the wedding: 'The Palace is gambling everything on Märtha', was *Dagbladet*'s front-page headline on 17 March. The strategy misfired, however, when scenes from a film made by her boyfriend – author Ari Behn (dubbed 'Big Behn' by some journalists) – were screened, despite his attempts to have this stopped, on TV2 showing him sniffing cocaine with 'Polish prostitutes' during a visit to Las Vegas. 'A royal roadmovie' was how *Bergens Tidende* described it all on 31 March (this title appeared in English), likening the travails of the Norwegian monarchs to the 'annus horribilis' of Queen Elizabeth in 1992. Press coverage was substantial and led to headlines such as 'Palace fears for its reputation' (*Dagbladet*, 27 March 2001). The debate on the future of the monarchy subsequently became particularly intense when an opinion poll published in *Dagbladet* on 4 April 2001 revealed that support for the monarchy had sunk to an all-time low, with only 59% supporting its continued existence and 23% expressing a preference for a republic ('Even they are more popular than ours', wrote the newspaper referring to Queen Elizabeth and Prince Charles).

The question of drugs also remained 'unfinished business' for Mette-Marit until just before the wedding. Despite their widespread availability and consumption among various sectors of society – and Norway is by no means exceptional in this regard – drugs continue, as elsewhere, to be invested with a highly emblematic taboo value by those occupying a range of supervisory functions in relation to Norwegian society as a whole. In the end some form of closure to the earlier drugs story was deemed necessary and – in a move suffused with heavy religious symbolism – a public confession by the 'sinner' herself on 22 August 2001 just three days before the wedding (whether motivated or not by the fear of further 'revelations', as was widely rumoured) pre-empted any potential future damage. Thus, in a truly intriguing battle of the euphemisms, while Haakon's 'overenthusiastic partying' had proved to be insufficient, Mette-Marit's even more oblique 'my life has been rather excessive', though saying nothing that everyone did not already know, removed the final hurdle to a remarkable fusion of discourses on the day of the wedding itself when the most important union of all took place between the monarchy, the fairytale, the fashion and PR industries and the politicians as, in a professionally managed PR operation, the glamorous Cinderella was presented as 'a model for modern women' and her triumph was even seen by PM Jens Stoltenberg (in an article in *Dagens Næringsliv* on 23 August) as the crowning glory of years of struggle for the equality of women.

Norway – 'a different country'?

There is little doubt that Norway is to some extent a rather 'different' country within a European perspective: the phrase 'a different country' ('et annerledesland') is a not infrequently used self-definition (Hovland, 2000: 106), and on 3 September 2000 *VG* in fact described Haakon as a 'different prince in a different land'. The continuing unwillingness of a majority of its electorate to vote for entry into the European Union is merely the most emblematic index of that difference, but another was, for a very long time, its terrestrial television system, which until 1992 consisted of a single public-service channel. Despite this, Norwegian society is now undergoing a process of somewhat belated but relatively rapid change – changes which many other Western European countries experienced ten or even fifteen years earlier. These changes include 'rationalisation' of the public sector, the privatisation of state-owned assets, the increasing globalisation of the economy (particularly noticeable in the banking sector), the widening gap between rich and poor with spectacular rises in top executives' salaries, a visible realignment of mainstream politics (even allowing for Norway's somewhat fragmented party system) around right-of-centre values and strategies (an article in *Dagbladet* of 4 April 2001 pointed out how, although the right-wing party Høyre had been out of power for the past four years, its policies had in fact been carried out for it by the slightly left-of-centre coalition government during that period). In short, what we are witnessing is the fragmentation of the old Scandinavian Model and the slow loss of influence and authority of many of the institutions on which it was based (not only the trade unions and indeed to some extent the government itself, but also institutions such as the church and the monarchy) and its replacement by a quite recognisable neo-liberal alternative, accompanied by a greater integration of the Norwegian economy into the European economy in general, making the country's old 'inward-looking' and 'isolationist' posture (much commented on in the press) appear less and less sustainable.

An interesting feature of press comment on the relationship between Haakon and Mette-Marit and what this might mean for the future of the Norwegian monarchy is the frequency with which this debate has been framed within references to the postmodern. For example, when the prince finally confirmed the relationship, *Dagbladet* of 13 May 2000 carried an editorial entitled 'Postmodern monarchy' where the author argued that 'A modern monarchy must at regular intervals seek new legitimacy by showing that it has value for society. This is not easy to do at a time when political debate is subdued to the point of silence, all political views are moving towards the centre and ideologies have died out... in the long run it's doubtful if [the monarchy] can be sustained as a weekly-magazine monarchy'. In an article on 4 April 2001 calling explicitly for a move towards a presidency, the same newspaper wrote 'we are living in a postmodern era where mystique and the irrational have a new place in people's philosophy'. Even when the term 'postmodern' was not expressly used, it was frequently implicit in the debate. Thus *Dagbladet* on 15 April 2000 saw the prince's relationship as constituting:

> The opening shot in a debate on the future of the monarchy. Haakon's courageous course of action can be the beginning of a comprehensive modernisation of the monarchy where openness, closeness to the people and a strong social commitment are important elements. But it can also be the beginning of the end because the throne is increasingly experienced as a piece of furniture from IKEA.

And an article in the same newspaper on 2 December 2000 entitled 'Engagement between fact and fiction' viewed the announcement of the engagement as follows (the references to Carl Ivar and Eli are to the leader of the Progress Party and his wife who had just recently received death threats; other references are to the fashion store H&M, and the American television programmes *Ally McBeal* and *The Sopranos*). The bold is in the original:

> And it came about at that time when the land was being carpet bombed by that high-price humanoid Claudia Schiffer wearing cut-price panties and bra from you know who, and when Billy died on Ally in the court room and Tony Soprano took a long holiday after strangling Pussy, and Carl Ivar and Eli received death threats from someone with perfect spelling who could therefore hardly be a member of their own party, and when it wasn't even raining any more in Eastern Norway – then came *The Engagement*.
> **And made it even more difficult to distinguish between fact and fiction in the half-light under the December sky.**

We are therefore facing the (at least lexical) conundrum whereby, as Norwegian society slowly but surely *postmodernises* – following Jameson's definition of postmodernism as 'the cultural logic of late capitalism' – there are increasing calls from broadly left-wing sources for a *modernisation* of the monarchy. This situation is not unique to Norway: as the systemic dysfunctions of modernity are increasingly exposed by the changing alignments of the postmodern, belated attempts to redefine it emerge in response to the threat.

Conclusion
At least three quite distinct positions can be recognised in Norwegian press coverage of the relationship between prince Haakon and Mette-Marit Tjessem Høiby:

(1) A traditionally conservative Old Right position which wants the monarchy to maintain its function as symbolic guardian of the family, the church and the unity of the nation: references to the monarchy's supposed 'unifying' function were much used by supporters of this view.

(2) A conservative left-of-centre position which wants a more 'modern' close-to-the-people style monarchy as symbolic guarantor of a more 'open' and 'democratic' society. This tendency actively applauded the princely couple's 'modern' and 'unconventional' lifestyle, and tended, for example, to reject or attempt to modernise the romantic discourse, as in the following article from *Bergens Tidende* (11 December 2000):

> The future queen has not been sitting at home in a castle knitting or reading books waiting for the noble knight to knock on her door... This has been a modern Cinderella-story.
>   While royals used to ride around on white horses in flowery meadows, Haakon and Mette-Marit trudge around Oslo's streets with takeaway coffees in cardboard cups.

(3) A more radical left-of-centre position which sees the monarchy as anachronistic, 'past its sell-by date' (a much used phrase), and incompatible with a modern democracy, and calls for the institution of a republic. This cause was championed by *Dagbladet* but also found expression in other newspapers. It also took the form of the setting up of an organisation entitled 'For a Republic in Norway' which invited Haakon to debate the proposition that Norway should be a republic by 2014 (*Dagbladet*, 3 April 2001).

It will be clear from the above that media coverage was less about Mette-Marit Tjessem Høiby than about 'Mette-Marit', a randomly occurring signifier over whose range of meanings – over the possible 'Mette-Marits' which might eventually stabilise – there was extensive discursive (and therefore ideological) struggle. When it became clear that the various elements of the conservative camp could not prevent the wedding from taking place, a gradual consensus emerged around a compromise whereby the fairytale princess marrying her handsome prince would signal the modernisation and renewal of the Norwegian monarchy while simultaneously symbolising the continuation and updating of certain traditional views of Norwegian society – specifically of that cosy little 'Annerledeslandet' where social cohesion remains strong, the distances between the various classes remains small, and a single mother from a working-class background can end up marrying a prince.

   There was, however, a fourth group, not so much of players as of onlookers. These were a clearly emergent globalising tendency, difficult to categorise politically since it transcends both the Old Left and the Old Right, but has overlapping points of contact with both the New Right and the New Left, which – failing threats to the integrity of the state as in the case of Belgium – has no interest in the monarchy at all: none of its spokespersons or members were ever involved in the media debate concerning Haakon and Mette-Marit at any point, not even on a single occasion, even though they were much in evidence in other sections of the newspapers analysed. Indeed, it must view these activities with some bemusement.

Debates on the Norwegian monarchy – or any other European monarchy for that matter – become therefore symbolic battlegrounds where the future shape of the nation state in an era of increasing globalisation is fought out by those who still retain a stake – either economic or symbolic – in that particular configuration. The fact that the end of monarchy is being actively debated in the Norwegian media and in certain other (albeit relatively restricted) sectors of Norwegian society is less a debate about its monarchy itself, and more a sign of its decreasing isolation and its increasing absorption – however gradual – into an economic system whose interest in the inherited rituals of the nation states is nil.

1   *Dagbladet* began life as a broadsheet, changing to a tabloid format in the 1980s. It has a very different feel from UK tabloids: see Klausen (1986).

8. The Netherlands:
The Prince and The Politicians

Introduction
The Dutch national press falls into two easily identifiable categories:

1. A group of daily newspapers, based mostly in Amsterdam and Rotterdam. These are all broadsheet in format and come under the heading of 'quality' newspapers. There is a detectable gradient of 'seriousness', going from the extremely sober and highly respected *NRC Handelsblad* at one end of the spectrum to the much more populist (and rather conservative) *Telegraaf* at the other. There are no daily tabloids, either in format or in style: despite its boisterous headlines, its garish colours and its un-self-critical tendency to regularly announce what 'the whole of the Netherlands' is thinking on any specific issue, the *Telegraaf* is far removed from UK tabloids such as the *Sun* or the *Star* or similar publications found in a number of other northern European countries (*Bild* in Germany, *Neue Kronen-Zeitung* in Austria and so on).

2. A group of weekly magazines, the so-called 'roddelbladen' or 'gossip magazines' (also referred to simply as the 'bladen' for short). There are four of these: *Privé*, *Weekend*, *Story* and the most recent addition *Party*. They all have roughly the same size (approximately two-thirds that of a tabloid) and normally come out on a Wednesday. As their unofficial generic title suggests, they are dominated by human-interest stories and gossip and scandal of all kinds. It is not unknown for readers of these publications to take all four of them. (There are, of course, many other weekly magazines, but they are more specialised and do not have anything like the readership of the 'roddelbladen.)

The account given below is based mostly on information taken from the dailies *NRC Handelsblad*, *De Volkskrant*, *Algemeen Dagblad*, *Het Parool*, *Trouw* and *De Telegraaf*, though additional information has also been taken from the 'roddelbladen'.

The Royal Engagement: Phase I – August 1999–February 2000
Issues relating to the Dutch royal family – or, more correctly, the Dutch Royal House, since a distinction is made between the two in the constitution of the Netherlands[1] – appear reasonably frequently in the serious press, which is by no means averse to covering aspects of their private lives since they are, as the highly sceptical *NRC Handelsblad* put it (16 May 2001), 'Big Brother with a family tree'. None the less, 'revelations' concerning their private lives would normally be limited to the gossip magazines or at the very outside to *De Telegraaf*. What made crown prince Willem-Alexander's friendship with the Argentinian Máxima Zorreguieta somewhat different was that, though rumours that he had a new

girlfriend had been around in the 'bladen' for some time, the news was broken not by *Privé* or *Weekend* – who had shown an inordinate interest in his immediately previous girlfriend Emily Bremers and indeed in all his many former girlfriends – but by the Amsterdam-based *Volkskrant*. The story was in fact broken by its Latin American correspondent Ineke Holtwijk on 31 August 1999 (she got the second name wrong, giving it as Zorroguita, but this was quickly put right), and she remained the main source of information on the subject for some time after that. The *Volkskrant* continues to be rather proud of this scoop, and published a long article on 14 April 2001 reminding its readers that it was first off the blocks with this particular piece of news.

Over the following few months, this emerging royal story followed the pattern of most other stories of this kind: intense activity among journalists from all sectors of the press to find out as many details as possible about the new girlfriend, her parents and family, her friends, her personal history and so on, all spiced up in this case by the fact that she came from a somewhat 'exotic' location. There were the usual grainy photographs shot at long distance using zoom lenses purporting to show 'the couple'. In a spectacular blunder the *Telegraaf* printed a photo on its front page on 2 September 1999 claiming it was the prince and his new girlfriend, only to have to retract these claims the following day (having already paid an undisclosed sum – rumours of 50,000 guilders, around £14,000, were doing the rounds – for the item in question). At the same time a well-oiled romantic discourse sprang into life: the new girlfriend was 'beautiful' and 'intelligent' (as indeed are all royal girlfriends – on 10 April 2001, for example, the Danish weekly *Her & Nu* 'revealed' that crown prince Frederik's as yet 'secret' Australian girlfriend was 'dazzlingly beautiful, clever and well-educated'), the prince was her 'dream prince', she was his 'true love', the friendship would hopefully lead to a 'fairytale wedding'.

A particularly Dutch characteristic of this story more or less from the outset has been a consistently high-profile political presence, with the flow of official information (as opposed to both good unofficial information and to gossip) being controlled by the Government Information Service (Rijksvoorlichtingsdienst, or RVD), and in particular its head Eef Brouwers. The Dutch constitution makes the Prime Minister responsible for the well-being of the Royal House, with the result that within days of the news of the friendship coming into the public domain Prime Minister Wim Kok found himself besieged by questions on this topic from both the dailies and the gossip magazines during his weekly press conference. After early stalling tactics, by mid-September 1999 he had acknowledged the existence of the friendship, conceding that it was 'special enough to merit announcing', a statement widely reproduced both in the press and on television.

In the first week of January 2000 it was widely reported that Máxima had accompanied the royal family on their New Year's visit to India. On 13 January *NRC Handelsblad* announced (on its front page) that preparations for the wedding were already under way, despite official denials from both Kok and the RVD. The following day it was reported that Máxima had started to learn Dutch. On 19 January she was photographed by reporters from the newspaper *Vrij Nederland* in a pub in Amsterdam called Tabac, widely known to be a haunt of journalists, in conversation with Professor Victor Halberstadt, a prominent member of the Dutch Labour Party (Partij van der

Arbeid, or PvdA) which was at that time the leading partner in the governing left-of-centre coalition, the so-called Purple Coalition, frequently referred to in the Dutch media as Purple-II (Paars-II) since it was at that moment enjoying its second period in government. Halberstadt was also an expert in public finance (Máxima has studied public finance in Argentina and was at that time working for the Deutsche Bank in its offices in New York), and it was widely speculated that this obviously stage-managed scene was to signal the start of an educational process preparing her for her new role in Dutch public life. As more and more information seeped into the public domain, the RVD finally officially acknowledged on 2 February 2000 that Máxima was not just *a* friend of the prince, but in fact his girlfriend.

No-one could possibly have been surprised by this piece of news. However, what this Dutch case makes more obvious than most others is the importance of official announcements in the energising of a certain range of discourses and practices. Thus in the week following this official announcement the name 'Máxima' was lodged over thirty times at the Benelux Trademark Office for a whole range of products from slimming aids to perfumes, while a mortgage advisor whose company just happened to be called 'Maxima' received 52,000 hits on his website in a week – though it transpired that none of them were from people actually looking for advice (Torre y Rivas, 2001: 23–4). The race also began for the first video clip of Máxima, since views of her until that point had been limited to photographs. On the day the announcement was made the commercial television channel SBS6 announced that it had secured video of the object of everyone's desire from friends of the family in Argentina via an Argentinian television station (despite attempts by the Zorreguieta family to prevent this from happening). So great was the pressure to achieve this scoop that when the pubic-service broadcaster NOS announced that it had also acquired this footage and intended to show it before SBS6, the latter threatened to sue it for 630,000 guilders (c. £180,000) if it did so, at which point NOS withdrew, showing the clip one hour after SBS6.

Nothing so terribly unusual in all of this, then: the by now fairly classical self-sustaining media mini-frenzy in pursuit of larger number of readers/viewers than the competition. But things were to change as conflicting points of view over Máxima's father's past slowly began to emerge.

The Royal Engagement: Phase II – March 2000–March 2001

As is well known, Argentina was subjected to a particularly brutal military dictatorship between 1976 and 1983, first under General Videla (1976–82) and then under General Galtieri, a period during which many thousands of people 'disappeared' and the daily protests of their mothers outside the government buildings in the Plaza de Mayo in Buenos Aires became known worldwide. While it was known when the story of Willem-Alexander's friendship with Máxima Zorreguieta broke that her father, Jorge Horacio Zorreguieta, though himself a civilian, had been first Undersecretary and then Secretary of State for Agriculture for part of that military regime from 1976 till 1982, what was to emerge subsequently were serious doubts in certain quarters regarding his own version of exactly how much he knew concerning the human rights abuses of the regime while he had occupied those posts.

In the initial period of news coverage of Máxima's background, references to her father – who is no longer active in politics, being now the chairman of the Association of Argentinian Sugar Producers – were generally positive. Ineke Holtwijk maintained in her early reports that, although he had indeed been a member of the Videla government in the late seventies and early eighties, he had been a relatively 'little fish' and 'his hands were clean'. A number of Argentinian sources were also quoted by newspapers such as *Trouw* and *NRC Handelsblad* to the effect that the father had had no part in the human rights abuses which had characterised the military regime, and that his post had been an essentially 'technical' one. Despite this, however, critical voices were eventually raised.

Trouw itself had already reported in the early part of 2000 that Máxima's father had, for example, called on the farmers in Argentina to support the Videla regime – thereby suggesting an active role in support of the military dictatorship – and quoted Argentinian public prosecutor Julio Strassera as saying that moral condemnation of his participation in the regime was entirely justified. In a front page article the same newspaper pointed out on 7 March 2000 that the 'further revelations... concerning the past of Argentinian ex-minister Jorge Zorreguieta cannot be ignored by Dutch politicians'. But it was from approximately April 2000 on that the temperature regarding this issue began to rise significantly. Thus Dutch historian Hermann Von der Dunk appeared on television demanding an investigation into the father's background, similar to that which had been carried out into the background of the German diplomat Claus von Amberg when he had married the then Princess (now Queen) Beatrix in 1966. Slowly but surely others joined in, mostly politicians and academics, claiming that a democratic country such as the Netherlands could not simply pretend that this was not a problem. Arguing that Máxima might well have absorbed her father's allegedly undemocratic views during her childhood in Argentina, they insisted that it was absolutely essential to know exactly where any future queen stood on fundamental issues such as democratic principles and human rights. As the tension mounted over the ensuing months, in January 2001 former UNESCO Ambassador Maarten Mourik lodged a report with the Dutch Public Prosecutor accusing Jorge Zorreguieta of 'crimes against humanity and torture' (Torre y Rivas, 2001, 55).

This situation was further complicated by the fact that, according to the Dutch constitution, any member of the Royal House must seek the approval of parliament before getting married or forfeit any claim he or she has to the throne (a number of members with rather distant claims on the throne have in fact done this in recent years). Eventually the leaders of all the Dutch parties with representation in the Second Chamber (the equivalent of the Lower Chamber in other countries with a bicameral system) took up positions which varied from suggestions that Willem-Alexander should give up the throne if he married Máxima, through demands that she should publicly condemn her father's past actions and clearly state her own adherence to democratic principles, to views that her father's past was irrelevant as far as her marriage to Willem-Alexander was concerned: in this order these were, broadly speaking, the position adopted moving from the left of the political spectrum to the right.

As the question of the prince's friendship with Máxima became increasingly politicised as a result of the controversy over her father's past, the most remarkable consequence of this development was the withering on the vine of all the other discourses which had been gradually burgeoning around the couple in the serious press: only the 'bladen' were able to sustain any kind of romantic discourse by concentrating, in their inimitable way, on the human-interest side of the story to the exclusion of all else. Elsewhere anything unable to relate to the political debate and its moral ramifications fell silent. As early as 22 June 2000 *Trouw* was already writing that 'things have been quiet around the romance between the Prince of Orange and Máxima Zorreguieta for quite some time now'. As fears of an 'English-style' royal scandal began to emerge politicians began to choose their words extremely carefully. Thus in November 2000 Wim Kok asked for 'discipline' from his cabinet in order to avoid the emergence of 'English circumstances', while on 2 January 2001 *Trouw* referred ominously to Máxima as 'our version of Camilla Parker Bowles'.

In fact, outside the political controversy the silence was all-embracing, or was occasionally replaced by hostility. Thus, for example, although the House of Orange-Nassau has an extremely lengthy history, no discourses relating to this emerged. No fashion designers pushed themselves forward to use Máxima as a pretext for talking about their ideas (on the contrary, *Privé* of 17 March 2001 felt able to attack her dress sense in very uncompromising terms), no PR-gurus offered to advise the couple on how to handle their relationship with the media (*Trouw* of 2 February 2001, on the other hand, described Máxima's unexpected presence at the Queen's birthday's celebrations on 31 January of that year as a 'premeditated PR-stunt'). No-one suggested that their relationship was good for Dutch capitalism or that it would improve the Netherlands' standing in the world (indeed, quite the opposite). When, in early March 2001, Willem-Alexander committed the spectacular gaffe of attempting to defend Máxima's father by referring journalists to a letter sent to the Argentinian daily *Clarín* exonerating him, only for it to emerge that the author of this letter was none other than General Videla himself, there was much talk in the media of Prime Minister Kok imposing a 'radio silence' on the prince. But it was already clear by then that a blackout affecting much more besides had already been in operation for many months.

As all others withdrew, the main sources of discourse during this period were politicians, academics, the occasional churchman, journalists and – on occasions to a quite surprising degree – letter-writers to the newspapers: indeed, on a few occasions some of the dailies dedicated their entire letters page to this issue. However, the inhibiting effect of the intense politicisation of the issue on some discourses was offset by the emergence of others relating not to so much to the relationship between Willem-Alexander and Máxima as to the moral framework within which her father was being judged. Thus references to the not entirely unblemished record of Dutch imperialism did emerge, as did criticisms of the Netherlands' commercial links with Argentina during the Videla dictatorship and of their willingness to send their national football team there to take part in the World Cup of 1978 despite worldwide condemnation of the regime. For example, in a long article in *Trouw* published on 2 February 2001, Latin-America expert Hans Vogel pointed out that 'At the time of the military junta the Netherlands was one of Argentina's most important trading partners. At that time no-one ever raised any problems relating to human rights'. In its edition of 12 February 2001 the *Volkskrant* carried a long interview with Freek de Jonge, who had been one of the organisers of the campaign against Dutch participation in the 1978 World Cup, in which he stressed the importance of keeping Jorge Zorreguieta out of the Netherlands as a symbol of support for all those who had suffered at the hands of the regime. And one of twelve letters on the subject printed in the *Telegraaf* of 15 March 2001 read:

> To everyone, press and politicians first, who are itching to join in our new national sport, competitive shooting at Willem-Alexander and his future family-in-law, I would say: make your own apologies first. Apologies for the role the Netherlands played in the international slave trade. Apologies for our colonial past. Apologies for the fact that in 1978 we found football more important than human rights or the mothers of the disappeared. Apologies for the fact that we still shake hands with all kinds of dubious leaders if they promise us orders for our economy. And when in this way we've taken the beam out of our own eye, we can start on the mote in someone else's.

As more and more time passed and a solution failed to emerge, accusations of hypocrisy were raised with increasing frequency against the government. In its edition of 31 March 2001 the *Telegraaf* returned to the same theme:

> The heightened emotions may also have been connected with the tendency of many here to wash their hands of a regime with which, at the end of the seventies and the beginning of the eighties, our country maintained many close links. By taking a tough stand on Zorreguieta senior their consciences can be salved.

This is, of course, very unappealing territory for professional politicians, and it soon became clear that it was as much in their interest as in the Royal House's to find a way out of the problem. It also became apparent that the simplest 'technical' solution lay in ensuring that Máxima's father – the focal point of the controversy – was not present during the wedding, thereby silencing many of the critical voices. Prime Minister Kok undertook to find an answer to the problem, commissioning an investigation into Jorge Zorreguieta's past by historian Professor Michiel Baud, and working with the royal family regarding the question of the father's presence. His efforts were rewarded with the official announcement of the engagement on Friday 31 March 2001 during which Máxima publicly expressed her sorrow over the brutalities committed by the Videla regime, asserted her own absolute commitment to democratic values, and announced that her father had voluntarily offered not to attend the wedding. The live broadcast of this statement on three extended television news programmes on the public-service channel Nederland 2 and the commercial channels RTL4 and SBS6 was followed by around 5 million people, approximately 30% of the Dutch population. This announcement took place when the foot-and-mouth crisis in the Netherlands was reaching its peak.

Towards the Royal Wedding of February 2002
If the official acknowledgement of the relationship on 2 February 2000 had had a notable effect in energising a wide range of discourses and practices, the discursive release triggered by the official announcement of the engagement just over a year later was truly

remarkable. After the self-imposed silence of many months, there was a veritable outpouring of text. The following day the announcement was front-page news in all the dailies. The *Volkskrant* dedicated three-and-a-half pages to the story, and the *Telegraaf*, for its part, had a 16-page special supplement on the event (though admittedly over half of these pages were made up of adverts) carrying the banner headline 'This is true love'. The 'bladen' brought out special editions the following Monday, two days earlier than usual and with more pages than usual (*Privé* offered twenty-four extra pages, including 'The Fairytale in Pictures'). All the discourses which had been suppressed during the long months of political wrangling over the affair came flooding through: indeed, many of these can be found the *Telegraaf*'s special supplement of 31 March alone. For example:
- the romantic discourse re-appeared in full swing, with constant references to the 'dream prince' and the forthcoming 'fairytale wedding'
- family trees, not only of the prince (tracing his roots back to 1120) but also of Máxima (tracing her roots back to 1749) appeared
- comparisons with previous royal couples and their weddings (complete with ancient photographs) were drawn
- advice was offered by famous designers on what the wedding dress should be like
- the importance of Willem-Alexander in contributing to the international reputation of the Netherlands through his membership of the IOC or his work in water management was stressed

As far as the historical discourse was concerned, a forthcoming television series on Willem-Alexander's great grandmother Wilhelmina gained an unexpected boost, while the *Algemeen Dagblad*'s magazine of 28 April 2001 carried an article comparing his grandmother Juliana to her sixteenth-century forbear Juliana van Stolberg. The long-suppressed PR discourse also re-emerged. Following the announcement of the engagement *Trouw* suggested on 4 April (somewhat sarcastically, it is true) that 'There is absolutely nothing wrong the with Royal House's PR... In other words, the admittedly somewhat controversial product "Máxima" was launched on to the market by Orange Ltd with overwhelming success', while the decision to hold the wedding in Amsterdam and thereby efface the memory of 1980 (see below) was described as 'a smart PR move by the monarchy' by *NRC Handelsblad* on 26 May 2001, and Máxima was even hailed by an alderman from Meppel as 'the new Lady Di' (*Het Parool*, 31 March 2001).

A variety of legal and constitutional discourses also arose regarding Máxima's future title, specifically whether she would be addressed as Queen Máxima or not (Dutch readers were no doubt entertained to learn that, in the strict terms of their constitution, Beatrix is not their 'Queen' but their 'King'). There was also considerable debate regarding the nature of the wedding ceremony, since the Dutch royal family belongs to the Dutch Reformed Church while Máxima is, and intends to remain, a Catholic.

Merchandising once again moved into top gear (Heineken promised a celebratory beer). Advertising in particular, long silent on this front, got in on the act with quite amazing rapidity. Thus Durex published a full-page ad in a number of dailies on 1 April describing itself as 'likely supplier to the court'. The national lottery also published full-page ads of a frog wearing a crown with the words 'kiss here' printed over its mouth.

Other companies such as insurers Centraal Beheer and coffee-maker Douw Egberts quickly brought out television adverts relating to the event. In fact a prize – the Golden Crown – was organized for the most creative and humorous ad relating to the royal engagement and wedding, along the lines of similar prizes awarded for ads relating to the eleven-city ice-skating race, the World Cup and so on. As the organiser of the prize, Peter Strating, put it: 'Believe me, every self-respecting advertising agency is now sitting thinking up a campaign' (*Algemeen Dagblad*, 31 April 2001).

There was also a considerable amount of writing on what might constitute Dutchness, and what particular challenges adapting to Dutch customs and Dutch ways of doing things – the so-called 'polder model' – would pose for a future queen of Argentinian origin. Much of this was essentially good humoured in tone as journalists speculated, for example, as to whether she would ever get used to delicacies such as the Hemaworst, a kind of smoked sausage from Hoogevens, and a wide range of anthropologists and others were invited to give their views on what Dutch culture might consist of (*Het Parool*, 2 April 2001). But some of it also took the form of a criticism of what was seen as the parochial nature of Dutch life, as when Wilfred Takken suggested in a lengthy review in *NRC Handelsblad* that, during the official announcement of the engagement, 'with charm and verve the worldly Máxima easily swept her family-in-law aside' (4 May 2001).

Not all discourses were playful, of course, or necessarily complimentary. It was suggested both on television and in the press that the timing of the announcement was a diversionary tactic to distract attention from the foot-and-mouth crisis. And a number of newspaper readers were less than delighted at the return of the romantic discourse. Thus a letter published in the *Volkskrant* of 14 April 2001 complained: 'What am I reading in my quality newspaper? Wherever she goes the air begins to sparkle. Young journalists, both male and female, wipe the saliva from your lips, stop wagging your tails and stay critical when gathering news'. Another complained that the paper had 'lowered itself to a disgusting tabloid level'. Other more explicitly political voices were raised. The Netherlands, for example, has a republican movement which was keen to have its say. They no doubt felt encouraged by the fact that, just before the announcement of the engagement, opinion polls showed that support for the monarchy had sunk to an all-time low over the preceding year, falling from 87% to 62% (*Algemeen Dagblad*, 30 March 2001).

A particular cause of concern was what would happen in Amsterdam on the day of the wedding, 2 February 2002. There had been disturbances both during Beatrix's wedding in 1966, when smoke bombs were thrown and her German husband was met with shouts of 'Claus raus' (the German for 'Claus out'), and during her coronation on 13 April 1980 when the forced eviction of squatters from Amsterdam led to widespread rioting on the day and to chants of 'geen woning, geen droning' ('no house, no queen'). The difficult relationship between Amsterdam and the House of Orange dating back to the sixteenth century was investigated by *NRC Handelsblad* (22 May 2001) and many police sources and spokespersons for 'alternative' movements were asked for their views on this subject. Serious questions were raised about the increasing restrictions on the right to demonstrate in the Netherlands which had been amply in evidence during the European Summit in Amsterdam in 1997.

But in a more general sense a variety of voices were raised questioning the continued existence of the monarchy at all. These were most noticeable in *NRC Handelsblad*. For example, a long article on 26 May 2001 entitled 'God, the Netherlands and the House of Orange' (a variation on the more common 'God, King and Country') took the view that 'Nowadays it is difficult to see the ideological trinity of christian supreme being, nation state and royal line in anything other than an ironic light', and went on to suggest that the monarchy was quickly becoming meaningless in an increasingly globalised world:

> What can the equation God, the Netherlands and the House of Orange still mean in the year 2001? It seems to me to have become a purely historical question. There is no doubt that the dynasty established by William the Silent is part of the answer to the question what made the Netherlands a nation. A difficult point here is that no-one has ever been able to state clearly what a nation actually is. It's true that as a result of European integration and the progress of international law this question is less relevant (at least in the Netherlands) than ever before, but even so, many are racking their brains over what, in view of the immigration of people from other cultures, is specifically Dutch. This is not without importance, if only to make clear to immigrants and their immediate descendants from whom 'integration' is required what it is that they are supposed to integrate with.

An article in the same newspaper of 25 May 2001 entitled 'Máxima, the musical' (playing on the fact that there is currently a musical running in the Netherlands called 'Diana') savaged the whole affair. The musical's theme, the author Paul de Leeuw announced, would be 'Love is blind', and in it Willem-Alexander would break away from his mother Beaconstrictor. To a chorus of journalists he would sing 'I love her dear, a letter I've here, hola hela, it's from Videla'. As Máxima begins to sing 'Don't cry for me, Netherlanders', the balcony caves in, seventy dead, and Willem-Alexander's nephew is named king. The author suggests it will run for twenty to twenty-five years before audiences of ten-to-fifteen year-olds looking for a feel-good ending.

Conclusion

Expressions of warmth towards Queen Beatrix of the Netherlands are not easy to find in the Dutch press. On the contrary, she is often described as 'determined', 'iron-willed', 'headstrong', even 'arrogant', or at times icily referred to by her nickname 'Queen Smile' (her son's nickname, on the other hand, being 'Prince Pils'). Even a cursory reading of press coverage makes it clear that much of this criticism has political origins. These views even surface from time to time in the 'bladen'. For example *Weekend* of 19 April 2000 carried a lengthy article claiming – quoting politicians who 'did not want their names made public' – to 'reveal' the true opinions many politicians have of Beatrix, these expressed by terms such as 'bitch' or 'shrew' or 'the witch from Noordeinde' (the Queen's offices are in the Palace of Noordeinde in The Hague). An article along very similar lines appeared in the *Volkskrant* on 2 February 2001. It suggested that:

> Recalcitrance in The Hague regarding the self-willed queen has increased in recent years. Because the discrepancy between the world of Queen Smile with her gushing opinion poll ratings and the day-to-day activity of civil servants, leaders and politicians who work with her is great.

An unidentified cabinet minister also opined: 'The more I have to do with Beatrix, the more republican I become'. And though opinion polls do indeed suggest that she continues to enjoy the respect of the Dutch people, she has not been immune to criticism from that direction either. Her decision to press ahead with her skiing holiday in Austria after the extreme-right FPÖ joined the Austrian government was (though apparently approved by PM Kok) heavily criticised (references to where she has 'left her skis' are now not uncommon in the Dutch press). And her decision to invite Máxima's parents to the Netherlands in November 2000 when the debate about her father's past was at its height was not one which appears to have won the approval of the population at large.

The political tensions surrounding Jorge Horacio Zorreguieta's past also surfaced at a time of growing discontent in certain (mostly left-of-centre) political circles in the Netherlands regarding the position of the monarch, and particularly her (for over a century now it has been 'her') role in the formation of the cabinet following a general election. Thus the Second Chamber had already decided that, as from the next elections, it will be it rather than the queen who will select the 'informateur' (the person who investigates the feasibility of any proposed cabinet formation). In a discussion on 'the modernisation of the monarchy' in October 2000 PM Kok made it absolutely clear that the monarch could not refuse to sign a bill passed by the Dutch parliament, while leader of the D66 party and member of the Purple Coalition Thom de Graaf published a lengthy article in the *Volkskrant* in the same month urging the politicians to have the courage to carry through a thorough modernisation of the monarchy as an institution.

Despite this, what the debate concerning the relationship between politicians and monarch also makes clear is that, with the exception of GroenLinks, the party furthest to the left of those with representation in the Second Chamber (and which is to some extent the re-embodiment of the former Dutch Communist Party), none of the current political parties feel that there is anything to be gained by championing the cause of the abolition of the monarchy in view of the lack of widespread public support for such a course of action. What there is quite clearly detectable interest in, however, is ways in which the fundamentally anachronistic institution of the monarchy can be changed in order to present a particular vision of democracy of which they, as professional politicians, are happy to be seen as (and, needless to say, to be paid for being) the official public representatives.

Our conclusion, then, is that the debate about Máxima's father was much less about his role in the Videla dictatorship than about clipping the wings of the Dutch Royal House – and in particular its queen's – and foregrounding democratic principles with which certain of its privileges – particularly regarding the formation of the cabinet – are glaringly incompatible. For all the swelling romantic discourse and the postmodern fun of the advertisers, this very modern debate between professional politicians and a would-be 'professional' monarchy (*Volkskrant*, 2 February 2001) appears to have been won for the time being by the politicians, in particular Wim Kok. Willem-Alexander and Máxima were described by *NRC Handelsblad* on 2 April 2001 as 'coming under his yoke' during the announcement of the engagement, and there was general agreement that it was the royal family, and Queen Beatrix in particular, who had had to make the greatest sacrifices. As the *Volkskrant* put it on the same day, referring to previous social-democratic prime ministers:

> And so, after Drees and Den Uyl, it is once again a social democratic prime minister who successfully asks the House of Orange to make sacrifices in order to ensure the continuity of the constitutional monarchy.

However, as in other European countries where the relationship between monarchy and democracy is at least to some extent up for debate, the vision of democracy championed by the politicians is one which stresses the closeness between official institutions (of which the monarchy and the parliament are the most emblematic) and 'the people' while marginalising any scrutiny of the relationship between parliament and big business. We are not suggesting that this debate is a pseudo-debate, but it is a partial one. Thus a long article in *NRC Handelsblad* (6 April 2001) contrasted the situation of Willem-Alexander as heir to the family business Orange-Nassau with that of other erstwhile Dutch family businesses (Philips, Océ, Van Melle, Douwe Egberts, DAF) which had modernised, floated on the stock exchange and internationalised. As these companies begin to transcend the national frontiers and the Netherlands itself is 'increasingly transformed by European rules and customs [of which] the loss of the guilder and the introduction of the euro is only one facet', the creaking structures of the Royal House remain as a 'national symbol' and solace to the populace. The debate is, therefore, also to some extent a vicarious one, where the taming of the exotic Máxima comes to do duty for the domestication of the globalising forces to which the Netherlands itself is increasingly falling prey. As *NRC Handelblad*'s article on 26 May 2001 put it: 'With the addition of this jet-setting member from the world of split-second international finance, the modern monarchy symbolises globalisation, in contrast to the stuffy, cozy and mysterious image which has for so long characterised the House of Orange'. A victory for the politicians, then, but what 'the people' have truly gained in their day-to-day relationship with 'the economy' is much less clear to see.

1   The Royal House consists of the queen mother Juliana and her husband Claus, and all their children and grandchildren together with their spouses. There are currently seventeen members.

PART THREE
CELEBRITY, ROYALTY AND POWER

9. Royalty and Celebrity

Royalty and the zero trajectory of celebrity

For six or seven years we'd been able to get stories about landmines in the Guardian, maybe in the Telegraph, we couldn't get the Mirror or the Sun or any of those papers to even be remotely interested. Within a day of Diana arriving in Angola, the landmines issue was on the front of every one of those papers.

(Rae McGrath, technical adviser, Landmine Action, Channel Five documentary on Diana, 22 May 2001)

Thus William is not only the next but one in line: he is the marketing future for the family firm. He has to be a dream prince, the wooer of his disillusioned contemporaries. Sweet William, to be sold, and sold successfully.

(Peter Preston, www.guardianunlimited.co.uk/monarchy, 18 June 2000)

The new edition of the *Collins Concise English Dictionary* published in June 2001 contained entries on David and Victoria Beckham, footballer and Spice Girl respectively; on television star Sacha Baron-Cohen, whose character 'Ali G' had been prominent if not for long in a niche of British television; television presenters Chris Tarrant and Anne Robinson; and celebrity chefs Jamie Oliver ('The Naked Chef'), Gary Rhodes and Nigella Lawson. These presences are an ambivalent sign of contemporary British culture.

They represent a socio-economic range of British society, some retaining a marked working-class identity, another a daughter of a former Chancellor of the Exchequer. If they are, by 2001, the product of some thirty years and more of the postmodernization of British society, we shall have to try to understand the phenomenon they represent by referring to several subsidiary processes in the transformation of modernity, among them not least some oddities, in Britain, with respect to changes in socio-economic stratification.

Along with the aestheticization of culture, and amidst its transformation into media culture, the 'Posh and Becks' phenomenon – their expensive residence dubbed 'Beckingham Palace'; Victoria, in a wordplay upon Diana's self-whimsy, the 'Queen of Herts' – can be misconstrued as a stage in the move toward so-called 'classlessness' in British society. Despite jocular suggestions by newspaper columnists and others of patently 'unsuitable' potential marriages for the heir to the next King, the distance between

Prince William and David Beckham – or more pointedly in this sense, Victoria Beckham – is so great in British accounts as to suggest something even more potent than class consciousness, something more to do with 'blood', 'breeding', genetic suitability and unsuitability.

Place this consciousness beside events in Norway – where crown prince Haakon was married in 2001 to Mette-Marit Tjessem Høiby, a single working mother from Kristiansand in the south of Norway, the father of whose three-year-old child had earlier been imprisoned for offences including possession of cocaine and drunk driving – and the limited integrative potential of British monarchy is starkly evident, its force as exclusion, rather than inclusion, underlined. 'Serious' speculation in the British media about a future wife for William limits itself to European royals, upper-class girls from England and occasional American heiresses. In serious terms, no alternative is contemplated.

'Beckingham Palace' is a double-edged observation in the context of British society. While recognizing enviously the wealth of the Beckhams, the jibe satirizes their 'social pretension' (whether or not they have any – the aspiration after all does not come from them, but from a parasitical media with which they are merely complicit).

Celebrity before and after the media age are very different propositions. In ancient Rome the audience of the Colosseum compared notes and opinions on the fighting skills of their favourite gladiators and gossiped about their sexual adventures. Roman emperors like many monarchs before them and after them were visible figures, interacting with the audiences at key points of the games when deciding the fate of participants. An audience of 50,000, which is what the Colosseum held, is not small when compared to the circulation of a regional newspaper.

The potential reach of celebrity grew as newspapers, and then the much more universal medium of cinema, appeared. Television, eventually the Web, extend the celebrity project further still. In the early stages of the media age the importance of celebrity was comparatively restricted. Yet Victorian and Edwardian Britain were already following press accounts of royal life in increasing detail.

In the course of a gambling scandal in 1891, the Prince of Wales reluctantly appeared as a court witness, in a period in which gambling at cards was the object of much social disapproval. Because of publicity resulting from the trial there was considerable public disquiet, the *Times* ominously recalling past royal misdemeanours: 'over the throne a black shadow of a ghastly spectre has fallen. Among us has risen a second George IV in the heir to the throne of this vast Empire' (June 15, 1891).

Twenty years previously and at a time during which Victoria's popularity had been sinking as the consequence of her lengthy mourning for Albert, the Prince of Wales had contracted typhoid, in December 1871. Edward's illness was further dramatized by its occurrence at the tenth anniversary of Albert's death, which heightened fear in the country. The Prince's illness and recovery repaired some atrophied bonds between public and monarchy, the *Times* observing afterward that:

> The fourteenth of December, ten years ago sadly memorable for one of the greatest of national calamities, the death of the Prince Consort, has this year given a Prince back to us.

The life's work of the Prince Consort was finished; that of the Prince of Wales is yet unfinished. (18 December 1871)

In Edward's day, and at the end of Victoria's reign, royalty became visible in the newsreel. Edward's popularity was enhanced by his sporting interests, his horses winning the Derby in 1896 (the year cinema arrived in Britain) and twice later, in 1900, when one of his horses also won the Grand National, and in 1909. As the forgiving, perhaps even admiring reference to 'bets placed on the gee-gees' by the Queen Mother in the *Daily Mail* eulogy examined earlier reminds us, and the Queen's enthusiastic commitment to racing likewise signals, equine culture continues to operate as a conjunctive symbol between royalty and populace, despite the forbidding exclusiveness of the Royal Enclosure.

The impact of these Victorian events was also international. The first Thanksgiving Day in Canada after Confederation, for example, was in 1872, to celebrate Edward Prince of Wales's recovery from the illness of the previous December. There is indeed a line which can be traced from press coverage of Edward's illness, and indeed accounts of the death of his father in 1861, to events in the Place de l'Alma road tunnel 125 or 135 years later but the transformations in the development of media culture from the 1960s suggest a continuity of sorts from (say) 1861 until the 1960s.

After this period both the general role of the media within culture, and the construction of monarchy as a process in itself, alter in nature.

In the wider world of celebrity, early film producers attempted to keep the identities of their actors secret for economic reasons until Carl Laemmle invented the star system with his protégée Florence Lawrence in 1910. In the 1920s and beyond in the golden age of Hollywood, stars attained great public visibility and their lives, real and imagined, became the focus of gossip and media coverage, so that they lived in the public view in two capacities, in their screen roles, and through what was known or invented of their private lives.

A perusal of the Collins English Dictionary of 1991, a decade earlier than the Beckham's inaugural edition, reveals entries not only for Richard Dimbleby, a media figure whose gravitas might have been expected to earn him some historical durability, but, for example, also for motor racing drivers Nigel Mansell, Alain Prost and Niki Lauda, celebrated primarily because of the capacity of the various media (particularly television) to display their feats – and their economic interest in doing so – but also for real abilities in their competitive field.

Random alphabetical samples reveal shifts in valorization. In 1991 under 'John' and in company with religious, royal and high-culture Johns (the apostle John, King John and Gwen and Augustus John) we find Barry John, the Welsh rugby halfback and Elton John, the pop star. The dictionary is understandably cautious with its Smiths, who, even when from the world of entertainment, are substantial figures of their era, Bessie and Maggie, who share the entry with historical figures like Adam and Sydney. But the inclusion of Harvey Smith, the showjumper, like the presence of the racing drivers above, seems to point forward ten years to an era in which worthiness for inclusion in dictionaries becomes a problematic judgement.

Let us note here that this inclusiveness seems to signal an increasing valorization of celebrity in itself. It is not that a great racing driver, footballer or pop singer – putting aside for a moment the secondary activity of celebrity – does not deserve to be known for a primary activity at which they excel (racing, football, or writing or performing music). Many such celebrities fulfil at least one further criterion beyond Daniel Boorstin's definition of celebrities as those who are 'known for their well-knownness':

> The hero was distinguished by his achievement; the celebrity by his image or trade-mark. The hero created himself; the celebrity is created by the media. The hero was a big man; the celebrity is a big name. (Boorstin, 1961: 61)

Boorstin in this vein can be read now, certainly in the anglophone world, as a prophet of the postmodern phase. It is that world recognized (wearily) by the Portuguese newspaper *O Independente* when it complains, in the wake of Diana's death:

> In the world we live in the 'new heroes' are invariably ephemeral and futile. The top model has replaced the philosopher, the television star has taken the place of the writer, any kind of playboy has taken over from the general or the admiral of the great battles. (5 September 1997)

It was remarked earlier in this study that Boorstin's work on the image is a 'hinge work', prefiguring postmodern turns of analysis in a context still not quite itself postmodern. It is possible that this distinction of Boorstin's, which still in some sense operates productively, has nonetheless been blurred since the manufacture of celebrity was stepped up toward the end of the 1970s, and massively by the end of the 1980s, when *Hello!* magazine and accompanying phenomena appear.

The problem is – to return to the phrase above about 'putting aside celebrity' – that celebrity now seldom remains a secondary activity and it cannot be put aside.

History may look back on David Beckham as an excellent footballer justly feared by opposing defences, a committed and energetic player and captain. But (in Boorstin's terms) his 'achievement' is – in a fashion not anticipated by commentators forty years ago – swamped by his celebrity. Celebrity has become a thing-in-itself. All we can do, in Boorstin's perspective, is to distinguish between celebrities of whom it can be said that achievement precedes celebrity, and celebrities of the sort defined in timeless fashion by Boorstin, who are known for being well known. In the end, the economic imperatives of celebrity, coupled with the strengthening grasp of media culture over the rest of culture, make of celebrity the primary virtue obtainable in British culture, though it achieves its full force when coupled with wealth.

There is a yet much bigger celebrity scene in Spain, and a thriving celebrity culture in Portugal. According to *Público* (1 September 1997), for example, in Portugal there are four 'revistas do coração' (women's celebrity magazines) with over 1 million readers (in a country with a population of around 8 million), while the top four daily newspapers have only 400,000 each. In Spain, celebrities also make up the largest section of women's magazines and there are daily celebrity programmes on most TV channels. There is even a category of 'related celebrities' – people who are famous only for knowing other people who are really famous. However, monarchy is less included in the celebrity category than in the UK (Lamuedra, 2001).

There are magazines about monarchy, even obsessed about monarchy, in other European countries too: *Points de vue* (France), *Das Neue* (Germany), *Billed Bladet* (Denmark), but given that the press of these countries generally do not carry royal stories in the dedicated manner of the British press, such publications have a specialist nature not possessed by *Hello!*. British tabloids can easily carry, during peak royal events, at least as many – or more – pages on royalty as any *Hello!* edition.

Celebrity is evolving, in its current phase having also been increasingly associated with ordinariness. By simply being very visible on television, the 'stars' of *Big Brother* were discussed in Britain in endless newspaper columns and chat shows, as well as in many other parts of Europe, for example, Germany, France, the Netherlands and Spain. They might find themselves in turn invited to become cultural producers. Newspaper or magazine columns are often written by celebrities either without prior 'achievement' or who have produced distinction in quite some other pursuit; the guests in radio and television chat shows are generally selected because of their current celebrity on radio, television or cinema, unless they are marketing a film or a book. The exploitation of these 'celebrities' is often very intense, partly because the duration of their commodity value is not great. No doubt the intensity of exploitation often hastens the decline of their viability, but being taken seriously by media and public alike, and particularly in Britain, is such an uncertain affair that there is some logic, on the part both of celebrities and media producers, in maximizing short-term exploitation. Boorstin observes that a celebrity is 'destroyed as he was made, by publicity': the press can unmake celebrities 'not by murder, but by suffocation or starvation': 'No-one is more forgotten than the last generation's celebrity' (1961: 187).

But which celebrity now lasts a generation? Placing celebrities in dictionaries in 2001 was a risky business. Even by 1991 the manufacture of celebrity in its postmodern form was perhaps fifteen years old, so it is not surprising that relatively temporary celebrities already make their appearance in the dictionary.

Key moments in the manufacture of celebrity in the UK include the fabrication of 'punk' in the mid-1970s, the first pop 'revivals' – for example Mod revivals – occurring in the late 1970s, and the anodyne products of the British popular music producers Stock, Aitken and Waterman from around 1984. Charles and Diana are married in 1981. William is born in 1982. In the United States we can find the manufactured Hollywood 'Brat Pack' in the early-mid 1980s. Prince Harry is born in 1984. *Hello!* magazine is launched in May 1988 (with an interview with the Princess Royal, who features on the cover).

We place these royal events in this context not in order to claim them as inevitable consequences of the economic crash of 1973 – which does in part explain the new phase of celebrity manufacture – but to indicate the pressures of the economic environment in which this royal marriage and its family cast develops and disintegrates; and also to note a matter to which we will return, which is that royal celebrities are of a different substance from most other celebrities. They endure.

There was a brief media frenzy over pop star Madonna's wedding in Scotland in December 2000. But major royal weddings in Britain possess a cultural importance which dwarfs other celebrity events. Even in 1981 the breadth and density of cultural response to Charles and Diana's wedding, in a variety of economic and political dimensions, was very striking. One area of production illustrates the scale of the response – all over England, special brews of beer were produced to celebrate the wedding.

To produce a drink in honour of an individual, or event, or even a sports team – as has happened in France with wine labels featuring football teams – is not unique. But widespread special brews of 'Wedding Celebration' and 'Royal Wedding' ales, when combined with a vast range of other comparable entrepreneurial ventures, speak of a relationship between royal family and populace unimaginable for any other celebrity group. Here is a capacity to mobilize interest on a far larger scale, and reach deeper into the public imagination and the culture – and the purse – than the most celebrated of pop or sports stars. Such practices collectively speak of the 'special place' of royalty and of a longitudinal dimension in which – in the brewing context – 'history', 'tradition' and 'loyalty' figure as elements, though at what level of social and cultural reality is a question to which we will return in the Conclusion. If these beers are drunk in pubs up and down the land, the implication of 'partaking' in the event is strong, the symbolism religious in origin.

The brews ranged from the small scale – The Village Blacksmith public house in Greenwich offering a beer brewed by the Tisbury Brewery, Wiltshire, each bottle of which was signed by Mr Winnington the publican – to the large, Berni Inns producing a special ale, Berni Royal Reception Strong Ale, available if you were eating at its chain restaurants. Slightly less monarchist Scotland produced one brew, Belhaven's Princess Ale and for balance, from Wales, there was Brain's Prince's Ale. England, from Mary Ann's Celebration Special of St Helier, Jersey, in the south, to Jennings Celebration Ale from Cockermouth, Cumbria, in the north, produced nearly fifty special brews. One beer, Llanelli's Felinfoel 1981 Prince's Ale was even produced in cans. (web.ukonline.co.uk/daymond/celebrationbeers).

Of course all this brewing is an economic activity and many purchasers of these bottles might have bought them because of aesthetic or economic considerations which had nothing to do with royalty. But that several dozen brewers thought it economically worthwhile to engage in the exercise is evidence of a cultural significance attaching to British royalty in 1981 which is not evidenced even by the innumerable posters of film, pop and sports stars on the bedroom walls of teenagers in 2001; one of the very differences being the demographic specificity, the restricted appeal, of royalty's show business, media and sport celebrity competitors, whether the Beckhams or those most assiduous of merchandisers, the late Kray Twins.

Multiply this activity of brewers by equally industrious exploitations on the part of a host of other producers (of crockery, calendars, tee shirts, confectionery and whatever else) and we find the wedding physically sedimented in the culture, on display shelves, in kitchens, and in dusty cupboards on a scale and with a breadth not paralleled by other celebrity phenomena. Madonna's wedding – and no female star of pop was more important than Madonna in the late twentieth century – was the merest splash in a highland pool by comparison: the Google search engine around six months after Madonna's wedding listed roughly forty times as many websites dealing with the twenty-year-old royal wedding, as Madonna's. *Público* noted presciently shortly after the fatal accident that 'In death, Diana sells more than when she was alive' (5 September 1997).

This royal effect can be found in other countries, too, as can similar questions about the motivation behind celebratory enterprise. Belgian magazine *Le Vif-L'Express* (3 December 1999) has an article entitled 'Who benefits from this marriage?' which goes into detail on merchandising relating to Philippe and Mathilde's wedding. The couple also merited a beer (called Prinseske') followed by 'postcards, posters, balloons, banners, chocolates, coffee, CDs'.

And in Britain, of course, this impact of royal events was never just a Diana effect, there having been merchandizing of royal events for much longer and benefits to third parties much more recently too: it was reported by the New Year of 2001 that St Andrews University had seen a 44% increase in admissions over the previous year as a result of its having become the chosen destination of Prince William. If William's appeal is increased by his resemblance to Diana as well as his status as her son, he has also very swiftly become a royal celebrity in his own right, as will be seen below. A fortnight or so after Diana's death, Spain's *Cambio 16* broods about the inevitability of William's burden even as it dares to question the need for royalty at all. It carries a front cover photograph of William and a sad-looking Diana; 'William: the heir to the myth', it observes. Inside are 12 pages of articles on monarchy, including "What use are kings and queens?" and "Isabel II or Isabel the Last?".

The speed with which William takes up the relay from Diana suggests about royalty a key fact of dual durability, the generic and generational capacity of royal families to reproduce their distinct form of celebrity, as well as the durability of royal individuals as celebrities in their own lifetimes. This particular reproductive force is the force of a whole apparatus.

Durability is a key feature in this comparison. Whereas the time-span of celebrity in the heyday of Hollywood could be considerable, there has been a tendency since the 1970s for the half-life of specific celebrity products to be shorter and shorter. The manufacture of celebrity has become increasingly more inclusive, its logical outcome being the 'anonymous' celebrities of late twentieth- and early twenty-first-century television shows such as *Big Brother* and *Survivor*. The temporariness of celebrity in the early twenty-first century is sufficiently marked that the compilers of dictionaries will be increasingly challenged by the speed with which fame surges and ebbs.

This has created and is still creating, certainly in the UK, an alteration in social and cultural values which needs a good deal of investigation by the social sciences, especially in the form of empirical research. We consider some comparative questions about Britain and Europe below. It may be that for historical reasons, as has been suggested above, Britain has offered easier purchase for the postmodernization of society and culture than continental nations. France, greatly exercised in the spring of 2001 by controversy around M6's 'télévision-réalité' production *Loft Story*, produces much more serious discussion and pointed criticism of this form of television than could be encountered in the UK. The press was also happy to emphasize its foreign provenance: 'This idea, inspired by "Big Brother" produced by the Dutch Endemol group', notes *Le Monde* (2 May 2001). *Loft Story*, like *Big Brother* offers, in one sense, ordinariness and a (limited) sort of participativeness which might be argued to represent the 'inclusive' aspects of postmodernity observed in the opening discussion.

For other commentators the nature of the 'interactive' involvement of viewers is not sufficient to counter a sense of gloom at the thought of the cultural restriction offered by this mode. Whatever may be deduced, the many pages of serious comment in newspapers like *Le Monde* and *Libération* on *Loft Story* suggests substantial cultural difference from Britain, in which the general media reaction was exploitative.

By the same token celebrity itself may be on a zero trajectory through its increasing 'ordinariness'. It is possible that non-royal celebrity will become so diffuse as to negate its own state. This is signalled in Britain by the appearance of working-class 'girl' and 'boy' pop groups whose ordinary backgrounds and discourses are the root of their success and celebrity; multi-millionaire footballers whose socio-economic origins make them acceptable to working-class fans; a profusion of working-class regional accents in (some domains of) television; a valorization of the 'ordinary' in working-class orientated soap opera — and in many other ways.

But there is nothing ordinary about the Royal Family, even over thirty years after Richard Cawston's TV documentary *Royal Family* (1969) inaugurated decades of increased public obsession with royalty. Its date, at the time when the world production system was already manifesting problems, and the economic crash of 1973 was approaching, suggests that *Royal Family* is a feature of a pattern of change, in which the postmodernization of British society will witness the replacement of many physical commodities, like cars and white goods, with media commodities. By the 1980s and the wedding of Charles and Diana, their relationship is literally the world's most significant media commodity.

Most commentators have seen *Royal Family* as a mistake. Royal biographer Anthony Holden comments, on a Channel Five film on Prince Philip, that:

> In the short term this film was an immense success, it boosted the ratings, made them seem human, much more so than before: in the long term of course it's been a disaster because it created this insatiable public appetite for royal titbits of every kind, that led to the disasters of the eighties and nineties in the next generation. (Channel Five, 8 May, 2001)

Peter Preston observes:

> Albert, Duke of Clarence, eldest son of Edward VII, was a sickly fool who died before he became a problem; George V spoke better German than he did English; Edward VIII was a dashing, randy dunce. Even the last King we had, George VI, wouldn't have cut the modern mustard: stuttering, chronically shy, a chain-smoker who didn't want the job because he knew he had only his doggedness for charisma. How did they get away with it? Because of deference. Because their frailties and incapacities were largely hidden – certainly from the denizens of impolite society. The media monarchy began 30 years ago, when the Queen allowed the BBC to peer genteelly behind the scenes and see her and her

brood as 'ordinary people'. Richard Cawston's sanitised film was the natural progenitor of William's date with photo-opportunity. From then on, the family were stars in their own endless soap.

(You can be a star or a king. But not both, *Guardian* 18 June 2000)

This view of the shift inaugurated by Cawston's film seems unusually consistent across a wide range of commentators:

Once you let the cameras into the private lives of monarchy the aura of mystery will be removed, they will become much more seen as ordinary human beings and this may make them temporarily popular but as soon as there's any grounds to criticize them they will become very unpopular and once you open yourself up to the media, the media will not rest until they've taken over in its entirety. So this was a very dangerous thing for the monarchy to do to humanize this semi-divine Institution, nothing but trouble could spring from it... (Sir Peregrine Worsthorne, TV interview, PBS, 1997)

Tom Nairn, writing in the late 1980s, cites a report of broadcaster David Attenborough having said of the effect of the film that 'trouble might ensue because once the tribesfolk had seen inside the headman's hut the mystery was gone, and they would tire of seeing it repeated':

So far all such fears have proved utterly groundless. No quantity of 'exposure' appears to do anything but create demand for more. The Royal glamour has appropriated and used the world of celebrity, not vice versa...the tirelessness of the Royal Romance lies somewhere else. That is, not so much in the trivia themselves as in their relationship to whatever lies behind. (1988: 36)

Nairn speculates that this 'thing' behind royalty is great and inexhaustible.

We can say of David Attenborough's attributed concern that after more than thirty years of royal disclosure there is so much mystery remaining and perhaps multiplying that there can be no fear of it seeping away. One of the effects of the huge increase in royal stories and 'revelations' is to create, as has been observed, inconsistencies and incoherences, evident half-truths and outright contradictions, which serve collectively to enlarge the domain of speculation, to expose royal 'revelation' as part-speculation and part-fabrication, to be sure, but nonetheless greatly to expand the field of narrative production. This creates more space for imaginative engagement, so that the 'headman's hut' becomes infinite. The (at least partially) conscious and purposive strategies of media producers swell public imagination further, especially through what we called in the opening section of the book 'serial realignment' which can pitch royal against royal, faction against faction, or individual against family.

In other European countries there are well-established, very strong, discourses of 'ordinariness' surrounding royalty – in Denmark, for example, Margrethe as the 'ash-tray' queen – but the reality of their lives is very different too.

In the UK, the distinction between celebrity and royal celebrity seems clear. Before returning to the matter, let us consider a media phenomenon which is constructed upon celebrity, namely *Hello!* magazine, both symptom and reproducer of a late-1980s culture in which 'style' and 'design' had already been played through by magazines like *The Face*. This was a culture ready to adjust its standards, as the British popular press had already been proving in advance. 'Human interest', 'personality', the interpersonal realm generally, become ever more important as commodities. Barriers or taboos of whatever kind, blocking their exploitation, are fragile, faced with an increasingly ruthless logic of capital. Where sexuality can be added to the mix the dividends on publicity are yet greater and by the end of the 1990s there is in truth little control left in the media system.

But *Hello!*, wishing to maximize its audience, avoids excess, except, of course, in the sheer volume of its coverage of royal families, Britain's most of all.

Monarchy, human interest and *Hello!*

> There was absolutely no writing about the Institution of the Monarchy in the sense of a great debate on should we have it or shouldn't we have it. In those years during the War and I would say – until the end of the 1950's – it was something that you didn't need to write about, you didn't need to argue about. It was reported of course because it did things like opening Parliament but it wasn't an issue. It was just a bonus, a blessing that you took for granted really like it was just something that we had and we're lucky to have.
>
> (Sir Peregrine Worsthorne, TV interview, PBS, 1997)

Not everything has changed since the 1950s.

Hello!'s website listing welcomes surfers to 'news and pictures from the world of celebrity, royalty and entertainment', making the distinction clear. Its daily Web version carries a central photograph under the banner, which will vary with events. For example, on successive days in June 2001 (12, 13–14 June) it carried alternating photographs of the Prince of Wales – at a fashion event with models and designers, and at the same venue with Camilla – on the 12th, and on the next two days, two alternating shots of Leila Pahlavi, daughter of the former Shah of Iran, under the headline 'Leila Pahlavi found dead in mysterious circumstances'.

The standard front-page Web format has a left-hand column listing generic features ('special reports', 'profiles') while on the right, the contents of the current week's issue are listed under 'highlights', which in the issue of 19 June 2001 begins with UK TV actress Amanda Barrie, who is on the front cover; memories of Anthony Quinn, Prince Harry playing polo, the Louis Vuitton Classic, an item on Rod Stewart, and, toward the tenuous end of celebrity, a piece on television's *Ballykissangel* star Colin Farrell. The centre column on the Web page lists daily events. On 12 June these include items on Madonna, Elle MacPherson, British TV star Denise Van Outen, Sharon Stone, Richard Branson, Frederick Forsyth, Geri Halliwell, Jennifer Lopez, the Duke of Edinburgh and Mick Jagger. There is also a Web link to a feature on 'the royal houses of Norway – discover the past and present of European royalty'.

The Web version of 14 June has items on Earl Spencer, Robbie Williams, Angelina

Jolie, Ursula Andress, Martina Hingis, John Travolta, Elle MacPherson, Charles and Camilla, Donna Karan, and Denise Van Outen. Some of these items remain across two or three Web editions.

In all cases we observe a mix of celebrities from the worlds of fashion, music, film and television, sport and, less frequently, big business, if it is personality-driven, as in the instance of Richard Branson. It is clear too that *Hello!* requires to stretch the definition of celebrity from international stars like Madonna to strictly local phenomena like Denise Van Outen. It is by no means the case that readers, in the increasingly niche-marketed world of the expanding media, will know who all these 'celebrities' are. For this reason, the magazine obviously welcomes the chance to run with frequency photographs of well-known representatives in each of its categories, for example, from the ranks of musicians, Sting, Mick Jagger, Elton John, or Paul McCartney, who are all recurring presences.

In fact the left-hand column clearly lays out the generic distinctions for us. 'All the news on: celebrities; actors and actresses; musicians; fashion and models; royalty and statesmen (sic)'.

Whenever there is a salient royal event it effortlessly takes precedence over other news, so that photographs of Charles and Camilla, or William, or the Queen and Queen Mother, belong in positions of prominence in *Hello!* quite naturally. On the Web page of 14 June royal references comprise Charles and Camilla, Harry, and of course the main photograph of Leila Pahlavi, and the item on Norwegian royal houses. On 12 June, in addition to the main feature on Charles and Camilla, and Harry's polo-playing, there features also the Duke of Edinburgh. By comparison, though Spain's ¡*Hola!* is often described as the 'unofficial Hansard of the royal family', Lamuedra (2001) finds that it has less coverage of royals and aristocrats than *Hello!*, 36% as against 51%.

Royalty generally, including the Monegasque and Norwegian houses, is of great interest to *Hello!* readers but the British monarchy is supremely rated. Running through *Hello!* is a constant dialogue about the British royals, like so many currents of awareness rising and falling from the collective unconscious of *Hello!*'s staff and readers. 'Earl Spencer: "Diana would never have married Dodi Fayed"' is the first item on 14 June. Close to the annual opening of Althorp, his English seat, the Earl is in the happy position of being able to generate publicity; help to sell *Hello!*; please the readers; and fulfil a holy obligation of British society to pay reverence to Diana's memory – and all at once.

The frequently unctuous breakfast news magazine GMTV of the same morning, 14 June, which aims at a downmarket audience, and successfully impersonates popular discourses in its presentation style, features the faithful James Whitaker of the *Mail* whose constant attachment to Diana leads him to attack the Earl over his convenient 'discovery' of a number of 'hidden' photographs of Diana discovered in the attic close to Althorp's annual reopening.

'It is exploiting his sister, don't doubt that', says Whitaker. Responding to the presenter's feed – 'but surely the Earl must have loved his sister!' – Whitaker ripostes: 'I'll bet he spins out his love of his sister over several more openings of Althorp'. We have had occasion in this book to point up the constructed and often apparently arbitrary nature of royal accounts and public myths of royalty. This is the same Earl Spencer who was applauded (in the mythic account, 'by the nation') for his tribute to Diana and his attack on the British Royal Family during Diana's funeral.

(It is also Charles Spencer who, according to Channel Five's documentary on Diana in its 2001 series, denies the beleaguered Diana's request to stay in a cottage on the Althorp estate with her sons after Camillagate because it would cause 'too much hassle with security'.)

Audiences do not, of course, read *Hello!* or watch GMTV or Channel Five in isolation. What all these accounts of royalty accomplish together is the impression of a national conversation on the subject, and on its innumerable sub-themes, which is in turn presented by the beneficiaries of royalty, the media, as evidence of cultural and psychological requirements in the audience which the media for their part are merely serving. In this account the media are deferring to their audiences' wishes. Over Diana's funeral, for example, the media, in this account, were 'led by the nation'. We return to this theme later.

Worsthorne's remark that in the 1950s royalty 'was just a bonus, a blessing that you took for granted really like it was just something that we had and we're lucky to have' is not always very far away from describing the state of affairs for *Hello!* in 2001, except that *Hello!* never takes royalty for granted. It has been noted that the media generally, and probably the British press in particular, offer readers a remarkably inconsistent and incoherent view of royalty. *Hello!*'s has been more even.

The literature and media studies-originated concept of 'mode of address' seeks to explain the manner in which media texts construct a relationship (the facsimile of a personal relationship) with their consumers: we were, until relatively recently in royal history, perhaps the early 1990s, intended to decode coverage of the affairs of the Queen Mother with warmth and affection: of the late Diana (when her 'affairs' meant personal or public business), with adoration: of Princess Stephanie, with sympathy and sadness (the mode of tears): of Prince Albert of Monaco and Prince Edward, with scepticism, mockery and impatience: of Prince Charles, with affectionate exasperation.

Squidgygate and Camillagate had substantial effects on these narrative constraints, and subsequent events (the Windsor fire, royal reactions to the death of Diana, Sophiegate) have caused even the account of the Queen herself to become blurred. Only the Queen Mother continued to enjoy the benefit of a reasonably stable discursive position in the 1990s and early in the new century, despite media talk of her overdraft at Coutts and isolated instances of media sniping by journalists conscious of the benefit of a *frisson* to be had from attacking a National Treasure.

The respectful idiom identified by Worsthorne in the 1950s remained characteristic of a particular set of publications aimed at specific demographic groups. Magazines such as *Hello!* would never have referred to Diana as Squidgy, since it would have been to break the mode of address on which the magazine's success is founded, which is one which unites magazine and reader in a sort of bland, drugged semi-attentiveness which is applied equally to everything within its view.

It cheered its readers up with a New Year spread (16 January 1993) of fourteen pages on Diana's holiday with William and Harry in the Caribbean ('A carefree Princess Diana: together with William and Harry for a sunny start to the New Year') and it remained very understanding during the separation crisis with fifteen pages on the November Korean visit ('Fulfilling their duties with dignity despite the pressures they're under', 14 November 1992) and in a spread on a Midlands trip by Diana later in the month loyally observed that 'Courageous in the face of constant rumour and speculation over the future of her marriage, Princess Diana lovingly fulfils all her public duties', 21 November).

Covering Diana's first post-separation tour (her 'first solo tour', as *Hello!* has it) at a moment when critique might conceivably have surfaced at some point across the '17 spectacular pages', the reporter notes that;

> more committed than ever, Diana put her own troubles behind her to help one of the world's poorest nations. Aware that her first solo tour since her separation from Prince Charles last year would be well-publicised, she chose to visit the Himalayan kingdom, known as the abode of the gods, because it has some very down-to-earth problems. She arrived in the Nepali capital, Kathmandu, to face five days of relentless scrutiny by the press. But in a supreme test of her stated resolve to make humanitarian causes her life's work she carried on regardless.

In a heroic refusal of irony, the magazine records in detail Diana's transformed view of her own circumstances:

> Wandering down a steep path dotted with cowpats, she dodged stray goats and buffalo. One family invited her inside their mud hut and, after looking around its bare interior, she came out and sighed: 'I shall never complain again'.

> (*Hello!*, March 13 1993)

This turned out, as the famous *Panorama* interview proved, among other instances, to be quite spectacularly untrue. In fact it is Diana's conversion of everything into the interpersonal domain which makes her such an appealing media figure in a period in which 'human interest' dominates more and more of the media, and during a marked increase in 'tabloidization' of media forms previously confident in their ability to survive with a relatively upmarket audience.

An 'orchid in the land of technology': the most famous interview ever

The *Panorama* interview was an example of precisely this trend, the current affairs series having been emblematic of the BBC's Reithian tradition, its original anchor Richard Dimbleby, the BBC's most distinguished commentator.

The interview of 20 November 1995 was variously received by the rest of the media, but tabloids and qualities alike concentrated on personal qualities. On the day after the interview the British tabloids constructed 'Diana the adulteress': by and large the tabloids seized on her admission of sexual intimacy with James Hewitt – 'Diana, Hewitt was my lover', says the *Sun* (21 November 1995). The quality newspapers concentrated on a variety of less sensational aspects of the interview: the *Guardian* chose to lead with Diana's insistence that she 'would not go quietly', but none was very interested in the politics.

There is a phrase of Walter Benjamin's from a quite different context – 'an orchid in the land of technology' – which, appropriated, summarizes the contradictoriness not only of Diana's position in relation to the media, but also dramatizes both a contradiction and a hypocrisy about celebrity. Jonathan Dimbleby said of Diana just after her death that 'sometimes I felt that she didn't know if she even existed' (Channel 4 television, 31 August 1997) and she may in a technical sense have been historically unique, a human being whose self was partly experienced through her own mediation, someone who was part object and part sign (suggesting the idea of a media cyborg) and whose selfhood and iconicity were indistinguishable. No-one in history was so much a product of the media as Diana and no-one was ever more governed by her own image. She signalled her awareness of this in the *Panorama* interview:

> question 'It's been suggested in some newspapers that you were left largely to cope with your new status on your own. Do you feel that was your experience?'
> answer 'Yes I do..um.. on reflection, but then here was a situation which hadn't ever happened before in history in the sense that..ah....the media were everywhere...'

That Diana was very often complicit in the intensity of her own media coverage is clear. Even her loyal admirer, the *Daily Mail*'s James Whitaker, speaking on a Channel Five documentary on her in 2001, and speaking of her successful attempts to upstage Camilla after the separation, recalls:

> I remember I was in the south of France at St Tropez (chuckle) with Diana, and she was besporting herself daily in front of the cameras in an array of bikinis and swimsuits and she made sure for six days that she was on page one of all (chuckle) the newspapers and Camilla if she got in at all was on about page fifteen, it was a wonderful game that went on. It was a declaration by Prince Charles that he wanted to celebrate fifty years of the woman he was in love with, Diana just cut the ground from under the feet all week and got huge pleasure in doing so, I watched it, it was a joy to behold.
>
> (Channel Five, 22 May 2001)

But no doubt they would have been there in any case. *Panorama*, in the event, was no more interested in serious questions about Diana's or the monarchy's function than the *Sun*. In a study at the time, it was found that out of a total of 147 questions and follow-ups, at most 10 could be seen to address any serious constitutional or political matters: of these, at best around 4 addressed matters of politics (Blain and O'Donnell, 1995). There are around two dozen discernible subtopics in the interview up until around question 120. These range from post-natal depression and bulimia to the separation and Camilla Parker-Bowles and are entirely in the interpersonal or emotional domain. Asked what right she has to seek to represent the British people, the Princess personalizes the response immediately ('I'm not a political animal, but ..I know that I can give love') and when asked if she thinks the British people are happy with her role she responds that 'I think the British people need someone in public life to give affection'. Asked about any impact she might have had on the monarchy's future, she responds by talking about her children.

At the only moment at which Diana talks about actual change in the conduct of the monarchy, the interviewer changes the subject: Diana says 'I do think that there are a few things that could change, that would alleviate this doubt, and sometimes complicated relationship between monarchy and public. I think they could walk hand in hand, as opposed to be (*sic*) so different'. It has taken until question 125 to get to this point. The interviewer deflects it, as though alarmed, by asking 'What are you doing to effect some kind of change?', which is such a leap in sequence as almost to be a non-sequitur: and Diana talks about how she takes William and Harry to see AIDS victims.

We will never know what she was going to say, alas – it might have been the most interesting part of the interview for *Panorama*'s usual audience.

The last 19 questions return to the personal territory of the first 120. Of course there was nothing about Diana which would lure a television editor, producer or interviewer into thinking that she would provide good copy on the subject of political modernity, but that *Panorama* of all BBC vehicles should have been content to leave the political world of the British subject occluded from the language and content of the exchange on both sides was remarkable. Nothing abnormal, inadequate or offensive was thereby deduced by the rest of the British media on the next day or thereafter.

On BBC's *Breakfast News* magazine on the next day, having dealt at vast length with the previous night's interview, the newsreader says 'Let's look at other news now. The Bosnian peace process hangs in the balance' (21 November 1995). 'The breakfast tables of the nation are locked in debate', we were informed, but this was in the item about Diana, not Bosnia. (This is a mythic Britain in which people eat breakfast, and together at tables in kitchens.) The BBC's court correspondent Jennie Bond illustrated the surreal complicity with the Diana project which was characteristic of the BBC when she observed that 'her willingness to talk about (her work with cancer patients) is a sign of her new openness' (6.00 News, 3 December 1995). The possibility that Diana, as was attested then and has been frequently evidenced since, was very, very keen indeed for the media to talk about this work must conceivably have entered Bond's consciousness.

That Diana might have been a phenomenon of manipulation did appear in other contexts, for example amidst interpersonal turmoil in the early 1990s. A Scottish *Daily Record*'s leader writer comments that 'The Princess of Wales has pulled off a palace coup. "Squidgy" can now have her cake and eat it' (*Record*, 10 December 1992), and Jonathan Cooper in the *Daily Express* gives a very different account from James Whitaker above: 'The words that spring to mind after years of contact with her are: manipulative, wilful, obstinate, self-obsessed, selfish. This year there is another: vengeful' (quoted in *Guardian*, 12 December 1992).

In fact four and a half years after the foregoing attack and for perhaps as long as a month prior to the fatal accident, she had been the object of relentless criticism from the

English tabloids in connection with her relationship with Dodi Fayed. Far from being presented as the 'people's princess' she was shortly to become, she was routinely portrayed as a high-living jet-setter, an 'upper-class bimbo' with more money than sense who was spending all her time holidaying with her lover when she should in fact have been spending more time with her children. The criticism was quite overt and explicit: a week before her death the *Daily Mirror* (23 August 1997) carries a feature headline 'He's Got to be Loaded to go Out With Me' on Diana's expensive tastes and on the same day a feature in the *Sun* is entitled 'Just Cossie Loves You: How many swimsuits does a girl with a new fella really need, Di?' (23 August) and begins 'As this is Diana's fourth holiday in forty days – it's stressful being Queen of Hearts...'.

And even *Hello!* managed to be critical, without moving beyond the bounds of respect, referring (26 July 1997) to 'the effect of (William's) mother's increasingly erratic behaviour on her sons' (McElhone 1998).

The events in the Place de l'Alma road tunnel at eleven minutes past midnight on 30 August 1997 swiftly silenced these reports, which had been recorded in Europe too. Portugal's *Jornal de Notícias* observes:

> But in the 'spectacle of death' the media introduced a new register. For years the spectacle of Diana was her futility: the love mismatches, the confrontations with her ex-husband's family, the infidelities promoted to the rank of example, the luxury clothes and jewels, the lavish charity banquets of hundreds of organisations. With her death Diana changed into an affectionate and protective mother, an unhappy woman pursued by her mother-in-law, a citizen concerned with the great evils of the world, available for causes as just and dangerous as the removal of anti-personnel mines. (5 September 1997)

We return to the specifically political dimension of Diana, so remarkably absent from media coverage, yet so ably constructed by it as an ideological force, in the Conclusion.

Was Diana a victim of the huge media apparatus which surrounded her? If so, perhaps only in the sense that such an unequal partnership between one individual and the highly potent and ruthless forces of the media must perforce turn pathological. Diana's media exposure was very often actively self-willed, especially when developing her reputation in the early 1980s and subsequently as a function of her warfare with Charles and the rest of the royal family. Though the theme of 'media intrusion' ran through her life, she courted the media relentlessly. While some evidence of psychological damage in her life seems unquestionable, not all of it stemming from her marriage, Diana made her suffering one of her themes, an aspect of her performance – particularly in the mid-1990s – and questions have since been raised about the authenticity of some of her claims. Her life, like that of many royal family members, was relentlessly hedonistic, and she had limitless privilege with which to pursue it. New Labour leader Tony Blair, in dubbing her 'the People's Princess' helped effect a most remarkable transformation. It is true that Diana had engaged in work which brought her into contact with ill and underprivileged people but the sanctified Diana who emerged after her death, was, like the 'outpouring of grief', a fabrication.

Nevertheless Diana's dependence on the existence of a mediated self, and her relationship generally with the media, may have had historically unique characteristics, as she herself seemed to think. Looked at superficially, it seems not unusual for celebrities to attempt constantly to renew their fame but almost invariably that is in the context of their sense of the brevity of celebrity, and further sustained by entirely practical considerations, such as the need to be popular in order to work in films, or the need to be seen in order to sell CDs. In Diana's instance there seemed to occur an accelerated symbiosis between her and the media which became uncontrollable, exhibiting bizarre symptoms in both parties which produced vicarious tremors in suggestible sectors of the media audience. There is a quasi-technical sense in which the possibility might be upheld, as suggested above, that Diana participated in an unrepeatable experiment in representation.

A unique set of factors surrounded her life and death. Some were specific and contingent (her telegenic and photogenic appearance, so emphasized by contrast with the rest of the 'firm'; her simultaneous royalty and distance from royalty). Weaknesses in British society in the 1980s and 1990s – its bad faith, its fractures, its demoralization and loss of direction – may have encouraged an escapism in some quarters for which Diana was a welcome resource. The period saw growths in new forms of emotional expression in Britain closely related to the media. There developed other entrepreneurial interests in the domains of the personal and the emotional. There was much attention given to Diana outside Britain and a subsequent effect of magnification of the phenomenon.

But the technical aspect of her uniqueness lies in the sheer scale of her imaging and its imprint not just on British and other cultures but on her own psyche. This was an extraordinarily imaged human being. The scale of image production in the 1980s and 1990s across several media was in any case colossal compared with previous historical periods. Diana was thereby reproduced technologically in a manner which was without precedent. Her own needs to be imaged seem in retrospect as nothing compared to the monstrous and incontinent desires of the media to capture her.

The impression on the subject left after scanning the endless vacant steppes of newspaper and magazine pages and the miles of videotape on Diana is of significant puzzlement, along with an epic cultural embarrassment. But the temptation to seek a single explanation for her phenomenon should be resisted. Probably something like the combination of factors above is the only explanation available.

But it is worth summarizing once again the specifically postmodern aspect of Diana as a phenomenon here, as we switch the focus in the Conclusion to the ideological aspects of her significance. Diana is produced by factors which most importantly include:

- the post-1973 phase of what Harvey (1989) refers to as 'flexible accumulation'
- a high degree of mediatization including development of new technologies
- a loss of public subscription to representative forms of democracy
- globalization
- diminution of the high/low culture divide (aspect of 'aestheticization' of culture)
- cult of celebrity (a further aesthetic feature)
- entrepreneurialism in sentimental realm

- 'Latinization' of British culture (patterns of grieving post-Heysel, Hillsborough, perhaps as sub-feature of globalization) (to which we return)

these factors being in addition to more contingent aspects of the phenomenon (such as the need for New Labour to replace the Conservatives as the 'sensible', non-ideological, natural party of government).

An 'orchid in the land of technology'? The elements of imbalance which quickly became evident in this relationship were clearly systemic. Ultimately they were driven by historical processes. It would be as idealistic to imagine that Diana produced her own history, including whatever personal misery she may authentically have experienced, as to imagine that Margaret Thatcher produced the ideological conservatism of the 1980s. However, in this perspective (as in any other) Diana is more readily imaginable as a victim than the alternative monarch from Grantham, in the end because above all it was Diana's relationship with the media which remains as the single truly significant fact about her, still a truly extraordinary fact.

But, as we suggest in the Conclusion, the sanctified Diana of the funeral period and after is as much a fabrication as the 'outpouring of grief', the latter an invention which suited a number of conservative interests in Britain, including its New Labour government. The 'outpouring of grief' did not happen. It was made up by the media and the government in a contingent partnership of interest. This displayed a sinister side. British broadcasters closed off information about the rest of the world, sealing Britain inside its own pathological space of royal obsession as effectively as any totalitarian régime closes down its country. This was all the worse because Britain was not in the grip of a royal obsession. The agenda of the broadcasters and the politicians was forced on the rest of the country.

Hello! William: resumption of the narrative

> *Today is the day after. Other princes and princesses are already being sought out ... 'The show must go on' (Jornal de Notícias, 5 September 1997)*

> *The show must go on. The polls exact their imperatives. The student prince at his computer is launched like the latest Blair plan for the NHS. William is served up on schedule like a paella from his oven.*

> (Peter Preston, Guardian, 18 June 2000)

On a Prince William website, an opinion poll, opened in the spring of 1999, offers surfers the chance to choose between two options, 'World Peace', on the one hand, and on the other, the less feasible alternative of 'having Prince William all to yourself'. At the time of writing, a gratifyingly responsible 43% (3047 votes) have so far voted for world peace but 57% have voted for exclusive possession of the heir to the throne (4061 votes, total votes cast 7108; *Pretty Fly for a Shy Guy! 1998–2000* kittywinky@yahoo.com). The flourishing Web culture surrounding the topic of William includes unexpected growths, such as of gay clubs focusing on William as a gay icon, if optimistically (there is even the claimed existence of a club called precisely 'Let's Hope William is Gay'.)

An opinion poll in *The Observer* newspaper (30 December 2001) discreetly focuses questions on the older generations of British royals, but does offer the interesting result that despite the Web culture and media attention William elicits, when asked who should succeed the Queen 'when she dies or abdicates', more respondents favour an elected president (25%) than the media-inspired idea that the succession should pass to William (19%). However the significant figure is that 55% of the population favour Charles, which means that 74% of the population still favour a royal succession. This poll admittedly predated revelations in mid-January 2002 about certain recreational proclivities of Prince Harry, but, as with Deputy Prime Minister John Prescott's fabled punch of the 2001 parliamentary election campaign, there is no guarantee that misdemeanours by public figures will be judged disfavourably by the British public.

The fact is that William is an invaluable miracle of resurrection for the media. Having reaped every conceivable market benefit from Diana's life, as well as much ideological opportunity – and then again from her death – the media are able to reproduce much of her value in her son, in whose features she can so plainly be read.

The gleeful headlines which had 'Wills stalked by Uncle', when Prince Edward's television production company appeared in St Andrews to film him, played on the comparative discretion displayed by most media producers over William's early student days. But this self-control has about it the quality of a temporarily blocked volcano, and the furore over Prince Harry's sadly routine teenage behaviour in early 2002 was a diversionary explosion, one which would not ease the pressure for long. (This intrusion was licensed by 'public interest' considerations, the actions of the unruly princeling apparently imperilling British society in some fashion not quite clarified by editors.)

Medieval St Andrews gained an unexpected role in the postculture of the age of *Hello!*. The 44% increase in degree applications noted above for the university compared with the next biggest British increase of 15.9% (against a background which could be found elsewhere of a drop of 12%): the British Council recorded a 'surge of interest' from young women, especially from the United States (Guardian, 26 January 2001). William was arriving to study Fine Art.

Whereas *Hello!* is invariably respectful, sometimes perhaps it reveals itself as capable of irony, though it isn't invariably easy to tell:

> During his first year William will be one of 130 students to study the Art of Renaissance Italy, including the works of Leonardo da Vinci and Michelangelo. Fortunately, if he needs to do any last-minute cramming the Queen could let him flick through the world's largest collection of Leonardo's sketches that she keeps at Windsor. (*Hello!*, 13 February 2001)

If read by the signals over his grandmother's Golden Jubilee, the media will do as much as possible to reconstitute William as a Diana-variant as soon as the time is judged right, and any woman with whom he forms a long-term relationship will need to be strong in character. (If the Web-based wishful thinkers are rewarded by any surprises about William's sexuality, his partner in that case had better be either indestructible or quite invisible.) The extent to which the media – in Britain at any rate – can rehabilitate monarchist discourses when it suits them, as over the Jubilee, wherein all memory of anti-monarchic criticism can be forgotten, is well evidenced. The right kind of William could yet come close to equalling his mother in media attention, even in the unlikely event that, as some commentators have claimed, he might decide to try to dispense with his royal identity, and cede succession to someone else.

The 'right kind of William' will to an extent, as we have demonstrated, be a discursive product (that is, because he is also an economic commodity, and an ideological device). It may be that the differential principle will require a good William and a bad Harry to play contrasting roles to their 'eccentric' father and the refurbished Camilla. Once dramatically 'suitable' or 'unsuitable' partners are identified for the boys, the next sequence of episodes can be constructed and exhibited to a grateful audience. Another small cohort of 'dissident' journalists from anything which may in the future remain of the quality press in the UK will then be able to come up with the novel idea of enquiring whether the monarchy's time is up.

Then with any luck it will be time for another jubilee.

CONCLUSION

10   Royal Power and Media Power

With assurance and stubbornness...groups, small communities, affinity networks and neighbour-hoods are preoccupied with close social relationships. This is also the case with respect to our relationship with the natural environment. Thus, even if one feels alienated from the distant econom-ic-political order, one can assert sovereignty over one's near existence...It is in the secret, the near, the insignificant (which escapes macroscopic finality) that sociality is mastered.

(Michel Maffesoli, 1996: 44)

...if the editor of the Sun says that he likes to keep the monarchy there because by attacking them he can get a good story which puts on readers, if that is the cynical attitude of the editor of the Sun to the monarchy – it says more eloquently than any words of mine that part of the media is rotten, corrupt...the fact that as a nation our fate should be in their hands fills me with horror

(Sir Peregrine Worsthorne, TV interview, PBS, 1997)

Haakon's courageous course of action can be the beginning of a comprehensive modernisation of the monarchy where openness, closeness to the people and a strong social commitment are important elements. But it can also be the beginning of the end because the throne is increasingly experienced as a piece of furniture from IKEA.

(*Dagbladet*, 15 April 2000)

Political modernity

The most striking fact among many comparative features of European monarchy, as we noted in the Introduction, is that Britain's is the only monarchy not required to justify itself by its contribution to political modernity. The other monarchies we have been studying here are clearly constructed in the public sphere as maintaining or augmenting or, as in the Spanish case, inaugurating and even saving, conditions of political modernity. In an ambivalent instance, in The Netherlands, the media are strongly sensitive about any impediment the performance and symbolism of the House of Orange presents to Dutch political modernity. As was seen earlier, the Spanish monarchy in relation to modernity has virtually a reverse symbolic function from the UK's. In Spain, when democracy was threatened by coup, 'the King was in his place, defending democracy when he needed to' (*El País*, 22 November 2000). Spain was in a sense inoculated against the postmodernization of its politics by

General Franco, and there is little sign of the dosage wearing off, despite changes to other aspects of Spanish culture. When democracy can still be felt as an acquisition which needs to be defended, monarchy is much more likely to remain politicized than become postmodernized.

Admittedly there is a hybridity in this domain affecting even Spanish monarchy – which is also sold as a media commodity – but the 'uneven development' discussed in Chapter 1 has placed an accent on the modern when the Spanish royal house is constructed by the Spanish media.

As established above, with changes in the nature of the Spanish bourgeoisie and the increased globalization of Spanish society, an unmistakable trend is emerging in Spain suggestive of prior British transitions toward a higher salience of consumption, and a repositioning of values. Spain will not in this sense 'become like Britain' given the very different historical trajectories of the two nations, but it is visibly postmodernizing in its different fashion. But just as royalty in Spain is not nearly so strongly implicated in the 'celebritizing' process as it is in Britain, likewise the Spanish monarchy's symbolic and (in the recent past) entirely practical underwriting of political modernity makes of it a different species of beast from its British counterpart.

In Belgium, we noted in broadcast coverage of the royal wedding of 1999 a group of discursive strands none of which makes any appeal to 'tradition' or 'history':

• The wedding has united Belgium.
• The wedding marks the beginning of a new and positive phase for Belgium.
• The royal family is extremely advantageous for Belgian industry and commerce.
• The royal family is a key element of Belgian politics in general.
• The royal family links Belgium with other countries on an international scale.
• With its openness and closeness to the population, the Belgian Royal Family is a model for the third millennium.

In the case of the Belgian wedding, and in stark contrast to the frenetic encouragement of royal mourning in Britain at Diana's funeral, a strand in the press coverage was starkly honest about the absence of crowds and the apparent thinness of Belgian monarchism, while permitting itself a reflexiveness about the motive for the celebrations which was in large part absent in the UK's rhetoric over the 'outpouring of grief' in 1997.

Though the Norwegian media do concern themselves considerably with their monarchy's history, this is explicable in terms of its relative novelty; this historical element in the Norwegian construction of its monarchy is offset by strong concerns about the monarchy's effect on trade and external relations, and by much public discussion of the monarchy's relationship with modernity. As in Belgium, 'closeness to the people' is an important Norwegian criterion of judgement about the monarchy and the media of both countries view the British monarchy as in this regard backward.

And at this final stage in the argument it is now worth making it quite explicit that 'monarchy' as a concept is in fact stretched very considerably when applied even to only those few royal houses which are our object of study. There may arguably be as many features differentiating the British monarchy from its European cousins as there are constituting a family resemblance. It seems clear, too, that it is the British institution which greatly differs from the others, even if each is finally a monarchic institution of its own kind.

There is a plainly visible parallelism of account when looking at Spanish or Norwegian reports, or indeed republican constructions of the British monarchy, for example from Germany or France. We append below examples of the German press adopting a very similar line of interpretation of British constitutional politics and political culture to those, say, of the Spanish press, and Swedish television. The view of Britain from outside, if 'triangulated', so to speak, from a variety of·points on the topography of the European political landscape, is consistently one of a backward country whose monarchy is its most appropriate emblem. This is a consistency both across time – we cite reports on this theme a decade apart in this book – as well as across national boundaries (see Appendix).

NRC Handelsblad's caustic description of its monarchy as 'Big Brother with a family tree' (16 May 2001) and *Dagbladet*'s gloomy and poetic rumination on how the 'The Engagement' made it 'even more difficult to distinguish between fact and fiction in the half-light under the December sky' (2 December 2000) remind us that the complications of postmodern culture impact on analyses of the political role of monarchy even in those nations which either began thoroughly to modernize in the nineteenth century or who are now like Spain completing a process begun and thwarted earlier in the twentieth century.

Der Spiegel's description, cited above, of Britain's failure to modernize politically, printed nearly a decade before *Stern*'s much publicized dissection of British woes in 2001, lists the problems with a simplicity seldom encountered in the British press:

> class barriers are higher here, privileges are passed on from generation to generation more easily than anywhere else in Europe: one percent of the population own 17 percent of the private wealth; two thirds of this wealth – a unique situation in the western world – was inherited ... Only in Britain can the feudal rites, and the luxurious games of the aristocracy be admired, as though nothing had happened, no French or industrial revolution, no World Wars. (23 November 1992)

A decade after this piece, and after the first period of office of a New Labour government, the gap between rich and poor in Britain has widened and the surest sign of social acceptance of the new British elites – of sport, the media, and generalized celebrity – was to be photographed, in the press, or in fashion magazines, or in *Hello!*, or in the pages of its demotic imitator *OK*, precisely with members of the old elites. By preference, of course, this would be one of Britain's astonishingly large corps of royals; failing which, some prominent member of its vast and thriving aristocracy.

In a country exhibiting such comparatively modern features as The Netherlands, it is almost touching, from a British perspective, that journalists and editors should concern themselves at all with the illogic of the survival of the House of Orange. In Britain, where the monarchy is a substantial symbolic barrier to political modernization, radical political comment in the early 1990s usually got no further than speculating about what would happen if Diana became Queen. After her death, in the late 1990s, the speculation turned to Camilla. A daring suggestion by British media standards is to wonder publicly if the monarchy should 'skip a generation' – the phrase is redolent of a belief in retaining monarchy as long as the planet holds life – though as we have seen it was still Charles who was favoured by the public at the end of 2001 as the next monarch.

The talk in some quarters of the media, that on the streets during Diana's funeral the public anger was such that the monarchy was threatened, is unconvincing. The public, first of all, has never been empirically demonstrated to have felt anything at all. If a number of quite possibly unrepresentative voices were heard railing at the Queen because of her 'invisibility' after Diana's death (and then only because of Scotland's negligible visibility factor) then they were upset because they were monarchists, not incipient republicans. There is no prior reason, however, to think that they meant anything much at all.

Britain is the country in which media fury erupted when an Australian prime minister once touched the Queen. 'I like the Queen says anti-royalist Keating', was one headline in an *Express* piece which began 'Australian leader Paul Keating, dubbed the Lizard of Oz for his republicanism, yesterday insisted he likes the Queen' (11 September 1993). However unsurprising views of this kind were in the *Express*, the sentiments were typical. There is only one logic of British culture where the British monarchy is concerned, and it is a logic stemming from its permanence.

When the tabloids in particular choose through their leaders, as distinct from rogue columnists with licence, to play their 'outsider' persona, where they define themselves against the 'establishment' or the monarchy, they perform an unconvincing mimicry of critique. On the same day in 1993 (after Camillagate) that the *Sun* says 'We're worried that we're being set up. Being given enough rope to hang ourselves. Wouldn't the Establishment just love that?', across at the *Daily Star*, the leader reads:

> Nobody could deny a serious rift between the heir and his future consort was of legitimate public interest. *Except the Establishment.* The marble-mouths, who hide their steel claws in velvet gloves, simply didn't want you to find out what – it is now clear – had been common knowledge for months in the snobby world of Royal circles and politics. *So they framed the newspapers.* (both 13 January 1993)

These propositions are extraordinarily audacious. To suggest (1) that the *Sun* and the *Star* are run in the public interest; (2) that the British press will ever face effective controls except over essential political information; (3) that relations between Charles and Diana mattered while Charles was yet years from the throne (except to editors); (4) that the editors of London newspapers and their proprietors are at odds with 'the establishment' – is a remarkable exhibition of nerve. (These propositions exhibit an absence of reality on a very large scale, demonstrating precisely why it is that formulations such as Baudrillard's 'third phase of the image' are required for the purposes of theorization. Sometimes 'false consciousness' is so great as to render the mere concept of ideology inadequate before it!)

Change, circularity, stasis

Does the British monarchy operate with a reverse effect from its European counterparts? The latter operate variously as a symbol of modernity or as a conduit for discussions about failings in modern development. There is a real question about Britain's potential to modernize politically at any pace and in a sustained fashion, despite recent constitutional change which seems to further the process and which did occur quickly after New Labour's election in 1997.

It is not that other signs of modernity have been absent in British life. The UK is a country which produces innumerable internet start-ups, design consultancies, advertising, public and corporate communications, and other 'knowledge economy' companies, which can deliver world-leading goods, products and services, and which has innovated in fields such as fashion and architecture, and was for long the most innovative culture in the world for the production of popular music.

In fact signs of British modernization have always been particularly mixed, as befits a country which cloned the world's first arthritic sheep. Britain in some respects entered the modern world very early and thereby helped develop it, and as we noted in Chapter 1, literary evidence of a modern consciousness – a correspondence with objective social and cultural development, presumably – is available in Britain probably as soon as, if not sooner than, anywhere else.

But in a postmodern perspective, it might be argued that failings in *political* modernization, specifically, lasted so long that modernization in politics was overtaken by postmodernization, the British moving directly from subjecthood under a broad ruling elite headed by the monarchy – skipping European-style citizenship along the way – to a new form of unempowerment and consumer subjection in the 1980s and beyond. A part of this curious set of phenomena is a continuing if slow 'modernization', actually occurring in places later than postmodernization, which within the 'dual coding' model poses no theoretical contradiction.

It is instructive, incidentally, to ask if the British can achieve citizenship – as a development from 'subjecthood' – by becoming European, or whether they can achieve a European identity only by acquiring British citizenship. To await the latter without a growing European dimension to British life can only be imagined as an interminable process.

Other amenities of the modern world, and subsequently of the postmodern world, may have substantially disguised the reality of this failure in citizenship. In a subtle version of that succession from modern to postmodern, the second phase indeed has to be seen as partial, in the sense that the current phase of 'subjection' must have characteristics of both the ideological age and the post-ideological age. 'Conservatism' can thereby be seen to contain both political-ideological and consumer-ideological constituents (of course both are political in the end).

Whenever the media surprise us and break ranks with the norm of political conservatism, retreat or recuperation are never far behind:

The monarchy remains symbolic of privilege over people, of chance over endeavour, of being something, rather than doing something. We elevate to the apex of our society someone selected not on the basis of talent or achievement, but because of genes. For all the lip-service that politicians of all parties pay to meritocracy, for so long as we have a hereditary monarchy, Britain enthrones and glorifies the exact opposite.

A republic will not happen overnight, and cannot happen without a referendum. But we now believe its time has come.

The Observer, July 30, 2000

While her subjects still hold the Queen in high esteem – 71 per cent think her hard-working and 81 per cent say she is a 'good ambassador for Britain' – an exclusive Observer poll reveals widespread public belief that perks enjoyed by the Windsors, including exemption from inheritance tax, should be curbed. And support for some minor royals has fallen to its lowest point ever.

Time to bin your kin, ma'am (on *Observer* poll)

The Observer, December 30, 2001

What a slippage there is here. The results of this *Observer* poll give little sign that the populace will soon take to the streets in realization of the aim outlined in the same newspaper's editorial 18 months earlier. In late January 2002 a BBC Six O'Clock News broadcast contrives to start an item with the address: 'Those of you looking forward to the Jubilee...'. At first encounter this is a rather extraordinary concept – to whom can this refer, unless it is addressed to fellow media producers? – but it is all of a piece with the BBC's monarchic project. Jubilee-building forms a logical and orderly succession to wedding-building, divorce-building and funeral-building.

And as we approach our final consideration of what might be at stake in these debates, we finally return to consider the hypnotic effect of the woman whose life still haunts accounts of monarchy across Europe. What was happening at Diana's funeral when the 'outpouring of grief' was asserted by nearly all media commentators in Britain as an observable fact? Since this has become a given of cultural history, we had better address the question head-on. In Chapter 2 we explored the 'constructedness' of the funeral. What we propose here is a developed explanation of its functioning, part-modern, part-postmodern in its reference.

New Labour's 1997 landslide victory swept away not only a nineteen year Conservative monopoly on political power but a whole series of discourses – but not, crucially, their related practices, New Labour effectively moving to occupy much of the political space left vacant by the disintegration of the Conservative Party. In their place came New Labour's 'new' discourses whose aim was to create a new consensus and thereby win the support of key sectors of the British establishment, also seen as crucial for Labour's electoral success. These 'new' discourses were discourses of 'caring', 'compassion', 'kindness', 'community', 'solidarity': in short, putting 'people' first. The term 'people' – as opposed to the 'individual' of the Conservative years – rose to new heights of public prominence. All of these elements would be highly visible in the period immediately following Diana's death, when the 'people's princess' – as opposed to the selfish and uncaring version of her being circulated only days previously – would be routinely associated with 'kindness', 'caring' and 'compassion'.

Not only might 'society' have been thought to be back on the agenda with the return of New Labour (not for long, as it turned out) but with the ditching of the Conservatives, notions of *unacceptable* divisions and *unjustifiably* unequal distributions of all kinds – notions which had been given no political legitimacy for almost two decades – might reappear. Such discourses were potentially threatening for those elite groups in the UK for whom old-Conservative 'One Nation' politics, and the more recent 'Primacy of the Individual' discourses of Thatcherism, had been variations on the theme of 'classlessness.'

'Diana' (the signifier) had the potential to be transformed into the discursive bearer of a return of *class* awareness and protest – of which there was certainly an element in the days after the funeral, in comments made about the Royal Family – since she had already been constructed as a positive value by the media during its sympathetic phases precisely through being, albeit royal, also extra-royal, even ordinary. The presence at her funeral of disproportionate numbers of gays and other groups suggests that she may have been a vehicle for a variety of specific sectors of British society, some of whom may have been disaffected. This might or might not have been significantly disturbing for Blair's project – it is doubtful whether or not there was enough in the country of a real response to Diana's death to constitute a disruption of Blair's project of continuity, though on the other hand such presences were effectively redolent of fracture (a Conservative product) rather than the harmony of New Labour. But New Labour's response was at any rate far from defensive – instead here was an opportunity to codify its slogans, almost indeed to personify them.

There seems to have been an effort of truly massive proportions by an ideologically conservative media to construct other forms of disgruntlement semantically as something else, as nation-uniting, classless grief. It is not difficult to see why. Political protest can be amorphous and unpredictable. Grief, on the other hand, has a clear and widely agreed set of symbols and rituals, standardised patterns of behaviour and decorum, and indeed even an agreed vocabulary. It is the scale of this (re)signifying effort which explains the hysterical concentration not only on images of grief whose extension in 'real life' was by most accounts rather modest, but likewise the hysterical concentration on the symbology of grief to the exclusion of all other interpretations.

Earl Spencer's Westminster Abbey speech struck an unexpected chord with 'the people' because the expression of his own personal grievance – that the British Royal Family had failed to appreciate his sister's and no doubt his entire family's qualities – happened to coincide on a *lexical* level with the recodifying of social dissatisfaction, or protest at the Conservative years, into grief. In this process what was no doubt in part resentment against the structures and preconceptions of the powerful in an unmodern society was resignified as anger at the unwillingness of the British Royal Family to join in the expressions of grief of 'ordinary people' for their 'representative', Diana.

Were the accident to have occurred in August 1998, as distinct from August 1997, we speculate that reactions would have been different. The discourse of the 'outpouring of national grief' was amongst its other functions a *political* compromise on the one hand both made necessary and enabled by the discourses released by the Labour victory in May 1997, and on the other made possible by the particular forms of commodification of the Royal Family now dominant in the substantially postmodernised culture of the UK.

Postmodernization may have also manifested itself more positively at the funeral than some interpretations of postmodern culture would allow. (Shortly we will turn to a last interpretative framework, suggested by Michel Maffesoli's subtle development of Durkheim's category of the 'social divine'.)

It was noted in Chapter 1 that some commentators take a generally more sanguine view of the postmodern world than Marxist writers like Jameson and Harvey. What is widely termed (in a New Labour usage) 'inclusiveness', has actually been a theme of postmodernism theory for some time, applicable to many areas of culture, in senses such as 'empowerment', 'democratization' and 'multi-culturalism', among others. (In fact in this sense the herald of the postmodern, located – as is often the case in foundational cultural movements – in visual culture, Pop Art, asserts 'inclusiveness' in a reaction against the 'exclusiveness' of its Abstract Expressionist predecessor.)

Some loss of distinction between high culture and popular culture referred to in Chapter 1 as part of the postmodernizing process carries with it (as a real world process) an element of 'inclusiveness'. Diana's funeral appeared to be a pop funeral, a youth funeral – a democratic funeral, even, because 'the people' were held to have finally forced its form – and some degree of readjustment of royal response likewise seemed popularly ordained, though we surmise that it was truly ordained by the media. After this, what kind of funeral? In fact, anything which one likes – a gay funeral, a multi-ethnic funeral: as we noted in Chapter 2, a BBC reporter saw Diana's death as reuniting Northern Ireland. In aspects such as its 'participativeness' – the applause which started outside the Abbey and found its way in – it fulfils some broad criteria of postmodern events in their positive conception (the fact that the applause rippled from exterior to interior, for example, being a loss of boundedness of the sort proclaimed by cheerier postmodernists).

As a result of the twin processes of the commoditization of culture and the mediatization of culture, there a certain arbitrariness with which we all have to live, these days, when negotiating media claims about the present and about history. Generically, that thought, as we illustrated in Chapter 1, now has a long pedigree. We have demonstrated how a *discourse of disrespect* may help to sell royalty as a media commodity. If it doesn't, as in *Hello!*, journalists can turn to a pastiche of a pre-1960s *discourse of respect*. *Sun* columnists being rude about Diana or the Prince of Wales have never provided much of a measurement of a 'loss of deference' or 'changing attitudes' in the UK. These phrases are too readily used in relation to a cultural landscape with little consistency.

Royalty, power and the institution of monarchy

In the UK, as we have ventured to suggest, we are only released from our feudal role as subjects of the British monarchy insofar as we are prepared to constitute ourselves as consumers of our monarchy (and consumers in general, of course). In the UK the position of feudal subjecthood of the British is traded, and only partially, for that of economic subjecthood. The nature of British 'citizenship' remains problematic.

Intriguingly, the Home Secretary's white paper on immigration *Secure Borders, Safe Haven* (Home Office, 2002) while retaining the practice specified by the British Nationality Act of 1981 of having applicants for British citizenship swear allegiance to the monarch, introduces a new requirement whereby applicants are to receive a pack including a statement of 'what it means to be a British citizen' and are to promise in a 'citizenship pledge' to uphold Britain's laws and 'democratic values'. This is an audacious development, apparently exceeding the capacity for the understanding of citizenship characteristic of the indigenous population. However the retention of the pledge to the monarch is a reassuring counterbalance.

British royalty has taken a quite different track from those of the Dutch and the Norwegians. The latter amble more or less harmlessly along the special lanes designed for cyclists in rational modern countries, even if occasionally offending by neglecting to choose, with due care, the long-term companions for their tandems.

To be fair, cycling is very dangerous in Britain. Britain's royalty wisely stay in their limousines, and the cavalcade forks onto two routes at once. They lumber along with archaic pomp on the low road. On the motorway, they roar onto the fast lane of consumerism. Only the Royal Family can do this. For them, the police clear the roads. (When Her Majesty, delayed by a learner driver, misses a fly-past in her honour early in 2002, the media are enthralled by the novelty that like 'us' the Queen can be delayed by Britain's pre-modern transport system.)

'The fact', says Sir Peregrine Worsthorne in an interview cited above, and speaking not of the Royal Family but of the media, 'that as a nation our fate should be in their hands fills me with horror'. It is the status of the claims precisely as 'fact' which must be our enduring concern along with his sense of 'the nation'. Let us reconsider what the nature of the relationship is which associates the force of the media; political power in Britain and Europe; the institution of monarchy; and that construction of royal 'personalities' – their attributes, their close relationships – which is 'royal families'.

We have not sought – of course – to imply that no forces obtain beyond 'political conservatism' and 'progressivism', or 'mediatization' and 'consumerization', in the historical processes linking people and their monarchies. Michel Maffesoli, speaking in a relatively optimistic tone about contemporary society, albeit from a French viewpoint, notes that 'even if one feels alienated from the distant economic-political order, one can assert sovereignty over one's near existence'. His *The Time of the Tribes* explores a tendency in postmodern culture for social fragmentation to be offset by novel forms of collective identity. Apparently insubstantial, coalescing as they do around the products of consumer culture, Maffesoli's 'tribes' nonetheless offer an intriguing and subtle alternative to an entirely dystopian model of political awareness – in other words a vision of a steady loss of community and engagement. By contrast, Maffesoli perceives periods of engagement and disengagement with conventional politics as a recurring historical feature:

...the physicist J. E. Charron showed how a black hole is a star whose increasing density gives birth to another space – a 'new universe', he said. Proceeding by analogy...we can formulate a hypothesis that at certain periods of history, when the masses are no longer interacting with those in government… the political universe dies and sociality takes over. Furthermore, I believe that this movement is a swing of the pendulum, proceeding by saturation: on the one hand, direct or indirect participation predominates: on the other hand, there is an increased emphasis on everyday values. In the latter case, one can say that sociality preserves energies which in the political reign tend to take place in public (1996: 46)

This perspective might indeed encourage a more optimistic reading of Diana's funeral or William's websites than we have achieved, a sort of increased social interaction holding together, outside the Abbey, or in the streets of St Andrews or outside Crathie Church, forms of energy which can be recycled more purposively in other circumstances. (Indeed, why might these activities not be as valuable as any other activities, just in themselves? For example, they appear not to be actually harmful, unlike much human action.)

Discussing the nature of spatial relationships in society, Maffesoli quotes Durkheim on 'the social nature of sentiments':

'We are indignant together', he writes, referring to the proximity of the neighbourhood and its mysterious, formative 'force of attraction'. It is within this framework that passion is expressed, common beliefs are developed and the search for 'those who *feel and think as we do*' takes place. (Maffesoli's emphasis, 1996: 12–13)

Whereas, says Maffesoli, the 'rational era is built on the principle of individuation and of separation', the 'empathetic period' is by contrast 'marked by the lack of differentiation, the "loss" in a collective subject: in other words, what I call neo-tribalism' (11).

We should at least give room to the possibility that there is something in the mediated interaction of royal families and their subjects or citizens, in the UK and Europe respectively, which is related to the search for 'those who feel and think as we do'. Apparently there was at least some 'being indignant together' in 1997 (even if for those of us in the cynical camp, only at the bad taste of the British media's over-reaction to a funeral). That we may be in an 'empathetic period' is not in doubt. Douglas (2000) notes parallels between responses to John F Kennedy Jnr's death and Diana's, and much puzzlement among North American and British reporters and commentators on the scale of the response to Kennedy's accident, as well as a piece on the 'People's Prince' from the National Enquirer. Can there be a new growth of community in all this?

Maffesoli's interest in proxemics, given what we might call the 'virtual contiguities' of the media, and given the actual physical congregations at royal events, is helpful in thinking about electronic societies. His notion elsewhere of what he calls an 'aloofness' from the political, and of the death of the political universe, followed by a resurgence of sociality, has some specific resonances in the United Kingdom of the last twenty years, as well as in Europe and the United States. However we would then need to define what forms of 'sociality' are available in these transforming societies, and whether the 'performances' of relationship, which are characteristic of imaginative interactions with royal families or other celebrities, may not in fact rather constitute negative evidence of wider wants in the social realm. (Perhaps even these latter 'performances' themselves take place much less frequently than their construction in the media might lead us to believe.)

What kind of 'empowerment' may be achieved on the part of members of a crowd applauding Earl Spencer's speech, or of members of a chat-room swapping gossip about William is hard to determine. There is certainly little empowerment to be comprehended in the vision of impoverished and besieged council house residents engaged in discursive sympathy for the royal family's lack of personal freedoms.

And there is one other fact to be introduced in this study, a curious fact which like so many instances in this book emphasizes difference between Britain and the European monarchies under examination.

Whether or not our present socio-cultural universe is 'depoliticized', it is in whatever case curious that there is so little public and media-based discussion in Britain of the institution of monarchy as distinct from its personification. As we have seen for example in the Dutch instance, it is a staple of European monarchic discourse precisely to devote some attention to the institution as a constitutional topic. Even in the instance of recent constitutional re-arrangements in Scotland and Wales, very major in the former case, only a very limited technical discussion takes place in the public realm, beyond the invisible quarters in which technical detail is drafted. In part, the relentless interpersonal, 'human interest' focus of the British media makes a more technical comprehension difficult to popularize, but no doubt there is only a small public appetite for such content, in turn partly determined by media-reading habits. There is little recent tradition of public discussion of constitutional arrangement in Britain, in distinct contrast, for example, to Spain, in which arrangements of the constitution have a much more vital post-war life of their own.

In the few public discussions in Britain which speculate about a republic, the idea seems so far-fetched that the most elementary formulations are all that are available. This is not surprising in a country so conservative that genuine outrage can be found in some quarters at the idea that Westminster's upper chamber should be elected. This absence of a public realm of constitutional debate – both at different stages of the cycle 'originated' and 'sedimented' in media debate – makes its own comment on the category of 'power' in its association with the concept of royalty in Britain.

In fact, it is with the concept of 'royalty' and not of 'monarchy' that the discussion of 'power' becomes associated, only for power thereby to disappear as a category. Nearly all debate in Britain which is potentially about issues of political empowerment in their bearing on the institution of monarchy, veer quickly into discussions about specific royal performances, fitness for succession, work rate – or truly and in fact nearly always, into discussions about how members of the royal family dress or behave in public or private. In a book whose survey of recent media constructions of royalty ends in the Golden Jubilee year it is worth returning to the beginning of the sovereign's reign to remind ourselves that this is not a new tendency:

> At the opening of today's thousand-year-old rite the Archbishop of Canterbury presented Queen Elizabeth to the people as our 'undoubted Queen', that is by hereditary right....It is easy to fall into hyperbole at such moments of mass emotion as this, but there is no exag-

geration here. Others of our Queens, Elizabeth I and Victoria, for example, have swayed the hearts of their people after a time, but Elizabeth II captured them from the start. She has done it not merely in virtue of her youth and grace, but because she joins to these qualities the high seriousness we have come to associate with the House of Windsor. That gravity was hers today, and perfectly attuned to the occasion. It made its subtle appeal to all hearts. It stirred the sense of a young woman set apart and dedicated and even a little lonely and greatly deserving a nation's affection and support.

(The Coronation of Queen Elizabeth, *Manchester Guardian*, 3 June 1953)

That quickly recuperated reference to the danger of hyperbole apart – hyperbole is the default mode for much of the media now – the focus on interpersonal characteristics, glamourized by a vaguely-sketched reference to givens of history, is perfectly in tune with the tributes lined up for the monarch's fiftieth year at the helm. Moreover, a strand of this description prefigures one of the much later discourses of Diana too, and of Margaret at her death, suggesting generic dimensions to her account which further bolster our sense of its constructedness (indeed this generic basis would implicate other figures such as Stephanie of Monaco).

We note below that the media are in the last instance a product of society, though they may also in another sense produce culture, and this account from the beginning of Elizabeth's reign is a further reminder that the postmodern phase of the construction of royalty in the media is continuous with a modern account.

Whether one focuses upon the occlusion of the political dimension as political ideology or as commoditization, what is significant about the media construction of the British Royal Family, as quite distinct from many available constructions in their respective national media of the Dutch or Spanish royal families, is the apolitical trajectory of debate. This explains the slight ridicule noted in the past by Nairn and others which attaches itself to those who reintroduce the political dimension to such debates. It likewise explains the real difficulty in the UK, as distinct from other monarchies we have discussed, of fitting 'power' and 'monarchy' into the same paradigm.

It is difficult to see anything other than an ongoing performance of marginal republicanism in Britain without serious debate about the institution of monarchy in its association with the framework of institutions producing power in British society. The final point to be made about the British media specifically is that in the end they construct something called 'the royal family' and confuse it with the monarchy. And royal families may be the subject of 'criticism', but since they are a human substance and the material for an interpersonal narrative, there is no possibility of sustaining a serious critique of their symbolic functioning if the address is so seldom to the institution of monarchy. A *consistent* and *long term* and *widespread* use of registers of critique of the monarchic institution, found in quantities constituting a critical mass in media commentaries in Europe, is absent in Britain

As we have seen, there are sporadic debates in serious newspapers (in any case not so much read in the UK); and a few British journalists have been producing critiques of the post-war phase of the monarchy since Malcolm Muggeridge found himself partly ostracized in Britain just a few years after the Coronation for criticizing the royal family.

There were vigorous assaults on British royalty in public debates in previous centuries. But the volume of attention to the British royal family as a personal narrative remains the accurate measurement of the political case – not minor changes in the overall tone, or voices from the periphery. We might revisit our conundrum about Europeanness and citizenship in Britain above – can the British achieve citizenship only by becoming European or can they achieve a European identity only by acquiring British citizenship? – and replace the terms, repeating a question from the Introduction in a slightly different form. Can the British achieve citizenship by reshaping or shedding their monarchy, or can they radically address the question of the monarchy only by first achieving citizenship? The achievement of citizenship, or the achievement of a republic, would, of course, as noted in the Introduction, be dependent on whether or not these processes are still historically available. The gloomy tendency within postmodernism theory might argue that the bell tolled a while back for both, and that 'post-citizenship' and 'post-republicanism' are now those mere replicas of political participation which the consumerized world has to offer.

Another answer to both questions is that politics usually moves across a broad front, and that if anything significant happens in Britain which constitutes change in the disposition of power, then these European, and participative, and monarchic, and yet other dimensions of the political and economic worlds, will all require to have undergone development first.

Maffesoli's 'swing of the pendulum' – though a potentially welcome thought to those depressed by the state of the political universe in the new century – is not really by itself as a concept so very reassuring. The 'death' of the political universe, if not over-reported, has been caused by new accelerating phenomena of the last thirty years. The socio-political and cultural situation we find ourselves in is novel. It is not clear if the metaphor of the pendulum is applicable. It is uncertain how much of what has happened to us is in any sense reversible. Writing in France, which brought its own solution to bear on the question of monarchy a while ago, and in a Europe where more of the indigenous white populations, at any rate, have been able to participate in a larger number of the benefits of modern political development than in the UK, it is possible to be more sanguine, perhaps, about 'depoliticization' than in the United Kingdom. The political universe has fewer signs of life about it in Britain and the USA than in Europe, though Europe, as we have noted, is producing symptoms of the ailment. One of the questions raised by this book concerns whether it is the British or European state of affairs which is more likely to prevail across the board over the longer term in the context of global economic and political circumstances. This is not to exaggerate difference or suppress similarity, but only to enquire whether differences which do exist will prevail, or flatten out, and in which direction.

What is certain is that the media will be an essential component of the process. In a state of affairs in which so much of whatever may exist, from nation to nation, of public debate about the disposition of political power takes place through media channels, the overall production of ideology will incorporate a large media-derived element. This will in individual national instances vary. The monarchies we have examined, to take one example of variation, deal seriously in their school education systems with questions of civics or citizenship, and of politics and history, to different degrees. In Britain, where discussion of the need for more 'citizenship' – related content in school education was still of a preliminary nature at the beginning of the new century, media production of ideology in the realms we have been examining may be relatively more important than ideology produced by the education system. In this sense the occlusion of serious debate about the monarchic institution in the British media system is of a piece with its generally low visibility as a topic.

It may be worth asserting that in this sense media culture, so much more important than it was thirty or forty years ago, and so much more influential though it is, is nevertheless in the final analysis a product of national socio-cultural forces which are even more determining, and endure amidst the facts of globalization. In other words, if the British media appear politically more conservative about their monarchy than European media systems do about theirs, that is because Britain is a politically more conservative country generally and over many more matters than the monarchy. Journalists and editors are produced by their cultures. Likewise, if the British media economically exploit their monarchy on a different scale from that on which the Belgian or Dutch media exploit theirs, that is in part because of much wider differences in the rate and scale of postmodernization across Europe.

So while in Spain and The Netherlands the media can still engage in much serious and developed debate about their monarchies, Britain's media with the smallest of exceptions continue to focus obsessively on the traits of royal personality. While the media in the European monarchies determinedly assert the value of their royal families as guarantors of political modernity, the British media speak proudly of tradition and continuity.

And as Britain's royal legions in a thousand images go back and forth through the doors of the Dorchester and the Ritz, 'brave' the cold at Klosters and warm up in the Caribbean and the Côte d'Azur, and as 'modernization' in British political parlance remains largely a slogan, it is difficult to see much compensation for the council estates in the distant prospect of William's wedding.

AFTERWORD

Calibration and Compliance In The UK: *Mourning, Celebration and Conformity In 2002*

Well, a funeral is a sombre occasion, but it's not all gloom and doom
  (David Dimbleby, Queen Mother's funeral, BBC Television)

As the British media have become steadily less concerned with the real world since the tabloid revolution of the 1970s, the processes of mediation themselves have also in part displaced the external world which was once more exclusively the object of attention of reporters and editors. In a recent TV news fashion, for example, reporters turn into lecturers and 'explain' the 'facts' of whatever situation they are addressing. They stand in front of a studio screen with captions and pictures summarizing what they have selected as the 'main themes'. Elsewhere, British reporters give location reports to camera, 'explaining' reality to us on the spot, by standing in front of it. This is in contrast (for example) to the relative invisibility of reporters on much French television news coverage, in which the imperative is to take cameras and microphones to the scene of events and make visible and audible the relevant locations or people.

In parallel with the postmodern supersession of objects by signs, British media attention is very easily caught by facts of media life, so that, for example, Tony Blair's relationship with the media during 2002 was at least as interesting to them as whatever might be left of the real world of British politics. There is a logic of what this volume earlier cited as 'representation crisis', whereby the very question of whether the media can, or cannot, report the world objectively becomes progressively outdated. The equivalent question now is over the functions of the media. Where in their repertoire does reportage belong? The status of this reportage function is not identical from country to country. The main question about 'objectivity' in the present day is one of how much room there is in the economy of the British media system for engagement with real life. Even on that most celebrated product of reality television, *Big Brother*, a fifteen-minute delay from life to screen enables cuts (which in the UK reach extraordinary quantities) to comply with rules of law and public 'taste'.

We have noted two chief motives behind the prominence of royalty in the media, namely one which is economic and one which is ideological. In the latter instance the ideological function in Britain has emerged as markedly different from its continental equivalent. Most likely the economic/entertainment drives were present as usual in the

Golden Jubilee year, but it is in the ideological domain that the stakes seem to have been raised. On the death of the Queen Mother and afterward, as the Golden Jubilee year picked up momentum, a tendency which had emerged at the death of Diana reappeared with a new creative energy. The desire to 'unite' Britain in 2002 within allegiance to the monarchy (as distinct from 1997's immersion in 'grief') verged on the feverish, most especially within the institutions of broadcasting.

The Jubilee coverage began tentatively, but became intensive, in particular after the Queen Mother's death. War in the Middle East; the potential for nuclear devastation in the Indian sub-continent; renewed serious conflict in Northern Ireland; and famine in Africa – all these and many other events were frequently displaced in the first half of 2002 by lengthy items, often high on the news agenda, on more urgent matters, such as the Queen's visit to Prince Charles's exhibit at the Chelsea Flower Show (Her Majesty seemed duly impressed).

There are some perfectly obvious explanations for over-reaction on television. Newpaper editors cater for consumers whose demographic profile is known to them, and they make judgements on that basis. The *Independent* or the *Guardian* and *Observer*, can be cooler toward royalty than the *Daily Mail* if they wish (as can the Scottish press, to a variable degree). Predominantly the English press is ideologically conservative, and its reporters, columnists and editors are either monarchist by calculation or even conviction (saving the presence of rhetorical devices for 'criticism', which we have analyzed above).

News programmes on BBC1 or ITN have to deal with a greater demographic spread in the audience, so that if they sound like the *Daily Telegraph* on royal matters, it is because they think that in a conservative culture this is less dangerous than sounding like the *Guardian*. And indeed the BBC and ITN do sound like the right wing press when covering royal matters. Were their ideological position (conservative and contentious though it is) on the European Union, or American foreign policy, so obviously mono-dimensional, then – even in Britain – that might be problematic for them.

In parallel, a process of recuperation occurred during 2002, in which a more traditional construction of the monarchy was marketed by palace scenographers, an impression strengthened rather than dispelled by some singularly British performances of 'modernization' (these involved innovations such as Prince Charles's address to the monarch as 'Mummy' during a Jubilee pop concert). The Prince's characterization of the Queen as 'a beacon of stability in the midst of change' seemed to encapsulate not only the predominant account of the monarch in media coverage, but the unreconstructed passion for the past which underpinned it. The BBC narrative at the Queen Mother's funeral kept returning to the theme of continuity, emphasizing how the Abbey had witnessed 'daily worship on this site for almost 1000 years', and other such invocations. The degree of consensus in media accounts to the effect that change is a negative value was very striking during the Jubilee year, given previous hiccoughs in the popularity of the Family, and wild talk of republicanism in some of Britain's quality newspapers in 2001.

The funeral of the Queen Mother both in its performance aspects (such as the photogenic positioning of the princes around the catafalque) and in its media realization, concentrated relentlessly on 'tradition', even where minting it freshly. A recurring theme in the account of the nation's loss was the sense of fracture in historical experience, the Queen Mother's death being depicted as a loss of connection with what was portrayed, not without contradiction, as an imperially monarchic past which was also vaguely communitarian (the Queen Mother apt to drop around for tea at moments of national crisis). Nonetheless, this regal/sympathetic past was instantly reinstated, in the Jubilee performances which followed, and along with its contradictions.

New habits associated with the 'mourning' of public figures have been consolidated since Diana's death, and in the instance of the Queen Mother's funeral there were widespread institutional displays of what was coded as 'respect' or 'affection' (an 'outpouring of affection' having picked up the relay from 1997's 'outpouring of grief'). Supermarkets closed, for example, or if open, stopped serving at tills. By 2002 the streets of Britain during royal events were routinely calibrated by television so that the strength of public feeling might be measured, and conformity assessed. The experience of those unwittingly caught up in these performances in public spaces was telling, subjects feeling themselves under strong pressure not to demur. Ceremonial forms of royal deaths in contemporary Britain have grown teeth. Compliance is further policed by the media.

'I should perhaps just mention that at 11.30 there will be a fairly widely-observed two minutes silence, that is as the Queen Mother's coffin is inside the abbey, and just at the start of the service', instructs David Dimbleby from his anchor position in the funeral coverage on BBC television. We are thus proofed against solecism, and discouraged from deviance. If the careless claims of 'loss of deference' in British society have any worth, then perhaps it is to the arrival of new forms of consumer conformity, or to other explanations, that we must turn, faced with the odd phenomena of 2002. Because, otherwise, deference seems in relatively good shape to be reconsidered as a primary explanation. The Queen's Golden Jubilee produced deference in superabundance, and it puffed out of the British media and its presenters in scented clouds.

Something really is needed to explain the frantic processes of participation-measurement which have become a feature of media coverage of royal events. When no-one is there, it is only that they have not yet turned up ('it's still quiet here, but several thousand people are expected later'). When three people, and not three thousand, are recorded by television at a key point on a route, they are framed in a close shot which deprives the surrounding emptiness of its impact, since public absence does not belong within the account.

Palace scenography can sometimes aid television, and was most impressive during the Queen Mother's funeral, but when all else fails, including the manipulation of the television frame, the integrity of the narrative demands bluffing, plain and simple. Even a respected veteran BBC reporter, rather isolated in a quiet Windsor on the morning of the Queen Mother's funeral, has problems keeping his facts unadorned, and his narrative is an interesting mixture of factual reporting and loyal improvisation. At first he is very direct in his account: '[...] At the moment Windsor is quiet, really exceptionally quiet. There's hardly anybody about...': but then the demands of the overall monarchist narrative assert themselves so that he then surmises that 'I think people are preparing to watch on television rather than come out onto the streets at the moment'.

Perhaps in fact they are having breakfast, playing with their children, or doing any of many hundreds of other things, for all he knows. At many moments like this in royal 'reporting', fiction replaces reportage. In simple terms, since he has not investigated what all these absent people are doing, he does not know what they are doing. Then, over closed shots excluding any empty space (evidently, nearly all the space is empty):

> There are a few hardy souls who have been gathering outside the, eh, castle, just on the right there you can see [names two people], they, they, came up from Brighton last night expecting to have to queue up to get a place, and eh, were really rather surprised to find themselves on their own, but since this morning others have been trickling in and bringing with them, you can see, they've put some flags there, there's also a wreath of red roses, eh, which has been hung up there, 101 red roses, and eh, it makes, you can see, the pattern, 101, little tribute to the Queen Mother.

We saw precisely this tension near the start of the book in accounts of Diana's funeral, the honest instincts of reporters warring with the editorial demands of narrative consistency. This reporter now launches into a new phase of conflict between objectivity and creativity, as the camera tilts down a statue of Victoria at the bottom of the hill:

> And the, down at the bottom of the hill, the statue of Queen Victoria has – overnight! – has suddenly found itself garlanded with flowers, eh, and down at the bottom there a little photograph of the Queen Mother, a few well-wishers have put their own personal tribute, but in general you can see if you look around the streets here, that they, they *are* empty, I think a lot of people will watch on television, then come out into the streets afterwards, to get some personal contact after they've watched the state occasion. The shops, the offices, even the local banks, they're all planning to close today, so it's even quieter than normal, their staff will be able to watch, and then they're coming in to start work at 2.00, so they can come in and they can see the cortège as it passes, or a little before 2.00, so that will proba-bly build up the crowds then, but this has been a funeral which has surprised us all as it goes along, so we'll wait and see what happens here in Windsor....

Like innumerable other reports from the funeral and Jubilee in 2002, this is a mixture of reportage and ideological reinforcement; and also an appeal to get involved – right down to correcting the initial estimate of the timing, in case you arrive too late. The central ideological thrust is that everyone, everywhere, is concentrating mentally on this one event, because of the importance of the royal family in their hierarchy of values. No-one in this account is simply making toast, or feeding the cat. Everyone is living in royal time and space. They are so upset that they will need 'personal contact' later.

Here in Windsor, albeit in the hands of this seasoned reporter, breakdown between the language and the pictures threatens the very narrative integrity he is struggling to uphold. For example, in this instance, the shot of Victoria's statue shows that there are

APPENDIX

A Note on Britain and Europe

We know, dear Sir, that you and other conservatives hate Europe and would like to seal up the Channel tunnel. You can do this. Many mainland Europeans feel the same in the light of BSE and foot and mouth.

Welt am Sonntag on Sir Peter Tapsell's comparison of Gerhard Schröder's vision of Europe, to Hitler's (quoted in *Guardian*, 19 May 2001)

The most complicated problem is the menu. The latest news is that Elizabeth II – like count Dracula – hates garlic, which is one of the most classic ingredients of Belpaese cuisine.

(*La Repubblica*, 10 October 2000, on the Queen's Italian visit)

The British royal family has horribleness built in. The richest of the rich, the most stupid of the stupid, the most irresponsible of the irresponsible.

(*Tribuna*, Spain, 14 December 1992)

The authorities reacted with swift brutality, slaughtering all 1500 sheep on the farm.

(UK Channel 4 News, on the subject of the German character, during a foot and mouth scare near Dusseldorf, 28 February 2001)

This book has been partly about differences between Britain and Europe. We append a note on the changing relationship between Britain and Europe as it has been mediated in recent times. It is clear that remarkable material differences persist between Britain and the rest of Europe, surpassing intra-continental differences. These differences are not surprising if the process called 'globalization' is treated with due care.

Globalization has been described succinctly as 'time-space compression' (Harvey 1989: 147) but subtle accounts have always avoided the implication of homogenization of culture, as in Roland Robertson's equally economical description of globalization as 'the twofold process of the particularization of the universal and the universalization of the particular', which avoids confusing 'increasing connectedness' with' increasing similarity' (Robertson, 1992: 177–178). The paradoxes of the globalizing world demand a recognition of the maintenance and reproduction of difference – even its growth – alongside the often more apparent developments in contiguity and networking. Differences between Britain and much of the rest of Europe remain marked, and that sense of difference has been finding its way more and more into both British and continental discussion.

Some objectively measurable spaces, like the distance across the English Channel from Dover to Calais, turn out in many contexts to be more important as symbols than they are as quantifiable journeys. It may be a lot further from Dover to Calais, in that sense, than from The Hague to Brussels, or even from Paris to Berlin. Britain began the twenty-first century not only every bit as apparently isolated from Europe as previously, but vigorously constructed as such, in discourse on both sides of the Channel and the North Sea.

We find the assumption very plainly at work in the Europe of the early twenty-first century that Britain is a backward country: but we will find this idea very hard to disentangle from symbolic structures which need careful investigation. The new century opened in a Britain whose landscape was flooded, whose road and rail networks were choked, whose towns were filled with litter, disaffected youth, drug addicts, petty criminals: its countryside was littered with the carcasses of slaughtered animals; and pyres of smoke, as journalists kept telling us, filled the skies. Actually, this was a very small proportion of the British landscape, but it was all of the television screens and newspaper photograph frames which such images filled.

European and other international observers were moved to speak in terms of plagues, even of a curse on Britain. Foot and mouth ravaged the country just after the rail system had been closed down by train disasters, which closely followed petrol shortages, which occurred at a time of freak rainfall patterns. The British Royal Family in this context was seen in Europe as an index of the country's wider plight. *Le Monde* (6 April 2001) wryly observing the Sophie Wessex scandal, noted that she was merely: 'Responsible for the latest scandal which is rising like a soufflé in the kingdom of the Windsors. ... "Wait till you see the Sunday papers!" says a local colleague licking his lips'. *Schadenfreude* has attended a significant quantity of European media comment on the serial plights of Britain and its royals – it is one of the kinder responses in the European repertoire, actually – and it was greatly in evidence in the first year of the new century.

More than one European politician spoke of the British government's 'mediaeval' approach to tackling the foot and mouth outbreak, or even of Britain's mediaeval state. (This overlooked the outbreak's association with Britain's nature as a globalized society, but perceived backwardness in Britain had been a refrain for some time overseas.)

We have earlier seen how *Der Spiegel*, writing before the royal marriage break-up

Figure 6. Juan Ballesta's cartoon in the Spanish weekly magazine Cambio 16 (2 April 2001) shows George Bush applauding as Tony Blair urinates on the European Union

on 23 November 1992, characterizes the country: 'The British empire collapsed, its once mighty industries are rusting, slums proliferate in the cities, the state is heavily indebted abroad, its place in Europe is uncertain'. *La Vanguardia* (10 December 1992) spoke of how 'Great Britain is today an island stripped of its overseas possessions and leaning against Europe with the worry of not knowing whether to join it unreservedly or to insist on retaining some vestige of its "splendid isolation"'.

A particularly sustained critical piece on Britain, in *Stern*, 'Der englische Patient – Great Britain in crisis. The country is as sick as its cattle' – gained its celebrity through a temporary fashion of the British media for reporting overseas analyses of Britain, not through any novelty in continental disdain for the UK (*Stern*, 25 May 2001).

The view which Europe takes of the United Kingdom, as we have already seen, is neither invariably comprehending nor unswervingly benign. Jean Baudrillard's pleasantry to the effect that five hundred years after America, England has 'yet to be discovered' (Gane, 1993: 208) seems to have become increasingly relevant as a descriptor of continental reactions to British culture and society, in the opening years of the new century. Britain's attitudes to Europe, meanwhile, are only too well understood by her EU partners – all of the monarchies we examine here are, with Norway's exception, of EU countries – and continue to cause them vexation. In this sense there is an important dialogic aspect to the relationships examined. Robertson (1992: 168) has noted a 'dialectics', produced by relationships between nations, as a trend observable over a very long period of time.

In the last quarter or so of the twentieth century, and now in the early years of the twenty-first, in a media-saturated, much more densely globalized culture, we find evidence of an intensified and far faster symbolic exchange; for example in 'dialogues' across national boundaries between newspapers during international events. This has been seen in many of the cross-national reports and evaluations of monarchy in earlier chapters.

There are currently mixed signals, from all the actors, about their responses to the EU, and Britain's relationship with it. On mainland Europe, depending where we look, there are signs of both warmth and pessimism about the European Union. Many have meanwhile detected in the UK a slow, partial and intermittent acceptance that the European question has become serious for the British, and that the consequences of being left outside the amenities of the European household might be grave. This still chiefly negative representation of the attitude to Europe of many social groups in the UK is probably accurate. Real enthusiasm about a European identity was as thin in Britain in 2002 as it had been in 1990. But government and big business has been in general increasingly serious about the European project; and in other quarters of British life – not least in popular and consumer culture, an important concern in this book – Europe is becoming more and more visible inside Britain's boundaries. New Labour's victory in the 2001 General Election was accompanied by much poll evidence to the effect that the British by and large expected Britain to join the euro, whether they much approved of it or not, and that likelihood sharpened after the new currency's introduction in Europe at the start of 2002.

That most British mass media output was often hostile to Europe, to the Union specifically, and to the former Community – and belligerent especially over the perceived national traits of Britain's neighbours – seemed axiomatic throughout most of the 1980s and 1990s. Perhaps in the very last years of the twentieth century the picture grew a little more complex. But a tone of sometimes frivolous dislike, or some mixture of fear and contempt, often continue to taint even those British media accounts of European matters which are designed for serious viewers and readers.

Despite some small signs of movement referred to above, Britain is still markedly unEuropean across a range of markers such as patterns of social stratification, cultural preferences, legal and constitutional safeguards, standards of civility, public behaviour and style, and political and cultural aspiration. The differences which invariably emerge from all cross-national comparisons – as is the case here, indeed, when we make comparisons within mainland Europe, let us say from Spain to Belgium – are nonetheless of a larger order of magnitude. They possess particular structural characteristics, when the comparison is between Britain on the one hand, and our group of European countries in this book, on the other. This study has proposed Britain as a special case on the evidence of the differential functioning of European monarchy with respect to questions of culture, and specifically, political culture. As the monarchies of Europe, in some instances in defiance of expectation, have arrived in the twenty-first century (whether by limousine or the cycle track) the idea that Britain as a country presents a special instance – a negative instance, too – has become widespread.

The overseas construction of Britain's apparent woe, symbolically fabricated as an amalgam of 'backwardness' and 'accursedness', had become the matter of fierce international exchange in the British press, and anguished debate on television, by 2001. This marked the appearance of what was almost certainly a genuinely unprecedented, overt, phase of defensiveness in British culture, amidst a growing number of indigenous British discourses, much evident a year or so later, of the superiority of European social and civic arrangements, including transport and health provision.

REFERENCES

Barthes, R. *Mythologies*, London, Jonathan Cape, 1972.

Barthes, R. *Image, Music, Text*, Glasgow, Fontana Press, 1987.

Baudrillard, J. *Symbolic Exchange and Death*, London, Sage, 1993.

Baudrillard, J. *Simulacra and Simulations*, New York, Sémiotext(e), 1983.

Baudrillard, J., *America*, London, Verso, 1989.

Bell, D. *The Coming of Post-Industrial Society: A Venture in Social Forecasting*, New York, Basic Books, 1973.

Berman, M. *All That Is Solid Melts Into Air*, London, Verso, 1983.

Billig, M. *Talking of the Royal Family*, London, Routledge, 1992, 1998.

Blain, N. and H. O'Donnell 'Royalty, modernity and postmodernity: monarchy in the British and Spanish presses', *Acis: Journal of the Association for Contemporary Iberian Studies* Vol.7 (1): 38–49, 1994.

Blain, N. and O'Donnell, H. 'The construction of European citizenship; monarchy and citizenry', paper to Belgian Linguistic Association/International Pragmatics Association conference on Political Linguistics, University of Antwerp, Belgium, December, 1995.

Blain, N. and O'Donnell, H. 'Constructing the People's Princess: The State of Britain and the Death of Diana', in C. Cornut Gentille D'Arcy (ed.), *Cultural Confrontations*, Zaragoza, University of Zaragoza, 1999.

Boorstin, D. *The Image: A Guide to Pseudo-Events in America*, New York, Harper Colophon Books, 1961.

Bourdieu, P. *Contre-feux*, Paris, Liber-Raisons d'agir, 1998.

Braudel, F. *The Identity of France*, volume one, 1986, London, Fontana.

Brunt, R. A. 'Divine gift to inspire'?, in Strinati, D. and Wagg, S. *Come on down? Popular media culture in postwar Britain*, London, Routledge, 1992.

Cardús i Ros, S. *Política de paper. Premsa i poder a Catalunya 1981–1992*, Barcelona, Edicions La Campana, 1995.

Cardús i Ros, S. 'Politics and the Invention of Memory. For a Sociology of the Transition to Democracy in Spain', in Resina, J. R. (ed.) *Disremembering the Dictatorship: The Politics of Memory in the Spanish Transition to Democracy*, Amsterdam, Rodopi, 2000.

Coward, R. *Female Desire*, London, Paladin, 1984.

Crook, S., Pakulski, J., Waters, M., *Postmodernization*, 1992, London, Sage.

Davies, J. *Diana. A Cultural History: Gender, Race, Nation and the People's Princess*, London, Palgrove, 2001.

Douglas, L. *Oh What a Beautiful Mourning*, unpublished dissertation, Glasgow Caledonian University, 2000.

Elias, N. *The Symbol Theory*, London, Sage, 1991.

Fussell, P. *The Great War and Modern Memory*, Oxford, Oxford University Press, 1977.

Gane, M. *Baudrillard Live: Selected Interviews*, London, Routledge, 1993.

Giggal, P. and Williamson, L. 'Media reporting of the death of Diana, Princess of Wales', unpublished empirical project, Glasgow Caledonian University, 1998.

González Cuevas, P.C. 'La invenció d'una tradició: visió histórica de la monarquia durant la transició democtàtica', in *Avenç*, no. 182, 1984.

Habermas, J. Modernity: an unfinished project, in Ingram, D. and Ingram, J. S., *Critical Theory: The Essential Readings*, New York, Paragon House, 1991.

Harvey, D. *The Condition of Postmodernity*, Oxford, Blackwell,1989.

Harvey, D. *Spaces of Hope*, Edinburgh, Edinburgh University Press, 2000.

Hawkes, T. *Structuralism and Semiotics*, 1977, London, Methuen.

Hebdige, D. *Hiding in the Light*, London, Comedia, 1988.

Hobsbawm, E. and Ranger, T. (eds.) *The Invention of Tradition*, Cambridge, Cambridge University Press, 1983.

Home Office *Secure Borders, Safe Haven – Integration with Diversity in Modern Britain*, London, The Stationery Office, 2002.

Hovland, B. M. *Kongelege jule- og nyttårstalar som nasjonale ritual. Tre skandinaviske eksempel*, Copenhagen, Nordisk Ministerråd, 2000.

Hutcheon, L. *A Poetics of Postmodernism: History, Theory, Fiction*, New York, Routledge, 1988.

Huyssen, A. *After the Great Divide*, Macmillan, London, 1984.

Huyssen, A. Mapping the Postmodern, in Jencks, C. (ed.) *The Post-Modern Reader*, London: Academy Editions/St. Martin's Press, 1992.

Jameson, F. *Postmodernism, or, The Cultural Logic of Late Capitalism*, London, Verso, 1991

Jencks, C. *What is Post-Modernism?* London, Academy Editions/St. Martin's Press, 1989.

Jencks, C. *The Language of Post-Modern Architecture*, London, Academy Editions, 1991.

Jencks, C. (ed.) *The Post-Modern Reader*, London, Academy Editions/St. Martin's Press, 1992.

Kermode, F. *The Sense of an Ending*, Oxford, OUP, 2000. First edition 1966.

Klausen, A. M. *Med Dagbladet til tabloid. En studie i dilammaet «børs og katedral»*, Oslo, Gyldendal, 1986.

Labany, J. 'Postmodernism and the problem of cultural identity', in Graham, H. and Labany, J. (eds.) *Spanish Cultural Studies: An Introduction*, Oxford, OUP, 1995.

Lamuedra, M. 'Spanish and British Women's Magazines: Classifying the unclassifiable – a blurred genre', paper presented at the Conference of the Association for Contemporary Iberian Studies, Essex University, 2001.

Lefebvre, H. *Critique of Everyday Life*, London, Verso, 1991.

Leus, K. and Veny, L. (eds.) *Het federale belgie in de praktijk. De werking van de wetgevende vergaderingen na de verkiezingen van 21 mei 1995*, Brugge, Die Keure, 1996.

Lyotard, J. F. *The Post-Modern Condition*, Minneapolis, University of Minnesota Press, 1984.

Maffesoli, M. *The Time of the Tribes*, London, Sage, 1996.

McElhone, C. *Commodifying Diana: Princess Diana, Postmodernity and the Mass Media*, unpublished dissertation, Glasgow Caledonian University, 1998.

Nairn, T. *The Enchanted Glass*, London, Radius, 1988.

National Enquirer, 'John: The People's Prince', JFK Jr Memorial Issue, 3 August 1999.

Norris, C. *What's Wrong with Postmodernism*, Hemel Hempstead, Harvester Wheatsheaf, 1990.

Norris, C. *Uncritical Theory: Postmodernism, Intellectuals and the Gulf War*, London, Lawrence and Wishart, 1992.

Noterman, J. A. M. *La république du roi*, Braine-L'Alleud, J. M. Collet, 1998.

References

PBS Frontline, interview with Sir Peregrine Worsthorne, transmitted 18 November 1997, transcript on www.pbs.org/wgbh/

O'Donnell, H. 'Mapping the mythical: a geopolitics of national sporting stereotypes', in *Discourse & Society*, 5:3, 1994.

Poster, M. (ed.) *Jean Baudrillard: Selected Writings*, Cambridge, Polity Press, 1988.

Resina, J. R. (ed.) *Disremembering the Dictatorship: The Politics of Memory in the Spanish Transition to Democracy*, Amsterdam, Rodopi, 2000.

Robertson, R. *Globalization: Social Theory and Global Culture*, London, Sage, 1992.

Rose, M., *The Postmodern & the Postindustrial*, Cambridge, Cambridge University Press, 1991.

Salmon, K. 'Spanish foreign direct investment, transnationals and the redefinition of the Spanish business realm', in *International Journal of Iberian Studies*, No 14:2, 2001.

de Saussure, F. *Course in General Linguistics*, Glasgow, Fontana/Collins, 1974.

Sondermann, K. *O Deutschland! Oi Suomi! Vielgeliebtes Österreich! Zur politischen und gesellschaftlichen Karriere vorgestellter Wesen*, Universität Tampere, Institut für Sozialwissenschaften, 1995.

Thompson, J. B. *Ideology and Modern Culture: critical social theory in the era of mass communication*, Cambridge, Polity Press, 1990.

Torre y Rivas, J. de la, *Máxima: Prinses van Oranje*, Naarden, Best Selling Books, 2001

Turnock, R. *Interpreting Diana*, London, BFI, 2000.

Williams, R. 'The Metropolis and the Emergence of Modernism', in Timms, E. and Kelley, D. (eds.) *Unreal City: Urban Experience in Modern European Literature and Art*, Manchester, Manchester University Press/St Martin's Press, 1985.

Vattimo, G. *The Transparent Society*, London, Polity, 1992.

Vattimo, G. *La società trasparente*, Milan, Garzanti, 2000.

Williamson, J. *Consuming Passions: the Dynamics of Popular Culture*, London, Boyars, 1985.

Wright, P. *On Living in an Old Country*, London, Verso, 1985.

INDEX